The Elements of Bankruptcy

Third Edition

Douglas G. Baird

Harry A. Bigelow Distinguished Service Professor
The University of Chicago

New York, New York
Foundation Press
2001

Cover Design: Keith Stout

Cover Art: Paul Klee, "Composition With Triangles"

COPYRIGHT © 1992, 1993 FOUNDATION PRESS
COPYRIGHT © 2001 By FOUNDATION PRESS
        11 Penn Plaza, Tenth Floor
        New York, NY 10001
        Phone Toll Free 1–877–888–1330
        Fax (212) 760–8705
        fdpress.com

ISBN 1–56662–868–7

TEXT IS PRINTED ON 10% POST CONSUMER RECYCLED PAPER

For Walter J. Blum

Contents

Introduction

Modern bankruptcy law is a domain with identifiable and coherent boundaries. In *The Elements of Bankruptcy* I offer an introduction to this world for lawyers and others who want to understand bankruptcy's fundamental rules and principles. My ambition is to show that modern bankruptcy law is at once rich, interesting, and accessible. This edition reflects the state of the law as of November 2000.

The first three chapters chart the landscape. Chapter 1 explores both the substantive provisions of the Bankruptcy Code and the procedural rules that govern bankruptcy cases. Chapter 2 looks at the rights of the individual debtor in bankruptcy. Bankruptcy law gives the individual a fresh start: the "honest but unfortunate" debtor can file a bankruptcy petition and walk away with the right to enjoy both future income and some existing property free from the encumbrance of debt. The nature of this fresh start, however, has proved elusive, so we will try to identify principles that are emerging from the burgeoning case law.

Chapter 3 examines the absolute priority rule, the basic principle of corporate reorganizations. Corporations enter into bankruptcy for reasons different from those of individuals. Firms already have limited liability under state law: when a corporation fails, its shareholders are not liable to the corporation or its creditors. By reorganizing under Chapter 11 of the Bankruptcy Code, an ailing but otherwise strong firm can create a sound capital structure. That corporation, like the individual, may discharge old debts through bankruptcy, but the reasons for doing so have nothing to do with protecting flesh-and-blood human beings from their creditors.

The different legal problems of financially troubled individuals and corporations are adjudicated in the same place—bankruptcy court—not only for historical reasons but also because they present similar administrative difficulties. In both situations, one needs to hold creditors at bay while sorting through the debtor's affairs, gath-

1

ering the assets, ascertaining the liabilities, determining wrongdoing (if any), and authoritatively establishing who gets what. The remaining chapters in this book focus on the way in which this process works.

Chapter 4 examines how rights originating outside of bankruptcy are treated inside of bankruptcy. For the most part, a creditor's claim in bankruptcy turns on what the creditor had outside bankruptcy. Chapter 5 shows how the Bankruptcy Code ensures that the debtor's assets available to creditors outside of bankruptcy are available to them inside of bankruptcy as well. Chapter 6 completes our examination of the basic rights and obligations of the debtor and those with whom it has dealt by examining *executory contracts*. An executory contract is one in which each party owes obligations to the other. Hence, it is at once both a liability and an asset.

An insolvent debtor may not transfer assets unless it receives fair consideration or reasonably equivalent value in return. This basic principle of fraudulent conveyance law, thus stated, is uncontroversial, but its effects are far reaching and may play themselves out in mysterious ways in the context of leveraged buyouts and intercorporate guarantees. This issue and the related issues of equitable subordination and substantive consolidation are the subject of chapter 7. Chapter 8 examines the law of voidable preferences. When bankruptcy is on the horizon, a debtor is no longer free to choose which creditors to pay. Existing preference law implements this idea through a complicated mixture of rules and standards.

When a bankruptcy petition is filed, creditors must cease their efforts to be paid, but the debtor must continue to deal with the rest of the world as before. The Bankruptcy Code tries to achieve both ends through the automatic stay, which is the subject of chapter 9. The following chapter explores the powers of the debtor in possession. When a firm reorganizes under Chapter 11 of the Bankruptcy Code, the old managers of a firm ordinarily continue to run it. Known collectively as the debtor in possession, they enjoy substantial powers. For example, they may, in the ordinary course of their business, buy, sell, and lease assets as well as borrow money. The final chapter looks at the process of creating and confirming a plan of reorganization.

This idea for this book grew out of my long and fruitful collaboration with Thomas Jackson, who introduced me to bankruptcy law when I was a student. The book itself took shape while I was giving a series of seminars at the law firm of Sonnenschein, Nath, and Rosenthal in the winter of 1991. In the years since the last edition, I have continued to learn from long conversations with many splendid judges and lawyers, including Donald Bernstein, Ronald Barliant, Steve Case, Frank Easterbrook, Russell Eisenberg, Robert Ginsburg, Ken Klee, Richard Levin, Robert Martin, John Schwartz, Ronald Trost, and Eugene Wedoff. Work with a number of colleagues, especially Barry Adler, Edward Morrison, Randal Picker, and Robert Rasmussen, has also helped me reshape this book. The careful eye and deft pen of my editor, Leslie Keros, put the manuscript in final form. Finally, I am grateful for the research support of the Lynde and Harry Bradley Foundation, the John M. Olin Foundation, and the Sarah Scaife Foundation.

Chapter One

A Road Map to Bankruptcy Law

The Structure of the Bankruptcy Code

The word *bankruptcy* derives from the medieval Italian custom of breaking the benches of a banker or merchant who absconded and left creditors unpaid. As the roots of the word suggest, the first English bankruptcy statutes were directed at merchant debtors, and they were viciously punitive. Indeed, their harsh character prompted one delegate to the Constitutional Convention in Philadelphia in 1787 to oppose granting Congress the power to enact uniform bankruptcy laws. Under English law, uncooperative bankrupts were hanged, and the Convention delegate feared that Congress might follow suit. For modern lawyers, the very incongruity of bankruptcy and the death penalty suggests, correctly, that bankruptcy law not be linked too closely with its seventeenth- and eighteenth-century English counterparts. We will do better by focusing on the law as it is today and turning to the history of bankruptcy law when appropriate.

Since 1978 the Bankruptcy Code has been embodied in Title 11 of the United States Code. Although easily located, bankruptcy law remains a common law discipline in which a lawyer must reason by analogy and constantly be aware of general principles. Bankruptcy law is neither mechanical in its application nor narrow in the range of problems it confronts. A client in bankruptcy can face every legal problem that a person can face outside of bankruptcy.

Bankruptcy law is built on nonbankruptcy law; as a result, the bankruptcy lawyer must understand both the applicable nonbankruptcy law and the ways in which bankruptcy law may change it. An example will help to illustrate this point. Suppose you represent a computer hardware manufacturer that has a patented process for making computer chips. Your client discovers that a competitor is using its process and that the competitor has also filed a bankruptcy petition. You need to know how the patent would be enforced outside of bankruptcy, and then look at how bankruptcy changes both the underlying right and the manner in which it can be vindicated.

This task is not as formidable as it might seem. Bankruptcy law changes nonbankruptcy law only when the purposes of bankruptcy require it. Ensuring flesh-and-blood individuals a fresh start requires

4

such a change, but surprisingly little else does. <u>In the absence of a specific bankruptcy provision to the contrary, bankruptcy takes nonbankruptcy rights as it finds them.</u> <u>Only the procedures change,</u> and these change only to solve the particular problems bankruptcy is designed to address. This is known as the *Butner* principle:

> Congress has generally left the determination of property rights in the assets of a bankrupt's estate to state law. Property interests are created and defined by state law. Unless some federal interest requires a different result, there is no reason why such interests should be analyzed differently simply because an interested party is involved in a bankruptcy proceeding.[1]

Butner thus allows us to draw from a complicated statute a single organizing principle. Knowing the outcome under nonbankruptcy law can go a long way toward understanding the problem in bankruptcy. <u>When a litigant seeks an outcome different from the one that would hold outside of bankruptcy, the bankruptcy judge will likely ask the litigant to identify the part of the Bankruptcy Code that compels the departure.</u>

We can begin with a sketch of the basic structure of the Bankruptcy Code. The 1978 Bankruptcy Reform Act restructured the bankruptcy courts and bankruptcy procedure. The substantive provisions of the 1978 Act put in place the Bankruptcy Code, which constitutes Title 11 of the United States Code. It has been amended periodically, with two major revisions in 1984 and 1994. Like other titles of the United States Code, Title 11 is divided into chapters. As we shall see, with the exception of Chapter 12, all the chapters of the Bankruptcy Code have odd numbers. Congress originally enacted Chapters 1, 3, 5, 7, 9, 11, 13, and 15, leaving the even-numbered gaps to accommodate future amendments. In 1986 Congress added Chapter 12, which deals with the special problems of family farmers, and deleted Chapter 15, which covered the United States Trustee. Provisions governing the United States Trustee system now reside in Title 28. Chapters 1, 3, and 5 contain provisions that generally apply to all bankruptcy cases. The remaining chapters set out different procedures for distinct kinds of bankruptcy cases.

The United States Trustee is responsible for overseeing the administration of bankruptcy cases. The United States Trustee should ensure that cases do not languish in bankruptcy court, a fate not un-

---

[1] Butner v. United States, 440 U.S. 48, 55 (1979).

common when the stakes are small and no single creditor has the incentive to investigate the debtor. This job is important not only to protect the general creditors but also to ferret out fraud, which often contributes to business failure.

Chapter 1 provides definitions (§101), tells us which parts of the Code apply to which kinds of cases (§103), and sets out eligibility requirements for each kind of bankruptcy case (§109). Chapter 1 also contains what appears to be a broad grant of power to the bankruptcy judge. Section 105 grants the bankruptcy judge the power to "issue any order, process or judgment that is necessary or appropriate to carry out the provisions" of the Bankruptcy Code. It is not, however, a mandate for bankruptcy judges to do whatever they find just or equitable. The power that a judge enjoys under §105 must derive ultimately from some other provision of the Bankruptcy Code.[2]

The heart of any code lies in its definitional section, and the definitions in §101 are the focal point of many disputes. The definitions of *creditor* and *claim*, for example, will play a central role in the bankruptcy of a firm that faces mass tort liability. Suppose a firm sold asbestos products in the past and is liable under state law to those who contract asbestosis and other diseases from being exposed to the asbestos it sold. Many of these individuals may not yet have shown any symptoms and will not for many years. Whether the firm can deal with the rights of these individuals in bankruptcy turns on whether these future victims are considered creditors and whether they have claims within the meaning of §101.

Section 101 also introduces us to the language of modern bankruptcy practice. It tells us, for instance, that the person whom a bankruptcy case concerns is a *debtor*. A person or a firm in bankruptcy is no longer called a *bankrupt*. Although that word retains some currency among lay people, among bankruptcy lawyers it sounds old-fashioned and precious. Section 101 defines most of the terms that apply throughout the Bankruptcy Code, but not all. One of the most important definitions in the Bankruptcy Code, that of *notice and a hearing*, is found in §102, which nominally deals with rules of construction.

Many provisions in the Bankruptcy Code allow actions to take place after notice and a hearing. One should not, however, assume that everyone must receive actual notice or that a hearing is required

[2] See Gillman v. Continental Airlines, 203 F.3d 203 (3d Cir. 2000); Barbieri v. RAJ Acquisition Corp., 199 F.3d 616, 621 (2d Cir. 1999).

in every instance. Section 102 tells us that we need to give only "such notice as is appropriate in the particular circumstances." Moreover, if no party requests a hearing or if a court finds there is insufficient time to have one, an actual hearing is not necessary. Over the years, a body of learning has developed around who needs to be notified at each stage and the consequences that follow if they are not.[3] As in many other contexts, the basic principles in bankruptcy track those outside. Most analyses begin with the observation of the Supreme Court in *Mullane v. Central Hanover Bank & Trust Company*:[4]

> An elementary and fundamental requirement of due process in any proceeding which is to be accorded finality is notice reasonably calculated, under all the circumstances, to apprise interested parties of the pendency of the action and afford them an opportunity to present their objections.

One section that is easy to miss is §104, which provides for indexing of many of the dollar thresholds elsewhere in the Bankruptcy Code. These thresholds are changed every three years through administrative regulation to reflect the consumer price index. Under §109, for instance, individuals wishing to file under Chapter 13 can have no more than a specified amount in unsecured claims. This amount was raised by administrative regulation in 1998 and will be raised again in 2001. Section 109 also sets out who can take advantage of various chapters of the Bankruptcy Code. Chapter 9, for example, deals with the debts of municipalities, and §109(c) tells us, not surprisingly, that only a municipality may file a Chapter 9 petition.

Section 109 is as good a place as any to see how the Bankruptcy Code works. To know whether an ordinary domestic corporation may be a debtor under Chapter 11, one looks first to §109(d). It states that to be a debtor under Chapter 11, one must qualify as a debtor under Chapter 7. Section 109(b) excludes some "persons" from Chapter 7, but does not mention corporations. This brings us to §109(a), which tells us that a debtor can enjoy the benefits of bankruptcy only if it is a person. Hence, a corporation is eligible for bankruptcy if it is a person. To know whether a corporation is a person, we must look to §101's definition. It tells us that *person* as used in the Bankruptcy Code includes a corporation. Section 101 goes on to define a corporation. That definition would be of use in a case in which, for example, we faced the question whether a business trust was a corporation.

[3] See, e.g., Fogel v. Zell, 221 F.3d 955 (7th Cir. 2000).
[4] 339 U.S. 306, 314 (1950).

There is no explicit requirement that a debtor be in financial distress or insolvent before filing for bankruptcy. Section 101 of the Bankruptcy Code defines insolvency as the condition that exists when a debtor's liabilities fairly discounted exceed its assets, but insolvency itself is not a prerequisite for bankruptcy for individuals or for corporations. Indeed, §109(c) specifies that a municipality must be insolvent to file a Chapter 9 petition. The absence of any mention of insolvency in other parts of §109 creates the negative inference that other debtors need not be insolvent to be eligible for bankruptcy.

The absence of such an explicit requirement makes sense. Suppose a firm has assets of $100, ordinary debt of $49, and a 50–50 chance of losing a lawsuit that would expose it to an additional $100 of liability. It is technically solvent: it has liabilities, fairly discounted, of $99 and assets of $100. Nevertheless, its ordinary creditors may recognize that there is a 50–50 chance they will not be paid. Hence, they will be restless and may trigger the kind of destructive race to assets that a bankruptcy proceeding can prevent.[5]

Moreover, insolvency may not be easy to measure at the outset of the case. When confronting the question whether a debtor can be put into bankruptcy involuntarily, the Bankruptcy Code uses a different measure of financial distress. Creditors can put a debtor in bankruptcy involuntarily only if the debtor is unable to pay debts as they become due. This benchmark is much easier to apply than an insolvency measure, and it overlaps with it substantially. Most loans include terms that accelerate a debtor's obligations under circumstances when it is likely that the debtor's liabilities exceed its assets. When the second condition exists, the first tends to follow. At one time, we distinguished between these two benchmarks of financial distress by calling the first "insolvency in the bankruptcy sense" and the second "insolvency in the equity sense."

None of this, however, should suggest that those in good financial health make use of bankruptcy law. Bankruptcy law tracks nonbankruptcy law, and a solvent debtor must pay all its creditors 100 cents on the dollar. When an opportunity for abuse exists (when, for example, bankruptcy's procedures offer a way to force a favorable settlement of an irritating antitrust suit), courts are likely to dismiss the case on the ground that it was filed in bad faith.[6]

---

[5] See In re Johns-Manville, 36 Bankr. 727 (Bankr. S.D.N.Y. 1984).

[6] See In re SGL Carbon Corp., 200 F.3d 154 (3d Cir. 1999).

Chapter 3 of the Bankruptcy Code deals with case administration. Sections 301 through 307 tell us how a bankruptcy case begins. Sections 321 through 331 set out the rules governing those who administer the bankruptcy estate. The court must issue an order before the debtor can hire lawyers or other professionals. Under §329 attorneys must file a statement with the court showing how much they will be compensated and the source of the compensation, even if they do not ask the debtor for payment. In addition, Rule 2014 requires that lawyers disclose all their connections with the debtor, creditors, any other parties in interest, and their accountants. Such disclosure is needed to satisfy §327(a), which requires that the debtor's attorneys be disinterested.

The disinterestedness requirement complicates the job of any lawyer who wants to continue representing a corporate client after it files a bankruptcy petition. If a firm owes its lawyer anything for services provided before the petition, the lawyer may not be able to represent the firm in the bankruptcy proceeding. By virtue of being owed money, the lawyer is a creditor within the meaning of §101, and hence may no longer be disinterested. Similarly, a lawyer who is paid for services already rendered outside the ordinary course of business within ninety days before the filing of the petition may be subject to a voidable preference attack, and this may also keep the lawyer from being disinterested. A lawyer who represents any of the firm's directors or shareholders personally may not be able to represent the firm in bankruptcy. A lawyer who sits on the firm's board, or who has partners who sit on the board, may also fail to meet this requirement.

Even if a lawyer herself has had no previous relationship with the debtor or creditors, she must ensure that none of her associates or partners has worked for them, either. Although a lawyer is not disqualified solely because of past representation of a creditor, see §327(c), determining when a lawyer is disqualified is not always easy. Here, as elsewhere in bankruptcy, it is often useful to begin with the nonbankruptcy baseline. In this instance, however, even identifying that baseline is difficult. Nonbankruptcy conflicts rules turn on whether one is representing a client in a transaction or in ongoing litigation. In bankruptcy, much of what goes on is negotiation, but litigation with almost any party is possible.

In all events, disclosure must be full. When a court finds that a lawyer is not disinterested or has failed to make proper disclosure, it can disqualify the lawyer, disallow fees, and force the lawyer to bear the expenses of any investigation triggered by the failure to disclose. One court imposed a $1 million sanction for nondisclosure notwithstanding a finding that the firm had done its work well. Indeed, in the same opinion the court found the firm's work so crucial to the reorganization that it wanted the firm to continue working on the case.[7] Nondisclosure can, in the extreme case, trigger the criminal sanctions imposed by 18 U.S.C. §152(3) for knowingly and fraudulently making a false declaration in a bankruptcy case.[8]

The duty to disclose is an ongoing one. Suppose that during the course of a case, your partners acquired new clients or new issues arose. You might discover, for example, that some of the firm's directors have perpetrated a fraud. You now must investigate all the directors, including the ones that are independent. At this point, you have to check to find out whether any of your partners or associates has done work for the principal employers of these directors. You have a potential conflict if you must lead an investigation of someone who is a senior officer of a major client. Sensitivity to such issues varies across different judicial districts and even among judges within the same district. This is an area in which all lawyers, but particularly young lawyers, need to be especially vigilant.

In a Chapter 7 case, the provisions of §§321 through 331 must be read in conjunction with §§701 through 705. The principal officer in a Chapter 7 case is the bankruptcy trustee. The trustee acts as the representative of the bankruptcy estate and is charged with managing the assets of the debtor and protecting the rights of creditors and others. The trustee, for example, has the power to bring actions the debtor could have brought outside of bankruptcy. Similarly, in a Chapter 11 case, the provisions of §§321 through 331 must be read in conjunction with §§1101 through 1109. For example, in Chapter 11 cases there is usually no trustee; instead, under §1107 the debtor in possession takes on the duties and responsibilities of the trustee. Bankruptcy Code provisions authorizing the trustee to take certain actions apply with equal force to the debtor in possession. In the case of a corporation, the old managers of the debtor corporation act as debtor in possession. Thus, when §363 authorizes the trustee to use, lease, or sell assets of the estate in the ordinary course of business

---

[7] See In re Leslie Fay Companies, 175 Bankr. 525 (Bankr. S.D.N.Y. 1994). For a general discussion of the law, see Bank Brussels Lambert v. Coan, 176 F.3d 610 (2d Cir. 1999).

[8] United States v. Gellene, 182 F.3d 578 (7th Cir. 1999) (lawyer at prominent New York firm sentenced to fifteen months in prison for failing to disclose his firm's representation of a major secured creditor in another matter).

without first obtaining court approval, it is also authorizing the debtor in possession to do the same.

Sections 341 through 350 set out a number of basic procedures. One of the crucial moments in the life of a bankruptcy case is the initial meeting of creditors that §341 requires. In a Chapter 7 case, for example, the creditors elect a trustee during the §341 meeting. They also decide, under §705(a), whether to form a creditors committee to monitor the course of the case. The bankruptcy judge is forbidden from attending the §341 meeting. Under the 1898 Bankruptcy Act, bankruptcy judges became closely involved in the administration of the bankruptcy case. Many thought that this involvement prevented them from having the degree of detachment needed to decide disputes between the parties. Since 1978, however, increasing concerns about the length of many bankruptcy cases have led to a number of changes, principally in §105, that have allowed bankruptcy judges to expedite cases, such as by holding status conferences. Bankruptcy judges, however, are not reverting to their earlier roles as much as they are adopting the case management practices that have become commonplace in federal district courts.

Because even the simplest bankruptcy cases take time, rules are necessary to allow the trustee (and the debtor in possession) to act and to keep the creditors from taking matters into their own hands. These rules are largely the province of §§361 through 366. By far the most important of these sections is §362, which imposes an automatic stay on all creditors. It requires creditors to cease all debt collection efforts the moment a petition is filed. The automatic stay looms so large that it is easy to forget that the stay is simply a presumption. The court can lift the stay whenever a creditor shows that there is cause or that its interest is inadequately protected. Moreover, a court has the power under §105 to stay actions that do not come within the scope of §362 so long as a policy embraced in some other part of the Bankruptcy Code justifies it. Sections 363 and 364 authorize the trustee (and hence the debtor in possession in Chapter 11 cases) to sell, use, and lease property and to borrow money. When these transactions fall outside the ordinary course of business, however, the Bankruptcy Code requires notice and a hearing and may impose other requirements as well.

A crucial step in any bankruptcy case is to identify the claims against the debtor and the assets owned by the debtor. Chapter 5 of the Bankruptcy Code tells us how to go about doing this. Sections 501 through 510 focus on claims against the estate. Among other things, this part of the Bankruptcy Code embraces the idea that the general creditors must bear the costs the debtor incurs during the course of the bankruptcy case. Under §507(a)(1) these costs are paid off first, and the remainder is divided among the general creditors. These costs, called *administrative expense claims*, include the expenses of the bankruptcy proceeding proper and those of running the business in the meantime.

Section 506 addresses the rights of a creditor who has properly perfected a security interest in collateral. (*Perfection* has a singular meaning in bankruptcy. To have a perfected interest a creditor must ordinarily give the world notice of the property claim. A mortgagee must typically record its interest in the local real estate records. A creditor with a security interest in personal property must typically file a financing statement in the secretary of state's office.) Outside of bankruptcy, a creditor with a properly perfected security interest in collateral is entitled to be paid to the extent of the value of the collateral before other creditors. As a general matter, properly perfected secured creditors beat (or, to use the words lawyers commonly employ, *prime* or *trump*) the rights of general creditors in bankruptcy as well. The secured creditor, however, has a right to priority only to the extent of the *value* of its collateral. It may not be able to take possession of the collateral itself. If the collateral is worth more than the amount of the debt (that is, if the creditor is oversecured), the creditor has a secured claim equal to the amount of the debt. In addition, §506(b) allows the creditor to enjoy interest on its claim during bankruptcy and also to be paid any reasonable expenses it incurs. The oversecured creditor, however, must have obliged the debtor to pay for the expenses in the security agreement.[9]

If the collateral is worth less than the amount of the debt (that is, if the claim is undersecured), the claim is bifurcated under §506(a). The creditor has a secured claim equal to the value of the collateral and an unsecured claim for the difference. It also has rights against particular assets by virtue of its security interest in those assets. In a simple Chapter 7 liquidation, the security interest—the lien—may simply pass through bankruptcy.

Suppose a bank lends a debtor $100 and takes a security interest in a piece of real property that the debtor owns. A subsequent recession causes the property value to drop to $25, and the debtor files a Chapter 7 petition. Because the debt exceeds the value of the land, the trustee cannot possibly benefit the general creditors by keeping the

[9] See United States v. Ron Pair Enterprises, 489 U.S. 235 (1989).

property. The trustee may therefore give the property back (or *aban-don* it, to use the language of §554) to the debtor. The Bankruptcy Code provides that the debtor's personal liability to the bank and all other creditors is discharged. The bank, however, remains free to foreclose on the land once it is in the debtor's hands because the lien survives (or passes through) bankruptcy. The doctrine of lien pass-through was first set out in *Long v. Bullard*.[10] The scope of this principle of lien pass-through, however, is more limited than it might appear because of special treatment provided for liens in Chapters 11 and 13.

Sections 541 through 560 establish what assets the estate has. These provisions are built on the central idea that one must begin with the set of rights and obligations that exist outside of bankruptcy and then identify specific bankruptcy policies that require departing from the nonbankruptcy baseline. Section 541 defines the central concept of the *property of the estate*. The trustee (or the debtor in possession) is charged with assembling the assets that are available to meet the creditors' claims and then distributing them. These assets, called the property of the estate, form the bankruptcy estate. Section 541 draws a sharp distinction between individuals and corporations. The future income of individuals does not become property of the estate, while the future income of a corporation does. Drawing this distinction is a crucial feature of bankruptcy's fresh start for individual debtors and it is the focus of the next chapter of this book.

In many cases, property to which the creditors of a debtor are entitled is property to which a third party lays claim. In these cases, the trustee may have to bring an action to vindicate the creditors' right to the property. If the debtor itself could have brought the cause of action, the property is deemed property of the estate under §541. In other cases, the trustee must exercise one of the so-called avoiding powers. Section 544(a) is the "strong arm" power of the trustee. Using it the trustee may, for example, set aside unperfected security interests. A creditor who takes collateral may not be able to take the collateral in bankruptcy if it has failed to record its interest through a public filing.

The avoiding powers also allow the trustee to set aside fraudulent conveyances, a power creditors generally enjoy outside of bankruptcy. These include transfers made and obligations incurred for less than reasonably equivalent value while the debtor was insolvent.

[10]117 U.S. 617 (1886).

They also include transfers made and obligations incurred with the intent to hinder, delay, or defraud creditors. §548. Another provision allows the trustee to set aside transfers that were made to a creditor on the eve of bankruptcy. §547.

The general provisions of the Bankruptcy Code in Chapters 1, 3, and 5 are not perfectly organized. A number of provisions could well have been placed elsewhere. Section 108, for example, gives the trustee a grace period for taking certain actions. Because the consequences of failing to take action often turn on whether the automatic stay is implicated, this provision is best read in conjunction with §362. Section 365, which deals with executory contracts, is perhaps the provision most conspicuously out of place. Executory contracts inherently involve mutual rights and obligations between a debtor and a third party. They are best seen as combinations of claims and assets. Executory contracts are claims against the estate because they give a third party rights against the debtor. They are simultaneously assets of the estate because they give the debtor rights against a third party. Because both claims and assets fall within the ambit of Chapter 5 of the Bankruptcy Code, the section on executory contracts belongs there. The failure to put §365 in the correct place should not, in principle, affect how it is interpreted, but its faulty positioning may have compounded the difficulties lawyers and judges have had in applying it consistently.

As the Bankruptcy Code has aged it has become increasingly fragmented, in part because of interest groups' success in obtaining amendments to it. Some sections that were once coherent have become long laundry lists. One cannot rely on first principles to explain why, for example, United States fishers deserve special protection from the trustee's avoiding powers in §546 or why HUD's debt collection efforts should be exempted from the automatic stay. When a federal agency is involved in a bankruptcy case, one needs to be especially alert to the possibility that the agency's enabling statute gives it special privileges in bankruptcy. Bankruptcy-specific provisions, however, can exist in other parts of federal law as well.

Some of the amendments that protect specific interests do reflect sound bankruptcy policy, but the groups that advance them do not invest the energy in pushing for their application across the board. An unsound lower court decision may lead to an amendment that protects a particular group in similar circumstances in the future. Courts, however, may invoke the maxim of *expressio unius*, holding that Congress meant for the unsound lower court opinion to become the rule for everyone else. Technology licensing is perhaps the most conspicuous example of a misguided opinion leading to a safe harbor—in this case for one type of executory contract—while also leading courts astray everywhere else.[11]

These problems should not cause us to lose sight of the big picture. One cannot look at the Bankruptcy Code in isolation. A general mandate, reinforced by 28 U.S.C. §959, requires that the trustee act in accordance with applicable nonbankruptcy law. A trustee enjoys the right to use property under §363, but the trustee must act consistently with applicable nonbankruptcy law. The trustee cannot use the debtor's chemistry laboratory to manufacture cocaine, nor may the trustee dump toxic waste on the debtor's property, not because of anything in the Bankruptcy Code but simply because these activities are illegal outside of bankruptcy.

The remaining chapters in Title 11 set out the different kinds of bankruptcy cases. As mentioned above, Chapter 9 is reserved for municipalities. Under §101, *municipality* means any political subdivision or public agency or instrumentality of a state. In addition to cities and towns, debtors in Chapter 9 may include water and power districts. Chapter 9 has not been widely used since the Great Depression, but cases involving it still do arise: one of the important bankruptcies of the 1990s was the case of Orange County in the wake of its speculative investments in derivatives and other exotic securities. The provisions of Chapter 9 are neither long nor complicated. What is most important to a lawyer handling a case under Chapter 9 is identifying what general provisions of the Bankruptcy Code apply in that chapter.

Individuals and corporations can usually choose to file under one of several different chapters. An individual debtor will most often choose Chapter 7 or Chapter 13. An ordinary corporation can file either a Chapter 7 petition or a Chapter 11 petition. The kind of bankruptcy petition that is brought depends on the goals of the person filing the petition. The court, however, enjoys a broad power to convert a case brought under one chapter into a case brought under another. Moreover, under §706(a) the debtor can convert a case that creditors file under Chapter 7 to one under Chapter 11.

As we will discover below in chapter 2, bankruptcy law gives the honest but unfortunate flesh-and-blood debtor the right to a fresh start. An individual who is hopelessly in debt can file a Chapter 7 bankruptcy petition, give up all nonexempt assets, and walk away

---

[11] For a discussion of the so-called *Lubrizol* problem, see p. 119 below.

from nearly all prebankruptcy obligations. Section 727 gives this debtor a *discharge*. Because future income of an individual does not become property of the estate under §541, the effect of §727 is to give the individual debtor the right to enjoy future income free of creditors' claims. Section 726 sets out how the debtor's property is divided among the creditors, but this section and others dealing with the administration of the estate in Chapter 7 often have little relevance in the case of the individual debtor. Many individuals filing Chapter 7 have no assets. The issue to litigate in these cases is the scope of bankruptcy's fresh start policy, not the division of the spoils among the creditors.

Chapter 13 also provides individuals with a substantive fresh start, but it takes a different shape. Chapter 13 allows an individual to keep all assets, but in return the debtor must create a plan under which creditors receive as much out of the debtor's future income as they would have received had the debtor filed under Chapter 7. The existence of Chapter 13 has led to a number of calls for reform. In modern times the largest asset for most individuals is the ability to earn money in the future. Perhaps for this reason, in recent years Congress has considered changing the way in which relief is given to debtors so that Chapter 7 would not be generally available. Instead, many individual debtors would have to repay at least a portion of what they owe creditors out of their disposable income for a number of years.

The question whether a debtor is entitled to all future earnings already arises under existing law. Section 707(b) allows the bankruptcy judge to deny a fresh start to consumer debtors "if granting of relief would be a substantial abuse." Courts must ask whether debtors with a high earning potential and an ability to pay back a substantial portion of what they owe engage in a substantial abuse when they invoke the bankruptcy laws, even if an accident or some other misfortune placed them in their current condition.

Like individuals, corporations may file under Chapter 7. In many cases, a corporation finds itself in Chapter 7 only after first having tried unsuccessfully to reorganize under Chapter 11. See §1112(b). These cases have nothing to do with giving an individual a fresh start. Chapter 7 offers no discharge to a corporation. In the typical corporate Chapter 7 case, the firm has ceased its operations or will cease them in short order. Any assets remaining after the secured creditors have taken what they can will usually go to the tax collector, who enjoys a special priority under §507(a)(8). The purpose of allowing corporations to file Chapter 7 petitions is not to give creditors assets but to assure creditors that the corporation has no assets. A Chapter

7 petition is the easiest way for corporate managers who are being constantly harassed to convince the firm's creditors that the firm has no assets and that their lawsuits are pointless. The bankruptcy process can offer scrutiny of the debtor's overall health that no individual creditor can match.

The Bankruptcy Code does not require that a firm in Chapter 7 be liquidated in the sense that all assets are broken up and sold piecemeal. To the contrary, the trustee is obliged to sell the assets for as much as possible, and sometimes this means selling the assets together as a going concern. In practice, however, we rarely see going-concern liquidations in Chapter 7. Corporate managers prefer the control and the presumption of continued operation that exists in Chapter 11. They will not file a Chapter 7 petition so long as they harbor any hope for the firm. If creditors seek to put the firm into Chapter 7 involuntarily, the managers will ordinarily be able to convert to a Chapter 11 case so long as they can show that the firm has a chance of survival.

Chapter 11 is the vehicle designed to straighten out the affairs of firms in financial distress. When the firm cannot continue as a going concern, Chapter 11 provides a mechanism for shutting it down and sorting out its financial affairs in a coherent way.[12] Chapter 11 is better suited than Chapter 7 for firms that are dissolving when there are problems beyond the simple sale of assets. Consider the following case. Apart from a secured creditor that has repossessed its collateral, the only other creditor is the Internal Revenue Service, which is owed Federal Insurance Contributions Act (FICA) and withholding taxes. The owner-managers of the business are personally (and potentially criminally) liable for these taxes, and they have filed Chapter 11 petitions as well. (Individuals are eligible for Chapter 11 relief, but apart from cases in which the debtor's affairs are tied up with those of a business, Chapter 13 or Chapter 7 is a more attractive place to resolve their financial problems.) We need to sort out who is going to pay what and on what schedule. In such situations, Chapter 11 is often the forum of choice for both the debtors and the IRS. If no one asks for the case to be dismissed or converted, the court is unlikely to do so.

In other cases, the firm as a whole may have no future, but discrete divisions may be salable. Chapter 11 is a mechanism that allows for

---

[12] See Samuel L. Bufford, What Is Right About Bankruptcy Law and Wrong About Its Critics, 72 Wash. U. L.Q. 829 (1994).

such sales and gives buyers confidence that they will acquire clean title. Finally, Chapter 11 provides a forum for a firm that will be kept in intact but needs a new capital structure. Past misfortunes may have left it unable to meet its obligations, but its assets are being put to their best use. By scaling back the firm's fixed obligations the creditors as a group are left better off.

Chapter 11 replaced Chapters x, xi, and xii of the old Bankruptcy Act. (The convention is to use Roman numerals for chapters of the 1898 Act and Arabic numerals for those of the 1978 Code.) In Chapter 11, the debtor in possession rather than the trustee ordinarily continues to run the firm. In many Chapter 11 cases, the assets are subject to the security interest of one large creditor. In such situations the general creditors are likely to play only a small role, if any. When the debtor is a substantial operating firm with a decent chance of survival as a going concern, enough may be at stake so that the general creditors will play an active role.

In theory, the United States Trustee chooses a committee of creditors at the start of every Chapter 11 case, but the committee is active only in cases in which enough is at stake. Section 1102(b) suggests that the creditors committee consist of creditors who hold the seven largest claims and are willing to serve. In practice, however, the United States Trustee often attempts to find a "representative" creditors committee. The creditors committee in Chapter 11 may also consist of the members of a committee organized by creditors before the case begins, if that committee is fairly chosen and represents the different kinds of claims that exist. The United States Trustee thus often looks well beyond the seven largest creditors because they may look more like each other than the class of general creditors as a whole. In the largest cases, there may be multiple committees of creditors as well as a committee of the equityholders.

Serving on a creditors committee can be a mixed blessing. Doing so ensures that one is close to the action and knows what is going on. But one may receive information that the debtor considers confidential, and this may interfere with a creditor's ability to act (such as its ability to sell its claim). Moreover, service on the committee is time consuming. Creditors committees in Chapter 11 cases (unlike committees in Chapter 7) can retain professionals such as lawyers and accountants, and the cost of hiring them is an administrative expense entitled to priority under §507. The creditors themselves, however, are not compensated for their efforts. Moreover, as a member of the committee, a creditor is charged with looking out not only for its own interests but also for those of the other general creditors.

Section 1104 allows the court to appoint an examiner, who may be given the powers of the trustee; the United States Trustee chooses the examiner, subject to court approval. An examiner may be retained simply to act as a mediator between the various factions. Examiners are sometimes appointed to investigate whether the debtor should bring a cause of action (such as a fraudulent conveyance action against shareholders) that the debtor in possession might not pursue as vigorously because of its conflict of interest.

One of the debtor's most important rights in Chapter 11 may be its exclusive right to propose a plan of reorganization for the first 120 days after the filing of the petition. If the debtor does not do this and the court does not grant an extension to the debtor, creditors are free to propose their own plans under §1121(b). If the debtor does propose a plan, it has another sixty days to secure its acceptance under §1121(c)(3). If more than one plan meets all the rules of Chapter 11, then §1129(c) directs the bankruptcy judge to consider the "preferences of creditors and equity security holders in determining which plan to confirm." The debtor can ask to have the exclusivity period extended, and creditors can ask to have it shortened. Terminating the exclusivity period can lead to the proposal and eventual confirmation of a liquidating plan of reorganization. From the perspective of a secured creditor, terminating exclusivity in such a case has the same effect as lifting the automatic stay.

In the first years of the Bankruptcy Code, extensions of the exclusivity period were granted as a matter of routine, often for years on end. In recent years courts have been more reluctant to leave matters to the debtor and more willing to cut the exclusivity period short or bring things to a close by lifting the automatic stay. Recognizing that they lack the ability to gather detailed information about a firm's operations, bankruptcy judges ensure that sensible decisions are made about the firm's assets by establishing clear benchmarks and taking decisive action when the debtor fails to meet them. At the start of the case, the principal lender may ask that the stay be lifted so it can foreclose on the collateral. The debtor's managers might argue that the stay should continue because the business can be sold as a going concern to another firm. The bankruptcy judge might turn down the secured creditor's lift-stay motion but rule that the motion will be granted six weeks hence if no buyer appears in the interim. In addition, objective markers suggesting that a firm is losing value, such as a failure to cover operating expenses or to pay insurance, taxes, or payroll, will lead the judge to dismiss or convert the case upon an appropriate motion. Such benchmarks, particularly those that the debtor sets for itself, allow the bankruptcy judge to exercise control without needing special knowledge or expertise.

Parties in Chapter 11 cases spend much of their time negotiating with one another, and §§1122 through 1129 establish the structure for these negotiations. These sections set out the procedural rights of all the players and their substantive rights in the event they fail to reach agreement. These various rights, the most important of which are in §1129, embody a general principle known as the *absolute priority rule*. This rule ensures that creditors in bankruptcy are paid according to their nonbankruptcy priorities, but it also has a large procedural component and its exact contours are complicated. The debtor's ability to impose a plan over the creditors' objection by satisfying the absolute priority rule is known aptly as the debtor's *cramdown* power.

Sections 1141 through 1146 govern the discharge of old claims and the implementation of the reorganization plan. Just as the discharge provision of §727 in the case of the individual debtor had to be read in conjunction with the exclusion of individual income from property of the estate under §541, the discharge provision in §1141 must be read in conjunction with the absolute priority rule. Together, the discharge of debt and the absolute priority rule implement the central aim of Chapter 11. They ensure that firms worth keeping intact remain so, despite the incentives each creditor has to look out for its own interest rather than the collective interest of all the creditors.

The Bankruptcy Forum

The Bankruptcy Code is designed so that the debtor's affairs can be sorted out in a single forum. Unlike a federal court sitting in a diversity case, the bankruptcy court has nationwide jurisdiction. Even a creditor who does not have the minimum contacts with California to make it amenable to suit in state court must still file its claim in the bankruptcy court in California if the debtor has chosen to file its petition there.[13] Indeed, many large bankruptcy cases are now filed in Delaware because proper venue for filing a bankruptcy petition includes state of incorporation and many large firms are incorporated under Delaware law.[14]

A number of constraints prevent the goal of a single forum from being fully realized. As our economy becomes increasingly global,

[13] See Harder v. Desert Breezes Master Association, 192 Bankr. 47 (N.D.N.Y. 1996).

[14] See 28 U.S.C. §1408.

firms are likely to have assets and creditors that are in multiple jurisdictions and thus beyond the power of the bankruptcy court.
Moreover, the law governing transnational bankruptcy is still largely
unformed. Section 304 of the Bankruptcy Code responds to problems that arise when an insolvency proceeding is brought against a
debtor in another country but many of its assets and creditors are located in this country. The creditors may want to vindicate their
rights in this country rather than pursue them abroad, but a representative from a foreign insolvency proceeding may file an ancillary case
under §304, asking the bankruptcy judge to enjoin creditors from
doing so. The court must balance the interests of comity (that is, respecting another legal system as well as the desirability of ensuring an
"economical and expeditious administration" of the foreign estate)
against the cost and inconvenience of forcing U.S. creditors to vindicate their rights in a remote and potentially inhospitable place.

The bankruptcy judge may be satisfied that the foreign insolvency
regime is not repugnant to the Bankruptcy Code and that U.S. creditors will not face discrimination in the distant forum. In such cases,
the judge is likely to exercise the power granted by §304 to stay the
collection efforts of creditors.[15] When the foreign proceeding does
not include fundamental guarantees of due process, however, defer-
ence will not be given to the foreign proceeding.[16] Left unresolved is
the appropriate treatment under §304 when the process is fair but
the substantive distributional rules depart significantly from those of
the Bankruptcy Code.

What happens when a large corporation has assets outside the
United States? Although there exists a general presumption against
applying U.S. statutes in foreign countries,[17] the bankruptcy estate
created by §541 extends to the debtor's entire property, wherever located. Thus, a U.S. citizen may not use the courts in a foreign jurisdiction to exercise control over a debtor in bankruptcy whose corporate headquarters is in the United States.[18] Similarly, a foreign credi-

---

[15] See, e.g., Haarhuis v. Kunnan Enterprises, Ltd., 177 F.3d 1007 (D.C. Cir. 1999)
(enjoining a breach of contract action in this country in light of an ongoing reorganization in Taiwan).

[16] See, e.g., In re Hourani, 180 Bankr. 58 (Bankr. S.D.N.Y. 1995) (court denies
relief to foreign representative when forum established by martial law provides insufficient assurance that process will be reasonable and fair).

[17] See EEOC v. Arabian American Oil Co., 499 U.S. 244, 248 (1991).

[18] See, e.g., Underwood v. Hilliard, 98 F.3d 956 (7th Cir. 1996); Hong Kong and
Shanghai Banking Corp. v. Simon, 153 F.3d 991 (9th Cir. 1998).

tor cannot pursue the collection of a debt discharged in bankruptcy, at least not if that creditor has assets in this country and subjected itself to the bankruptcy court's jurisdiction.

A multinational corporation may have its corporate headquarters in one jurisdiction, the bulk of its assets in another, and its creditors in another still. When the firm encounters financial distress, creditors (or the debtor itself) may bring an insolvency action in more than one jurisdiction. Suppose a parent corporation headquartered in Great Britain uses assets of its U.S. subsidiary to repay a French bank several weeks before entering bankruptcy proceedings in both Great Britain and the United States. The person charged with representing the firm's creditors (the trustee or debtor in possession under U.S. law) wants to recover the payment made to the bank. The insolvency laws of Great Britain, like those of the United States, limit creditors' ability to enjoy preferential payments on the eve of bankruptcy. Because the contours of British law are slightly different from those of the United States, the debtor has a better chance of success under U.S. law.

This situation presents two distinct questions: First, is the debtor is free to bring the action in either forum? Second, will the court hearing the action apply its own law, the law of the other jurisdiction, or a mixture of the two? The court might, for example, permit the preference action if either jurisdiction allowed it or only if both did.[19]

The ability to sort out the debtor's affairs in a single forum is limited even if the firm's activities stay within domestic borders. First, Article III of the U.S. Constitution limits what bankruptcy judges can do given that they do not have life tenure. Second, the jury trial right in the Seventh Amendment limits the ability to resolve disputes expeditiously. Third, the sovereign immunity a state enjoys under the Eleventh Amendment limits the bankruptcy court's power to resolve disputes even when the state is merely asserting its rights as a creditor. Let's look at each of these constitutional limitations more closely.

In eighteenth-century England, the Chancellor appointed commissioners to do much of the work of gathering and administering a bankruptcy estate. Because they were not judges, what these commissioners did cannot be considered an exercise of the judicial power.

---

[19] For one effort to sort through such issues, see Maxwell Communication Corp. v. Société Générale, 93 F.3d 1036 (2d Cir. 1996).

Modern bankruptcy judges likewise oversee the administration of the bankruptcy estate. They do not enjoy lifelong appointments and cannot exercise judicial power within the meaning of Article III.[20] Disappointed litigants have a right to de novo review in the district courts for matters that are not central to the administration of the bankruptcy case. But for matters that are central to the case, litigants are entitled only to appellate review. A second rationale for limiting the judges' power rests on an idea imported from administrative law. Because bankruptcy law is created entirely by Congress, a ruling under it (as opposed to a decision on matters involving other legal issues) constitutes an adjudication of public rights that an Article III judge need not decide.[21]

The Seventh Amendment requires that the right to a jury trial be preserved in federal court for suits at common law when the amount in controversy exceeds twenty dollars. Many of the questions in a bankruptcy case, including whether a particular person has a claim against the debtor, would be the basis of suits at common law if brought outside of bankruptcy. It does not follow, however, that all such claims give rise to a right to a jury trial. A bankruptcy court is a court of equity, and it has the right to use "chancery methods" to decide matters that are central to the bankruptcy process.[22] Other actions, such as fraudulent conveyance suits against third parties, retain their common law character and must be tried by jury unless both parties consent to have the judge decide the dispute.[23] Under 28 U.S.C. §157(e), if a right to a jury trial exists, the bankruptcy judge may conduct the trial only by special designation of the district judge and only if the parties again give their express consent.

The Constitution affects the forum in which bankruptcy disputes are tried in a third way. A state can also appear as a simple creditor. For example, it may allege that the debtor owes sales taxes. Alternatively, the debtor may argue that a provision of the Bankruptcy Code, such as §1146, entitles it to a refund of taxes it has already paid. Were the state a private party, it would, of course, be subject to the power of the bankruptcy court. A state, however, is immune from suit un-

[20] See Northern Pipeline Construction Co. v. Marathon Pipe Line Co., 458 U.S. 50 (1982).

[21] See Crowell v. Benson, 285 U.S. 22 (1932).

[22] See Barton v. Barbour, 104 U.S. 126, 134 (1881).

[23] Granfinanciera v. Nordberg, 492 U.S. 33 (1989).

der the Eleventh Amendment unless it waives its sovereign immunity, and waivers of sovereign immunity are not lightly inferred.[24]

In *Gardner v. New Jersey*, the Supreme Court held that "[w]hen the State becomes the actor and files a claim against the fund, it waives any immunity which it otherwise might have had respecting the adjudication of the claim."[25] Section 106(b) of the Bankruptcy Code reflects the doctrine of *Gardner*, and *Gardner* may still be good law.[26] States may avoid this disadvantage by choosing not to file a claim in bankruptcy court or by filing a claim that is unconnected with the action that the debtor wants to bring against it. The broad language of §106(a) likely reaches beyond Congress's power over states (but not other governmental entities). A state is not subject to the power of the bankruptcy court unless it has filed a claim with the bankruptcy court and the matter in dispute is tightly bound with the resolution of this claim.[27]

For all these reasons, the debtor's affairs may not all be resolved in a single forum. Nevertheless, most of what we shall study plays out in the bankruptcy court and is subject only to appellate review. It is useful to spend some time to see how the rules of procedure bring this about, despite the limitations outlined above.

Federal district courts have original and exclusive jurisdiction over all "cases" under Title 11.[28] The entire process the bankruptcy petition triggers is considered a "case" and thus may be filed only in a federal district court (as opposed to, say, a state court). Section 1334 also gives the district courts original (but not exclusive) jurisdiction over all "civil proceedings" arising under Title 11 or arising in or related to cases under Title 11. A controversy such as a fraudulent conveyance action that takes place in the course of settling a debtor's affairs is considered a "proceeding."

---

[24] See Florida Prepaid Postsecondary Education Expense Board v. College Savings Bank, 527 U.S. 627 (1999); College Savings Bank v. Florida Prepaid Postsecondary Education Expense Board, 527 U.S. 666 (1999).

[25] 329 U.S. 565, 573–74 (1947).

[26] See California Franchise Tax Board v. Jackson, 184 F.3d 1046 (9th Cir. 1999); Georgia Department of Revenue v. Burke, 146 F.3d 1313 (11th Cir. 1998); DeKalb County Division of Family and Children Services v. Platter, 140 F.3d 676 (7th Cir. 1998).

[27] See Mitchell v. Franchise Tax Board, 209 F.3d 1111 (9th Cir. 2000); In re NVR, 189 F.3d 442 (4th Cir. 1999).

[28] 28 U.S.C. §1334.

Bankruptcy jurisdiction can extend to parties who are neither creditors nor debtors when the dispute is related to a case under Title 11. The reach of related jurisdiction has been broadly defined. Courts sometimes seem to ask simply "whether the outcome of the proceeding could conceivably have any effect upon the estate being administered in bankruptcy."[29] A claim that a creditor has against a guarantor of the debtor that would have no impact on the estate is an example of an action that falls outside the jurisdictional reach of §1334.

Bankruptcy courts are adjuncts of the district courts, and §1334 must be read in conjunction with §157(a) of Title 28. Section 157 allows the district court to "refer" any or all bankruptcy cases to bankruptcy judges. It also provides that the district court may refer any or all proceedings arising under the Bankruptcy Code, or arising in or related to a bankruptcy case, to bankruptcy judges. In all district courts this practice is firmly institutionalized. Bankruptcy petitions are, as a practical matter, filed in the bankruptcy courts. The purpose of this circumlocution is to ensure that the dictates of Article III are satisfied. The bankruptcy judge is not acting autonomously and is not exercising judicial power because the bankruptcy judge is merely an adjunct to the district court. Just as a court of equity can appoint a special master, the reasoning goes, the district court can choose to delegate bankruptcy cases to bankruptcy judges.

The idea that the district courts have jurisdiction over bankruptcy cases and proceedings is not entirely a formal fiction. Although everything is routinely referred to the bankruptcy courts, §157(d) gives the district judge the power to withdraw the reference in any particular case or proceeding, in whole or in part, for cause. The district court can act either on its own motion or on a timely motion of any party. Although district courts rarely want to hear bankruptcy disputes, they have withdrawn the reference in some important cases.

Withdrawal of the reference is mandatory after a timely motion when "resolution of the proceeding requires consideration of both Title 11 and other laws of the United States regulating organizations or activities affecting interstate commerce." This provision has been read narrowly, as it must be, given that so many disputes in a bankruptcy case involve consideration of federal laws that affect interstate commerce. Courts frequently use a substantial-and-material test:

---

[29] Kelley v. Nodine, 783 F.2d 626, 634 (6th Cir. 1986). See Lindsey v. O'Brien (In re Dow Corning Corp.), 86 F.3d 482 (6th Cir. 1996).

withdrawal is mandatory only when the issues presented require a significant interpretation of federal laws, not when what is presented is the straightforward application of federal law to a particular set of facts. A difficult controversy involving the reach of CERCLA or some other equally complex statute is potentially a subject of mandatory withdrawal, but even then the district court may remand to the bankruptcy court for submission of proposed findings of fact and conclusions of law under §157(c)(1).

Once a case is referred to a bankruptcy judge, many decisions are subject only to appellate review by the district court. Section 157 tells us that bankruptcy judges "may hear and determine all cases under the Bankruptcy Code" referred to them, subject to appellate review under 28 U.S.C. §158. *Case* is used in the technical sense here and refers only to the process that begins with the bankruptcy petition. Individual disputes arise during the debtor's course through bankruptcy are *proceedings*. When these proceedings are central to the administration of the case (or, to use the term in Title 28, when they are *core*), the bankruptcy judge is again subject only to appellate review. Core proceedings include confirmation of plans, matters concerning the administration of the estate, and the allowance or disallowance of claims against the estate. Section 157(b)(2) contains a list of core proceedings, but this list is not by its terms exhaustive.

What remains are noncore proceedings. A typical example is a lawsuit that the debtor has filed against some third party. For these, the bankruptcy judge is subject to de novo review. The bankruptcy judge must submit proposed findings of fact and conclusions of law to the district court. The district court can make a final order only after reviewing de novo those matters to which a party has objected.

Under 28 U.S.C. §158(a), the district courts have appellate review of final judgments, orders, and decrees from the bankruptcy court. The district courts also have jurisdiction to hear appeals from interlocutory orders and decrees, but in these cases leave of the court is required. It is not clear whether this means parties must obtain permission of the bankruptcy judge, the district judge, or both.

The courts of appeals have jurisdiction to hear appeals from final decisions, judgments, orders, and decrees under 28 U.S.C. §158(d). Determining a final judgment for purposes of 28 U.S.C. §158(d) has proven difficult. Suppose there is a final judgment in the bankruptcy court, and the district court hears the appeal and remands to the bankruptcy court. Courts are divided on whether an appeal can be taken to the court of appeals. Section 158(d) does not tell us explicitly whether it is sufficient that the bankruptcy judge's decision be final or whether the district court's decision must be final as well. Most courts recognize that a district court's order generally is not final if it remands the dispute to the bankruptcy court, especially if the remand requires the bankruptcy court to make factual findings or exercise its discretion.[30]

The uncertainty in the meaning of finality in §158(d) can put lawyers in the awkward position of having to choose between appealing a decision that may prove to be interlocutory or waiving the right altogether if it later proves to have been a final order. Section 158(d), however, does not displace the ordinary rules governing appeals from the district court, and §1292(b) mitigates this problem to some extent. This section allows a court of appeals, in its discretion, to review an interlocutory order, provided the district judge finds that at issue is a controlling question of law as to which there is substantial ground for difference of opinion and that an immediate appeal may materially advance the ultimate termination of the litigation.[31]

This review of appellate review of bankruptcy court decisions, however, is somewhat misleading. Appellate review takes time, and most of the important decisions in a bankruptcy case—whether the firm should be shut down or whether the managers should be given another month to turn the operation around—are time sensitive and thus essentially unreviewable. How long to wait before taking action becomes a moot point well before the appellate court can hear the case. When a bankruptcy court approves an asset sale or lease transfer, those who object have no chance of having the decision overturned unless the sale itself is stayed pending the appeal. Even if the case is not formally moot (and it often will be),[32] the reversal of the decision does not itself affect the validity of the sale. See §363(m). Similarly, reversal on appeal of an order approving debtor-in-possession financing does not affect the rights of the postpetition extender of credit who acts in good faith, and appeals of such orders are often moot because a court can fashion no meaningful relief.[33] Such provisions are necessary to enable debtors to sell assets or borrow while the case is pending. No one will do business with a debtor in bankruptcy if deals can be undone after the fact.

[30] See Stuart v. Koch, 109 F.3d 1285 (8th Cir. 1997).

[31] Connecticut National Bank v. Germain, 503 U.S. 249 (1992).

[32] See L.R.S.C. Co. v. Rickel Home Centers, 209 F.3d 291 (3d Cir. 2000).

[33] Boullioun Aircraft Holding Co. v. Smith Management, 181 F.3d 1191 (10th Cir. 1999).

The practical effect of all this is to grant the bankruptcy judge enormous power. From the perspective of financial institutions that have done business with the debtor in the past and expect to continue to do business with it, Chapter 11 is an attractive venue only if the decisions of the bankruptcy judge are predictable. For this reason among others, Delaware has become the venue of choice for many large firms in bankruptcy.

The Bankruptcy Rules establish the procedures used in the bankruptcy courts. They do not change the substantive rules of the Bankruptcy Code, but they do affect how the issues are shaped. For example, they distinguish the types of hearings that take place before the bankruptcy judge. One type of hearing, called an *adversary proceeding*, is conducted under much the same rules as any other civil dispute. Many sections of the Federal Rules of Civil Procedure that govern pleading, joinder, depositions, interrogatories, and summary judgment have been incorporated into the bankruptcy rules governing adversary proceedings. We learn from Bankruptcy Rule 7001 that adversary proceedings include those to compel someone other than the debtor to deliver property to the trustee, to determine the validity of a lien, to object to a discharge, or to obtain an injunction or equitable relief.

Whenever an actual dispute before the bankruptcy court is not an adversary proceeding, it is a *contested matter*. Among the most common is a motion to lift the automatic stay. The procedures for contested matters are more streamlined and are set out in Bankruptcy Rule 9014. For example, no response is required in a contested matter unless the court orders an answer to a motion. The court, however, has the power to invoke the more elaborate rules for adversary proceedings in contested matters when appropriate.

Bankruptcy courts also have the inherent power under §105 to impose sanctions in order to maintain control of their courtrooms and of their dockets.[34] Moreover, Rule 11 or its counterpart under the Bankruptcy Rules, Rule 9011, is available at every stage of bankruptcy litigation. In addition, §362(h) of the Bankruptcy Code explicitly grants the bankruptcy court the power to award actual and punitive damages to an individual injured by any violation of the automatic stay.[35]

---

[34] See In re Volpert, 110 F.3d 494 (7th Cir. 1997); Caldwell v. Unified Capital Corp. (In re Rainbow Magazine), 77 F.3d 278 (9th Cir. 1996).

[35] Courts, however, are divided on whether "individual" in this context means only flesh-and-blood human beings. Compare Maritime Asbestos Legal Clinic v.

In the next two chapters, we switch our focus to the two major principles that animate bankruptcy law—the fresh start policy for individual debtors and the absolute priority rule for corporate debtors. We then return to look at various provisions of the Bankruptcy Code in more detail.

LTV Steel Co., 920 F.2d 183 (2d Cir. 1990), and Jove Engineering v. Internal Revenue Service, 92 F.3d 1539 (11th Cir. 1996), with Cuffee v. Atlantic Business & Community Corp., 901 F.2d 325 (3d Cir. 1990).

Chapter Two

The Individual Debtor and the Fresh Start

Creditor Remedies and Debtor Rights

We live in a society in which extensions of credit are woven into the fabric of everyday life. The telephone company becomes our creditor every time we make a call; we become indebted to the electric company every time we turn on a light switch. Few of us could pay for our education or buy a house if credit were not readily available. Although it is a fact easily overlooked in the study of bankruptcy law, most people pay back every penny they owe.[1] Creditors seldom have to resort to the legal process. Many, if not most, people pay their debts not because of the threat of legal compulsion but because they care about their reputation. They do not want to carry the stigma of being a deadbeat. Others repay their debts simply out of a feeling of moral obligation.

Not everyone is honest, however, and some would not repay their debts if creditors did not have the ability (even if usually unexercised) to call on the state to coerce repayment. Without the ability to enforce their rights, creditors would be less willing to lend. Nevertheless, those who fail to pay their creditors are most often not those who are dishonest but rather those who find themselves in dire financial straits caused by circumstances ranging from improvidence to bad luck. For this reason, American law has always put limits on creditors' ability to use the legal process.

In the seventeenth century, English law frequently treated debtors as miscreants who deserved whatever fate befell them. As one judge of the period observed:

---

[1] This point is easy tc show. If a lender is to survive, it must set its interest rate at a level that accounts for default. The component of interest that compensates lenders for the risk of default therefore cannot exceed the difference between the rate they charge and the risk-free rate, the rate the U.S. government must pay its creditors. This difference rarely exceeds 10 percent. Hence, lenders could not survive unless they were paid back at least ninety cents on every dollar lent. In fact, they receive much more.

> If a man be taken in execution, and lie in prison for debt, neither the plaintiff, at whose suit he is arrested, nor the sheriff who took him, is bound to find him meat, drink, or clothes; but he must live on his own, or on the charity of others; and if no man will relieve him, let him die in the name of God, says the law; and so say I.[2]

Even in the seventeenth and eighteenth centuries, however, American lawmakers tried to balance the rights of creditors and debtors. They wanted creditors to be confident enough that they would be repaid to lend in the first place, but our lawmakers also wanted to protect debtors from excessively zealous creditors. Laws governing creditors' ability to use law to recover what they were owed have always been tempered with a concern for the debtor's procedural and substantive rights.

In colonial America, a debtor's greatest procedural protection lay in the right to insist on a trial by *a jury of the vicinage*, a jury chosen from among the debtor's neighbors. The debtor's right to insist on a jury trial under state law and the absence of any similar guarantee in the federal Constitution was a focal point of the ratification debates in 1788 and 1789 and was in large part responsible for the Bill of Rights.[3] Today a debtor's procedural protections lie elsewhere.

Due process requires that a debtor have an opportunity to be heard. A general creditor cannot unilaterally seize the debtor's property after declaring a default. The debtor must have the chance to appear in court and contest the creditor's claim that there has in fact been a default. A secured creditor may seize collateral without going to court first, but only if it can do so without a *breach of the peace*. A secured creditor may repossess a car that is parked on the street, but the secured creditor cannot enter the debtor's premises without permission or without first going to court. Once a secured creditor repossesses assets, the subsequent sale must follow the procedures set down in Article 9 of the Uniform Commercial Code. A creditor who fails to follow these procedures is liable for any losses arising from its actions. In addition, the secured creditor may also lose its right to a

---

[2] These observations of Justice Sir Robert Hyde are quoted in Peter J. Coleman, Debtors and Creditors in America: Insolvency, Imprisonment for Debt and Bankruptcy, 1607–1900, at 5 (1974).

[3] The importance of debtor–creditor relations in the debates over the Constitution and the adoption of the Bill of Rights is recounted in Charles W. Wolfram, The Constitutional History of the Seventh Amendment, 57 Minn. L. Rev. 639 (1973).

deficiency judgment, its right to sue the debtor and recover the amount by which the proceeds from the sale of the collateral fall short of the amount of the debt. Other laws limit coercive debt collection practices such as harassing telephone calls to the debtor, the debtor's family, or the debtor's employer.

In addition to enjoying procedural protections, the debtor also enjoys a set of substantive rights. These, too, have changed and expanded over time. Even in colonial America, creditors were not able to reach all of a debtor's property through the judicial process.[4] Laws that exempted some property from creditor seizure (or *levy*) became widespread in the nineteenth century. Among the most common were statutes preventing a creditor from seizing the debtor's homestead. Laws also protected the debtor's tools of trade, as well as assets, such as clothes and household furnishings, that had little value in anyone else's hands. Laws limiting creditors' ability to reach a debtor's paycheck also became commonplace. Today nearly all states sharply curtail a creditor's ability to garnish wages, the procedure by which creditors force employers (or other third parties) to give them money that such parties would otherwise pay the debtor.

These laws form the backdrop against which bankruptcy works for individual debtors. Outside bankruptcy, creditors are limited in what they can do. A creditor cannot take the clothes off the debtor's back, nor can the creditor take so much of the debtor's paycheck that not enough is left to provide for the debtor and the debtor's family. Modern exemption statutes also insulate pension funds and the like from creditors' reach, and other state and federal statutes, although not formally denominated as exemption statutes, have the same effect. Creditors, for example, cannot garnish social security checks. The income social security gives a debtor is in effect an asset of the debtor that creditors cannot reach.

Most exemption statutes simply establish a presumption. A debtor can waive the right to protect property from the creditor's reach by giving that creditor a security interest in the asset. We want to protect the debtor's home from creditor levy, but we understand that the debtor would never be able to borrow enough to pay for a house if the lender could not foreclose on it in the event of default. In recent years, we have seen some limitations on creditors' ability to take exempt property as collateral. It is, for example, an unfair credit

---

[4] In colonial Virginia, for example, creditors could not force a sale of the borrower's land. See Coleman, *supra* note 2, at 191–92.

practice to take a security interest in household goods unless the creditor provided the credit used to acquire them.[5] Moreover, the debtor is also unable to grant security interests in other kinds of property that, although not typically called exempt, nevertheless share the same attributes, such as government entitlements and spendthrift trusts. Creditors generally can, however, take security interests in property that they enable the debtor to acquire (commonly called *purchase money security interests*), even if the property is otherwise exempt from creditor levy.

Bankruptcy's Fresh Start Policy

As mentioned earlier, the individual debtor in bankruptcy is typically honest but either unlucky or improvident. The debtor's spouse may have suffered from a catastrophic illness, for example, or the debtor may have lost a well-paying job and was unable to cut back on expenses before being overwhelmed by debt. Often the debtor has no assets on which the general creditors can levy. If the debtor has a house or a car, it is subject to a security interest. The secured creditor will be able to reach such assets inside of bankruptcy as well as out, so the general creditors cannot look to them for payment.[6] All the debtor's other property consists of items such as clothes and household goods that are exempt from creditor levy. If general creditors are to receive anything, they must look to the debtor's future earnings. Garnishment laws already limit the amount of each month's check that can be reached to pay the debt. The effect of bankruptcy law is to go further and insulate all the debtor's future income from creditors, not just part, provided the debtor cuts square corners. Bankruptcy law allows creditors to scrutinize the debtor's affairs and, assuming no misbehavior is found, provides the debtor with a fresh start.

Our bankruptcy law works tolerably well for individual debtors. The earnings that bankruptcy removes from creditors' reach are ordinarily not sufficient to pay them what they are owed. The requirement that those seeking a fresh start give up any nonexempt assets limits the number of opportunists who might take advantage of the system. In addition, §707(b) of the Bankruptcy Code allows the bankruptcy judge to deny debtors a fresh start if the fresh start would

[5] FTC Unfair Credit Practices Regulations, 16 C.F.R. §444.2(4).

[6] In some cases the secured creditor may make an accommodation for the debtor providing the debtor reaffirms the obligation.

work a substantial abuse of the bankruptcy process. The unscrupulous could, of course, attempt to hide assets, but those who seek the protection of bankruptcy law must disclose the whereabouts of all their assets and submit to questioning from creditors. Debtors who are not forthcoming lose, among other things, their right to a fresh start. The ability to scrutinize the debtor's affairs is of substantial benefit to creditors, many of whom stop pursuing the debtor once they satisfy themselves that the debtor cannot repay them. The procedure that bankruptcy law puts in place reassures creditors that the debtor does not have other assets and that nothing is being hidden from them.

The current system works in large part because filing a bankruptcy petition imposes costs even on debtors who have no nonexempt assets. The most obvious cost is that the debtor will find it harder to borrow in the future.[7] The other costs of bankruptcy are more difficult to measure, but they are, in all likelihood, more important. There is the social stigma that attaches to those who do not pay their creditors. Many individuals would see their own filing of a bankruptcy petition as a confession of failure. One can argue that neither stigma nor guilt should follow in the wake of a bankruptcy petition, but the fact that they do deters most from filing bankruptcy petitions until their financial situation is desperate.

Lenders recognize the force of stigma and guilt, and for this reason they are willing to lend even to those who have no assets other than their ability to earn money in the future. Indeed, the push for changes in bankruptcy law during the late 1990s came largely in response to a significant increase in filing rates that economic models based on past behavior did not predict. Moreover, survey data showed that increasing numbers of debtors entering bankruptcy learned about the possibility of filing for bankruptcy from their neighbors. Social norms can change suddenly and discontinuously, and fears of such a change may have brought about the legislative push. Filing rates, however, slowed in the late 1990s, and so did the calls for change.

The discussion above makes the fresh start in bankruptcy seem somewhat easier to justify than may in fact be the case. Creditors are not as likely to be repaid when debtors have a right to a fresh start because stigma and other extralegal sanctions will not deter everyone. This in turn raises the cost of borrowing for everyone. A right to

---

[7] Immediately after filing the petition, however, the debtor may find it easier to borrow. At that moment the debtor will have no creditors and will not be able to take advantage of bankruptcy's fresh start again for six years. §727(a)(8).

a fresh start in bankruptcy is a kind of insurance. All debtors pay a higher rate of interest at the outset and, in return, the creditor bears part of the loss that arises when a particular debtor falls on hard times. One must ask if it makes sense to make this "insurance policy" part of every debt contract.

A number of different factors determine whether a given risk is insurable. No insurance company will sell a policy that will pay someone's gambling losses in Las Vegas. Once a person had such a policy, of course, that person would gamble more recklessly than ever. (This is called the *moral hazard* problem.) Moreover, those who seek such a policy and are willing to pay its premium are the ones most likely to have large losses. (This is called the *adverse selection* problem.) The insurance that bankruptcy's fresh start gives the individual debtor creates both moral hazard and adverse selection problems. If you can get a fresh start when you encounter financial disaster, you might be tempted to borrow too much. Similarly, if lenders have to raise their interest rates to compensate themselves for the risk of a bankruptcy's fresh start, the debtors most willing to pay the high interest rate may be the ones most likely to get the benefit of the fresh start. The argument in favor of bankruptcy's fresh start must begin not with the claim that these problems do not exist but that they do not loom large enough to destroy the market for consumer loans or bring about dramatic distortions in it.

A right to a fresh start in bankruptcy is more like fire insurance than gambling insurance. Individuals are more apt to be careless when their house is insured, and arsonists are especially eager to buy fire insurance, but a thriving market exists for such insurance nevertheless. Individuals may become less careful when they have fire insurance, but not significantly so. Moreover, rules can be written to ensure that arsonists do not enjoy the benefits of insurance. Similarly, individuals have so much to lose when they go broke that the existence of a right to a fresh start is not apt to make them significantly more careless. Finally, the rules governing the fresh start screen out many of those who would use bankruptcy to avoid paying their creditors.

None of this, however, explains why individuals are not free to waive their right to a fresh start. Individuals are free to decide whether they want to pay for fire insurance, but they are not similarly free to waive the right to a fresh start (and save the premium associated with it). Debtors must "buy" the right to a fresh start whether they want to or not. Like any other kind of insurance policy, the debtor will ultimately have to pay for it. To justify the law as it exists today, one has to explain not only why the fresh start makes sense—why it is insurance that lenders want to sell and borrowers want to buy—but why we refuse to allow individuals to waive their right to it at the time they borrow. After all, such borrowers might well enjoy a more favorable rate because their willingness to waive their right to a fresh start may signal to the lender that they are extremely reliable.

We would, of course, want to ensure that the waiver of the right was a willing one, and the disclosure requirements would have to be quite stringent. Nonetheless we are reluctant to allow the waiver, and the source of this reluctance is not easy to identify. It is naïve to assume that lenders would insist on waivers because of their superior bargaining position. A lender with the upper hand in the bargaining will demand as high an interest rate as it can. The presence or absence of a right to a fresh start will not keep a creditor from using its bargaining power. To be sure, at a given interest rate a lender would rather make a loan without a right to a fresh start than with one. So long as the moral hazard and adverse selection problems are not too large, however, a lender should be willing to give borrowers a right to a fresh start in return for a higher interest rate. A lender with or without bargaining power should be willing to offer any terms for which the borrower is willing to pay. To explain the nonwaivability of bankruptcy's fresh start policy, one must look elsewhere.

Our belief that the right to a fresh start should not be waivable may result from a recognition of two distinct problems—the effects that our financial misfortunes might have on others and our own inability to assess risks correctly at the time we borrow.[8] Our own financial failure will affect others. Even if a coolly rational borrower reasonably thought the right to a fresh start was not worth its price, we might want to prevent that borrower from waiving that right. Financial failure would impose costs not just on the borrower but on family, friends, and society at large. The second problem starts with the observation that individuals are not coolly rational, certainly not all the time. Even if firms are adept at assessing risks, individuals may still not behave rationally when they borrow.

The temptation to borrow at a lower rate in return for waiving the right to a fresh start might be hard to resist at the moment we take the loan. Nevertheless, we would prefer not to be tempted in the first

---

[8] For an excellent discussion of the question of why it might make sense for the right to a discharge to be nonwaivable, see Thomas H. Jackson, The Fresh-Start Policy in Bankruptcy Law, 98 Harv. L. Rev. 1393 (1985).

place. Think of Ulysses, who ordered his crew to chain him to the mast of his ship and not to release him when they sailed passed the Sirens, however much he might protest. The prudence that would lead us to insist on the right to a fresh start might desert us at the crucial time.[9] In addition, we might be ill equipped to judge the likelihood of hard financial times in the future. We may not fully realize that while the chance of any particular financial reversal might be small, the chance of any one of these events coming to pass may be much larger. A substantial body of empirical literature suggests that people consistently underestimate this kind of risk.[10] One should not, however, assume that these justifications for forbidding the waiver of the right to a fresh start are unassailable. Their most significant failing is that they prove too much. Many other activities, such as skydiving and cigarette smoking, might be banned for similar reasons.

In considering the nonwaivability of the right to a fresh start, note that it is closely connected with the question of limiting the borrower's right to grant security interests in exempt property. One may prohibit the both the waiver of the right to a fresh start and the creation of security interests in household goods (other than purchase money interests) on the same grounds. Moreover, we may except some loans, including educational loans, from discharge for the same reason that we allow purchase money security interests in exempt property. Those who make purchase money loans enable debtors to acquire exempt property in the first place. Similarly, those who finance education increase the debtor's future earnings. (An economist would say that such a lender financed the acquisition of an asset called "human capital.") We may need to allow lenders to reach this "asset" to ensure that they make the loans.[11]

The Availability of the Fresh Start

In this section we examine how Chapter 7 of the Bankruptcy Code gives honest but unlucky individuals the ability to free themselves

[9] See Jon Elster, Ulysses and the Sirens: Studies in Rationality and Irrationality (1979).

[10] See Daniel Tversky & Amos Kahneman, Judgment Under Uncertainty: Heuristics and Biases, 185 Science 1124, 1129 (1974).

[11] One should not press this point too far. The government guarantees many educational loans, and the default rates are much higher than the norm. This source of credit is much less driven by market forces than are other sources of credit.

from past debts in return for giving up whatever nonexempt assets they own. Section 109(b) tells us that an individual may be a debtor under Chapter 7, and §301 states that an individual may commence a case on that individual's own initiative. Section 541 provides that the filing of a petition under §301 transforms assets (including exempt assets) that the debtor owns into property of the estate, but §541(a)(6) creates an exception for the individual debtor's future earnings. Future earnings are an asset, indeed the most valuable asset most of us possess. Nevertheless, future earnings do not become property of the estate, and §§727 and 524 of the Bankruptcy Code keep creditors from reaching any assets, such as future earnings, that are not property of the estate. Section 727 gives most individual debtors a discharge for most kinds of debts, and §524 prohibits a creditor whose debt has been discharged from engaging in any act to collect property from the debtor.

We are, of course, painting here with a broad brush. Section 727 contains a number of exceptions that ensure that the debtor is merely unlucky and has not defrauded creditors. In addition, §523 excludes some debts from the discharge. On the other side, §§524 and 525 broaden the scope of the discharge beyond prohibiting creditors from trying to collect debts. The core idea, however, is straightforward. The effect of these sections together is to allow the debtor to insulate future income from the reach of creditors, but at a price. The debtor enjoys future earnings, but creditors are entitled to enjoy all the debtor's assets, subject only to rules on exempt property codified in §522.

The Bankruptcy Code does not require that individuals be insolvent before they are eligible for bankruptcy. Such a requirement is unnecessary anyway. Debtors whose existing nonexempt assets vastly exceed their debts have nothing to gain from filing a petition. If such a person filed a bankruptcy petition, that person's assets would become part of the bankruptcy estate under §541. That debtor's assets are, by assumption, worth more than the debtor's liabilities. In bankruptcy, therefore, the assets of the bankruptcy estate should be sufficient to pay the creditors in full.[12] The picture can become more complicated, however. An individual's creditworthiness depends on both the value of that individual's existing assets and the capacity that individual has to earn income in the future. An individual might well

---

[12] In the rare case in which this happens, the remaining assets of the estate are returned to the debtor. §726(a)(6).

be insolvent in the sense that liabilities greatly exceed the value of existing assets, but the individual may nonetheless be solvent if we take the value of future earnings into account. The paradigm is the young urban professional with accumulated debts from several years of free spending. Such debtors may prefer to file for bankruptcy and continue their free-spending ways rather than adopt a more sensible life-style and pay the creditors what they are owed. The absence of a solvency requirement (broadly defined) means that such individuals face no explicit bar on obtaining bankruptcy's fresh start.

Whether such individuals should be able to enjoy a fresh start, however, turns on how one justifies it. On one hand, a right to a fresh start may be seen is part of the social safety net: it prevents debtors with overwhelming debt from becoming public charges. One would therefore be reluctant to give a fresh start to individuals such as urban professionals who could pay off creditors out of future income. On the other hand, if the right to a fresh start exists because individuals have poor impulse control, one could argue that everyone, even ur-ban professionals, ought to be able to free themselves from bad deci-sions made in the past and start over again. For this reason, a right to a fresh start may make sense even in the case of someone who could pay back creditors out of future income.

Section 707(b) of the Bankruptcy Code permits the court, acting on its own motion or that of the United States Trustee, to dismiss a Chapter 7 petition filed by an individual debtor "whose debts are primarily consumer debts if [the court] finds that the granting of re-lief would be a substantial abuse." Courts will dismiss the case when, for example, the debtor has exhibited a lack of good faith and honesty in dealing with creditors. In addition, some courts have used this sec-tion to deny a fresh start to debtors who had the ability to pay credi-tors out of future earnings. Under this view, filing for bankruptcy when one has the ability to repay creditors is, without more, a sub-stantial abuse. Because §707(b) does not expressly incorporate an ability-to-pay test, however, some courts have found that an ability to pay creditors back out of future income does not, by itself, render a debtor ineligible for bankruptcy; instead such courts look to the to-tality of the circumstances.[13] Even in applying that test, however, courts have placed heavy weight on a debtor's ability to repay.[14]

---

[13] Compare Zolg v. Kelly, 841 F.2d 908 (9th Cir. 1988), with Green v. Staples, 934 F.2d 568 (4th Cir. 1991); In re Krohn, 886 F.2d 123 (6th Cir. 1989).

[14] See In re Rubio, 249 Bank. 689 (Bankr. N.D. Tex. 2000).

The question whether individuals who are able to pay debts out of future income should enjoy the right to a fresh start is conceptually important, but we must keep this issue in perspective. First, the issue is not central to the day-to-day operation of our bankruptcy laws. The majority of debtors in bankruptcy are not in fact able to repay their creditors in full out of future earnings merely by cutting back on their life-style.[15] The typical debtors in bankruptcy are those just hanging on to a middle-class life. They make less than the median income and have nonmortgage debt that is twice their annual income. Indeed, much of the debate centers not so much on the typical debtor, but rather on how much the law can or should do to curb the abuses that undoubtedly do take place.

Some support means testing in principle, but think any implementation would do little to prevent the abuses that take place now and would hamper the ability of those who are the "honest but unfortunate" to obtain a fresh start. Consider the following case. A 65-year-old widow returned to the workforce several years ago after her husband became ill with cancer. She makes $32,000 a year as a secretary, and she has not taken a vacation in several years. She rents a one-bedroom apartment and owes $60,000, much of which stems from medical bills for the care of her late husband. The remaining debt consists of unpaid credit card bills, mostly for household goods and groceries. Interest runs at 15 percent. The widow is behind in her payments, collection agencies call at home and at work, and they are now threatening to garnish her wages. In implementing means testing, both the U.S. House and the U.S. Senate passed bills that would have made the widow's use of Chapter 7 presumptively abusive.

In debating these and other issues, however, we should avoid overstating the need for a fresh start. Denial of a right to a straight discharge of debts in Chapter 7 does not necessarily lead to catastrophe. Debtors who cannot use Chapter 7 still enjoy the protection of state and federal nonbankruptcy exemption laws. Because of the limits on garnishing wages that exist in every jurisdiction, denying a debtor a right to a fresh start is not the same as giving creditors the ability to take away all of a debtor's future earnings. Moreover, individuals who are unable to file Chapter 7 petitions often can file Chapter 13 petitions. Chapter 13 allows debtors whose debts fall below the dollar

[15] Teresa A. Sullivan, Elizabeth Warren & Jay Lawrence Westbrook, The Fragile Middle Class: Americans in Debt (2000).

limits in §109 to keep their existing assets and gives them a discharge if they pay creditors what they can out of their disposable income over a period of three to five years.

The extent of the fresh start a debtor enjoys may depend largely on the amount of property the debtor can keep after receiving a discharge. Some state laws put no dollar cap on the property that can be exempt from creditor levy. In Texas, for example, a debtor's homestead is exempt from creditor levy. Texas limits the size of the homestead (one acre) but not its value.[16] Debtors might use bankruptcy to discharge their debts even though they could pay them back in full without great sacrifice. One can again argue that a debtor who could pay creditors by selling a large house and moving to a more modest home should not be able to take advantage of Chapter 7.

Exempt property raises another issue as well. Assume that a debtor's ownership of nonexempt property does not itself make seeking relief under Chapter 7 a substantial abuse, but that the debtor acquired the exempt property on the eve of bankruptcy. Mere conversion of assets with the knowledge that one is putting the assets beyond the reach of creditors is not itself objectionable. But if one acquires the asset on the eve of bankruptcy solely to prevent creditors from reaching assets, courts may well find that there has been a transfer of property with the intent to hinder, delay, or defraud creditors within the meaning of §727(a)(2). For example, in one case a 90-year-old debtor, shortly after being named in a personal injury suit, bought a newly built house, added extras until his assets were exhausted, and immediately filed a bankruptcy petition. He had previously been living in an assisted-care facility and lacked the income needed even to pay property taxes on the house.[17]

Individual debtors (and the lawyers who advise them) should know what kinds of prebankruptcy planning are legitimate and what kinds are not. In the absence of a clear rule, one must rely on common sense. Fortunately, here as elsewhere in bankruptcy law, common sense will take one far. A judge is not apt to be sympathetic to a debtor who acquires an expensive harpsichord, for example, especially if the debtor does not know how to play it.[18]

Section 727 lists other actions that deprive the debtor of a fresh start. For the most part, these actions are bad acts that undermine

[16] Tex. Stat. Ann. §41.001.

[17] See Jensen v. Dietz, 217 F.3d 1006 (8th Cir. 2000).

[18] See, e.g., Panuska v. Johnson, 124 Bankr. 290 (Bankr. D. Minn. 1991).

the rights of creditors, such as making it impossible for them to understand the debtor's affairs by destroying or failing to keep financial records. §727(a)(3). If, however, the debtor is a poor recordkeeper to begin with (that is, the debtor is honest but unfortunate), the debtor should still be a legitimate candidate for a discharge. Courts typically do not use the financial records exception to deny a fresh start to such a debtor.

The exceptions to discharge under §727 are largely a product of history. The discharge was originally introduced into bankruptcy law to secure the debtor's cooperation; the intent was not to give the debtor a fresh start but to offer a carrot that would induce the debtor to cooperate with the creditors and help them assemble the debtor's assets.[19] This explains why a debtor who makes a fraudulent conveyance cannot obtain a discharge, but a convicted murderer can. (Whether, however, the murderer can obtain a discharge for the civil claim that the victim's heirs might have is a different question that we confront later.) In addition, §727(a)(8) requires a debtor to wait six years between one fresh start and the next. This limitation on the right to a fresh start does prevent the deliberate wrongdoer from abusing the right, but the limitation also can work in the debtor's interest because it can make it easier to borrow. Creditors who lend to someone who has just emerged from bankruptcy know that the debtor cannot file a bankruptcy petition before they have a chance to be repaid.

The Scope of the Fresh Start

As we have discussed, the individual debtor's fresh start derives from two sources. First, the Bankruptcy Code ensures that a debtor who gives up existing assets can prevent creditors from reaching any of the debtor's future earnings or assets acquired with them. Second, §522 of the Bankruptcy Code, which works in conjunction with nonbankruptcy state and federal law, allows a debtor to keep exempt property. Although the basic features of the fresh start are clear, they are complicated by the interaction between bankruptcy and nonbankruptcy law. What becomes property of the estate is entirely a question of federal bankruptcy law, but what property is exempt depends greatly on state and federal nonbankruptcy law. Because the

---

[19] The Statute of 4 Anne ch. 17 (1705), which instituted the discharge in bankruptcy, was in fact called "An act to prevent frauds frequently committed by bankrupts."

definitions of exempt property and property of the estate are not co-ordinated, one is forced to define each of them without being able to rely on the fresh start. The fresh start is the sum of the two, but each must be worked out independently.

The debtor can keep assets, regardless of whether they are exempt, if the assets do not become property of the estate under §541. Principal among these assets are earnings from future services within the meaning of §541(a)(6) and assets held in a trust that the debtor cannot reach under nonbankruptcy law, as stated in §541(c)(2). To understand how difficult it can be to determine future earnings, consider the situation in *FitzSimmons v. Walsh*, a case dealing with a partner in a law firm whose practice generated substantial income.[20] A partner's future income from a law practice does not derive exclusively from the partner's own future work. Future earnings from a law practice are generated in part by existing assets, such as employment contracts with the associates in the firm. Earnings also come from the partner's past efforts. There are accounts receivable and a client base that has been built over time. A partner's role at a law firm might consist only of rainmaking and may end once the client decides to retain the firm. An associate might perform all the subsequent legal work. None of the income derived from prepetition clients would qualify as the partner's future earnings within the meaning of §541(a)(6). In *FitzSimmons*, the Ninth Circuit required the bankruptcy court to examine the facts of the case and determine exactly what earnings of the law practice would be attributable to services that FitzSimmons performed personally after the filing of the petition.

Some courts have valued a practice by asking how much would have been realized in the event that the debtor had sold the practice.[21] But one must identify the kind of nonbankruptcy sale that provides the relevant benchmark. (An outright sale would obviate the need to make an estimate, but if the individual files in Chapter 11 and plans to continue to run the business, an actual sale is not in the cards.) A lawyer or doctor who sells a practice usually, as part of the sale, agrees to vouch for the buyer, introduce him to clients or patients, and perhaps work with him through a transitional period. In addition, the new buyer will ordinarily insist on a covenant not to compete. Hence, the amount for which a cooperative debtor could

[20] 725 F.2d 1208 (9th Cir. 1984).
[21] See, e.g., In re Prince, 85 F.3d 314, 323 n.5 (7th Cir. 1996).

sell the practice outside of bankruptcy may not be the relevant benchmark. A better approximation might be the amount the practice would fetch if the debtor ceased all connections with the business but remained free to open a competing practice.[22]

Problems also arise with the effect that the discharge has on liens and other rights that third parties have in the debtor's property. Suppose a bank lends a borrower $100,000 and takes a mortgage on the borrower's $150,000 home. The discharge prevents the bank from pursuing its claim against the borrower, but the discharge does not cut off the bank's lien on the property. After the Chapter 7 proceeding is over, the bank can still foreclose on the property if the borrower is in default. As noted in chapter 1 above, liens pass through bankruptcy. To ensure that a debtor enjoys a fresh start, however, bankruptcy law has carved out several exceptions to the doctrine of lien pass-through. For example, a right of redemption under §722 allows the debtor to extinguish liens on property intended for personal, family, or household use if those liens secure dischargeable consumer debt. (The debtor, however, must pay the secured creditor an amount equal to the value of the property.) In addition, the debtor is entitled to avoid judicial liens in exempt property and nonpossessory money security interests (other than purchase money interests) in some kinds of exempt property such as household goods and tools of the trade under §522(f). Finally, and most important, liens on the debtor's future earnings do not survive bankruptcy. The Supreme Court established this principle in *Local Loan Company v. Hunt*, which held that an assignment of wages did not survive discharge.[23]

The bankruptcy of Tia Carrere raised the same problem as *Local Loan Company* in a different guise.[24] Carrere, an actress, wanted to escape from a long-term contract with ABC requiring her to appear on *General Hospital*, a daytime television soap opera. A clause in that contract prevented her from becoming a regular on *The A-Team*, a prime-time show. The court had to ask if bankruptcy's fresh start freed her from the unfavorable employment contract. If Carrere had foolishly borrowed money from ABC and lost it all, she would have been able to file a bankruptcy petition and keep her earnings from whatever job she happened to take. Similarly, if a creditor of Carrere's had garnished her wages, the garnishment would not survive

---

[22] See Ackerman v. Schultz, 250 Bankr. 22 (Bankr. E.D.N.Y. 2000).

[23] 292 U.S. 234 (1934).

[24] In re Carrere, 64 Bankr. 156 (Bankr. C.D. Cal. 1986). Carrere ultimately lost.

bankruptcy. Conceptually, Carrere's promise not to appear else-where or indeed any covenant not to compete is the same. ABC has what amounts to an ownership interest in Carrere's future income stream. *Local Loan Company* establishes that such interests do not survive bankruptcy. To be sure, if one can discharge a covenant not to compete in bankruptcy, it will be harder for actresses like Carrere to find jobs in the first place. ABC would be less willing to take on new actors if it is not able to keep them. But this does not distinguish *Carrere* from *Local Loan Company*. Any limit on the doctrine of lien pass-through reduces debtors' ability to commit themselves and hence makes it less attractive for others to enter into agreements with them.

In this case and in others like it, the structure of the Bankruptcy Code makes it hard to confront such questions head on. The agreement with ABC falls within the definition of an executory contract under §365, but the Code deals with this question imperfectly. To resolve the issue courts often rely on such factors as whether the debtor's filing was in good faith. Such an approach makes it difficult to craft coherent principles and apply them consistently.[25] We return to this question when we discuss executory contracts in chapter 7 below.

Section 541(c)(2) looks not at future earnings but at a kind of property held in trust that is beyond the reach of both the debtor and the creditors at the time the petition is filed. The paradigm is the spendthrift trust. A parent might establish a trust for a child prone to impulsive spending and provide that the child could not convey future income from the trust in exchange for a fixed sum today. Non-bankruptcy law respects such provisions. Section 541(c)(2) tells us that bankruptcy law respects them as well. If a restriction on the transfer of a debtor's beneficial interest in a trust is enforceable outside of bankruptcy, it is enforceable inside of bankruptcy. The Bankruptcy Code does not limit the reach of §541(c)(2) to only those trusts that are denominated spendthrift trusts. It applies equally to any beneficial interest in a trust that has the crucial attribute of being beyond the reach of the debtor or the debtor's creditors.[26] Many trusts that are beyond the reach of creditors are not beyond the reach of the debtor. A debtor might establish a retirement plan, which, under nonbankruptcy law, creditors could not reach. The debtor, how-

---

[25] One can see this by comparing the opinion (and the result) in *Carrere* with Cloyd v. GRP Records, 238 Bank. 328 (Bankr. E.D. Mich. 1999).

[26] Patterson v. Shumate, 504 U.S. 753 (1992).

ever, is able to withdraw funds from such a plan (albeit with a tax penalty). For this reason, the assets of the retirement plan become property of the estate. The debtor is able to enjoy it after discharge only if the plan's assets are exempt property within the meaning of §522.[27]

After discharge, the debtor enjoys, free from the claims of the creditors, everything that the debtor would ordinarily enjoy in the absence of bankruptcy other than property of the estate. Future income is the most conspicuous example, but there are others. Consider the right of a spouse to take a statutory share of the decedent's estate rather than what was bequeathed in the will. The spouse has this right under nonbankruptcy law, and this right is not property of the estate, so the spouse retains this right notwithstanding the bankruptcy.[28]

The fresh start has one final component. In addition to allowing the debtor to keep everything that is not property of the estate and to nullify liens on future income under the principle of *Local Loan Company*, the debtor is also able to keep exempt assets. The Bankruptcy Code provides a list of exempt property that debtors can keep as part of their fresh start. States, however, can—and most do—decide on their own which of the debtor's assets should be beyond the reach of creditors in bankruptcy.[29]

State exemptions vary in detail according to jurisdiction. Some are firmly rooted in the nineteenth century and include such things as homesteads, church pews, and the family Bible. Modern exemption statutes also include pensions and insurance policies. Property that is exempt for purposes of §522(b)(2) may extend beyond what a state explicitly calls "exempt." For example, exempt property may extend to all property that the state has put beyond the reach of a debtor's creditors and that otherwise has the attributes of exempt property, whatever label the state (or substantive federal law) applies.

The most controversial issue concerning exemptions is not the type but the value of the property that can be exempted. Some states, notably Florida and Texas, exempt a debtor's homestead without a

[27] Lowenschuss v. Selnick, 171 F.3d 673 (9th Cir. 1999).

[28] See In re Brand, 251 Bankr. 912 (Bankr. S.D. Fla. 2000); In re McCourt, 12 Bankr. 587 (Bankr. S.D.N.Y. 1981).

[29] The Constitution gives Congress the power to pass only uniform laws on the subject of bankruptcy. The Supreme Court has held, however, that deferring to state exemption statutes does not prevent a bankruptcy statute from being uniform. See Hanover National Bank v. Moyses, 186 U.S. 181 (1902).

cap; others provide similar treatment for some insurance and pension plans. Suppose a wealthy investor lives in a large house in Florida that he owns outright. He might file for bankruptcy, discharge all debts, and still be a millionaire. So long as he was a Florida resident and owned the house at the time he borrowed, creditors have nothing to complain about. They can take this risk into account. A more complicated issue arises if the debtor bought the expensive house on the eve of bankruptcy or moved to Florida only after borrowing the money and after encountering financial trouble. One must draw a line between permissible prebankruptcy planning and transfers made with intent to delay, hinder, and defraud creditors.

When the popular press singles out examples of bankruptcy abuse, it often points to debtors that take advantage of a state's generous exemption laws. These laws, however, are part of bankruptcy only because Congress has deferred to state law. Despite calls for curbing bankruptcy abuse, political forces in the states with generous exemptions have pressed strongly to keep them intact.

When a state does not opt to have nonbankruptcy exemptions (both state and federal) govern exclusively, §522(b) gives the debtor a choice. The debtor can either take advantage of the nonbankruptcy exemptions or keep the property listed in §522(d).[30] The largest exemption in §522(d) is the $16,150 federal homestead exemption. But §522(d)(1)'s homestead exemption must be read in conjunction with §522(d)(5), for §522(d)(5) gives the debtor $850 plus up to $8,075 of the unused portion of §522(d)(1) to apply wherever the debtor wants—the so-called wild card exemption. Conversely, the $850 from §522(d)(5) can be combined with §522(d)(1) to give the debtor a $17,000 federal homestead exemption.

Section 522(d)(3) exempts $425 per item for household goods, subject to a cap of $8,625 (not counting the wild card). Other §522(d) exemptions include the debtor's interest in household goods, health aids, tools of the trade, and a motor vehicle, as well as the debtor's right to receive alimony, support payments, life insurance payments, veteran's benefits, and victim's compensation payments. Some exemptions are limited in scope or amount, while others are not.

Beyond the definition of exempt property, §522 also allows the debtor to "avoid the fixing of" certain liens on such property. This power exists whether the debtor uses the special bankruptcy exemp-

---

[30] As we have seen elsewhere, (in §109, for example), the dollar amounts are adjusted by regulation every three years. The figures here are those in effect in November 2000.

tions or the state and federal nonbankruptcy exemptions. More precisely, §522(f)(1)(A) generally allows the individual debtor to free exempt property from most kinds of judicial liens, including liens created by levy on behalf of a general creditor. Not included are liens that secure an alimony or child-support obligation. Moreover, §522(f)(1)(B) allows the debtor to avoid a nonpossessory, nonpurchase money security interest in specified property (see example in paragraph below). That property, listed in §522(f)(1)(B)(i), (ii), and (iii), turns out to be some of the same type of property as that set forth in §522(d). For example, §§522(f)(1)(B)(i) and 522(d)(3) both refer to household goods. The words in §522(f), however, do not necessarily mean the same thing as the ones in §522(d) because the former implicitly refers to property exempt under nonbankruptcy law, and arguably incorporates a nonbankruptcy definition, while the latter is a special term of bankruptcy law.

The difficulties that arise in understanding both the fresh start policy and the relationship between state and federal law have spawned a great deal of litigation. Especially complicated is the relationship between exempt property and liens. Section 522(f) gives the debtor the power to remove some kinds of liens on exempt property, such as a nonpurchase money security interest in household furnishings. This lien-stripping provision operates only on property a state deems exempt, and some states exempt only property that is unencumbered by a security interest. Suppose a debtor seeks to avoid an interest in a $200 sofa that secures a $150 loan. Under state law, household furnishings are exempt only to the extent of the debtor's equity interest in the property. In this case, only the $50 difference between the value of the sofa and the amount of the security interest would be exempt property. The secured creditor can argue that its collateral does not include the debtor's equity in the property and, because only the debtor's equity interest is exempt, its collateral is not exempt and its security interest therefore cannot be avoided. The Supreme Court, however, rejected that argument in *Owen v. Owen*,[31] and its holding in that case has since been codified in §522(f)(2). States have the power to decide what property is exempt, but whether a debtor can avoid a lien on such property is a function of bankruptcy's fresh start policy.

[31] 500 U.S. 305 (1991).

Defining Discharge and Nondischargeable Debts

A debtor who files a bankruptcy petition is entitled to a discharge of prepetition claims. The debtor is not free of obligations incurred after the filing of the petition. Moreover, some prepetition burdens remain notwithstanding the discharge because they are not "claims." For example, criminal sanctions such as imprisonment survive bankruptcy. A felon enjoys a discharge, but the discharge does not secure release from prison because the state's right to imprison someone is not a claim. Nor can a debtor use a bankruptcy filing to evade a child-custody order.

It is important to understand exactly what it means to discharge a debt. At a minimum, a discharge gives the debtor an affirmative defense to a suit on a prepetition claim. The effect of a discharge, however, is much broader. Section 524 prevents a creditor from making any efforts to collect payment from the debtor once the petition is filed. How the discharge affects future interactions between the debtor and the creditor, however, remains unclear.

A debtor may need to deal with the creditor after bankruptcy. For example, a debtor might seek a transcript from a school that had made loans to the debtor that were discharged in bankruptcy. The school and the debtor battle over whether the school has the right to refuse to give the debtor the transcript. The school has no duty to engage in further dealings with the debtor, but it is withholding the transcript solely because the debtor has not paid a debt that has been discharged.[32]

The discharge applies only to the debtor. Section 524(e) provides that the discharge does not relieve any third party from an obligation on the debt. A typical example is a guarantor whom the creditor can sue directly.[33] Complications arise, however, when the debtor has an insurance policy and the victim of an accident needs to sue the debtor to recover under the policy. The question is whether §524 bars an action against the debtor when the victim seeks to recover only from the insurance company. Most courts have held that §524 does not prevent victims from recovering in such cases. These courts reason

[32] Compare In re Heath, 3 Bankr. 351 (Bankr. N.D. Ill. 1980), with Johnson v. Edinboro State College, 728 F.2d 163 (3d Cir. 1984). Note, however, that limitations on the dischargeability of such loans may play a role in the way that school transcript cases are decided. For a discussion of these and other complications, see Najafi v. Cabrini College, 154 Bankr. 185 (Bankr. E.D. Pa. 1993).

[33] See Terwilliger v. Terwilliger, 206 F.3d 240 (2d Cir. 2000).

that because the debtor is not personally liable, such actions against a debtor do not interfere with the fresh start.[34]

Section 525 limits the ability of two parties, the government and the debtor's employer, to discriminate against those who have filed bankruptcy petitions, even though they may never have been creditors of the debtor. A state's discrimination against a debtor may take the following form. Before filing for bankruptcy, a debtor injures someone in a car accident and fails to pay the judgment that resulted from the subsequent tort suit. The state suspends the debtor's driver's license, and the debtor files for bankruptcy. The tort obligation is discharged, but the state refuses to reinstate the debtor's driver's license. In *Perez v. Campbell*, the Supreme Court confronted a case such as this in which, under the relevant statute, the state would not reinstate the debtor's driver's license until the judgment was satisfied, notwithstanding the discharge.[35] The Supreme Court held that a state statute designed to ensure that tort judgments were paid was inconsistent with bankruptcy's fresh start policy.

The principle of *Perez* has been codified in §525, which prohibits "governmental units" from denying licenses or otherwise discriminating against someone solely because that person is in bankruptcy or has not paid a debt discharged in bankruptcy. One should not extend *Perez* too far, however. For example, the doctrine of *Perez* should not apply if, under the relevant statute, the state would not reinstate the driver's license until the debtor offered proof of financial responsibility regardless of whether the debtor had paid the tort obligation.[36] This requirement, unlike the one in *Perez*, does not have the effect of inducing the debtor to pay an obligation that has already been discharged.

The reach of *Perez* may be limited for another reason as well. Conditioning a debtor's right to a driver's license on repayment of a debt is ultimately no different from giving a creditor a lien on some other valuable asset of the debtor. We know from the doctrine of *Long v. Bullard* that such liens survive bankruptcy so long as they do not at-

---

[34] See, e.g., Houston v. Edgeworth, 993 F.2d 51 (5th Cir. 1993); Green v. Welsh, 956 F.2d 30 (2d Cir. 1992); Owaski v. Jet Florida Systems, 883 F.2d 970 (11th Cir. 1989). But see Citibank v. White Motor Corp., 761 F.2d 270 (6th Cir. 1985). These cases arise only when the victim is entitled to the proceeds of the insurance policy (and not the bankruptcy estate).

[35] 402 U.S. 637 (1971).

[36] See Duffey v. Dollison, 734 F.2d 265 (6th Cir. 1984).

tach to future earnings. In other words, one cannot extend the reach of *Perez* without cutting back on the reach of *Long v. Bullard*.

Although the Bankruptcy Code defines claims broadly and a discharge affects even those who are not creditors, there are limits on the scope of the discharge. A debtor may be eligible for a discharge under §727 but still have some debts that are not dischargeable. Section 523(a) contains a list of nondischargeable debts. We have already noted one of these. Debtors who need to borrow to finance their educations often have no other assets. The only asset they can give to lenders is an interest in their future earnings. They can do this, however, only if such debts are not dischargeable. Section 523(a)(8) provides for this result.

To ensure that creditors have a chance to participate in the bankruptcy proceeding, a debtor does not receive a discharge of an ordinary claim unless the debtor includes the debt on the schedules it must file with the court and otherwise complies with procedures that ensure that each creditor is notified of the bankruptcy and has the chance to make a timely filing of a proof of claim. §523(a)(3). If a creditor does not know about the bankruptcy and has no chance to share in the assets, it is able to pursue the debtor after bankruptcy. In many cases, however, the debtor has no nonexempt assets; filing a claim is a pointless exercise, and the trustee advises the creditors not to bother, telling them that they will be notified if assets are later found. In such cases, an omitted creditor has not lost any right. As no other creditor was ever given a deadline, there was never a point at which any filing it might have made would have been untimely. Hence, one can argue that such a debt is discharged along with the others.[37]

The other nondischargeable debts in §523 fall into one of two categories (or sometimes a mixture of both). Either the debt arose out of bad conduct, such as a deliberate tort, or the debt in question is thought to be particularly important. Debts of the latter kind include child support, alimony, and many tax obligations. The dischargeability of tax obligations arises frequently in the case of an un-

---

[37] This reasoning is set out in In re Mendiola, 99 Bankr. 864 (Bankr. N.D. Ill. 1989), and has become widely adopted. See, e.g., Judd v. Wolfe, 78 F.3d 110 (3d Cir. 1996). For a discussion of the problem, see Lauren A. Helbing & Christopher M. Klein, The Emerging Harmless Innocent Omission Defense to Nondischargeability Under Bankruptcy Code §523(a)(3)(A): Making Sense of the Confusion Over Reopening Cases and Amending Schedules to Add Omitted Debts, 69 Am. Bankr. L.J. 33 (1995).

successful businessperson. Too often individuals fail to pay withholding taxes in the waning days of the business. Their money is used
to pay suppliers and workers enough to keep the operation open a
few weeks longer. The responsible manager of the business is personally obliged to pay these taxes, regardless of whether the business is a
sole proprietorship or a corporation. These tax obligations (depending on when the tax is assessed) are typically not dischargeable.
For this reason, as well as many others, taking stock of the debtor's
tax position and issuing the appropriate warnings are an essential part
of advising a debtor who is in financial trouble.

Section 523(a)'s "bad act" exceptions deny a discharge to debts
that were not incurred simply as a result of improvidence. For example, under §523(a)(2) debts incurred through false pretenses or false
financial statements are not dischargeable. For the same reason,
§523(a)(2)(c) limits the ability of a debtor to borrow and spend when
bankruptcy is imminent and the debtor's good faith is therefore suspect. The *fresh cash doctrine* has been a recurring issue in litigation
under §523(a)(2). Suppose a debtor has a loan from a bank. The
debtor encounters financial difficulties and returns to the bank for an
additional loan, which the debtor obtains through false statements.
The bank will argue that if the second loan is consolidated with the
first, there is only a single debt and that §523(a)(2) makes the entire
loan nondischargeable. Courts are divided on whether the whole
loan is nondischargeable or only the fresh cash portion, the part that
was obtained with the false statement.

The other exceptions for bad acts are largely self-explanatory.
Section 523(a)(4) deprives the debtor of the fruits of wrongdoing
while the debtor was acting in a fiduciary capacity. The difficulty
here is deciding what is and what is not fiduciary. An unsettled issue
is whether selling collateral and spending the proceeds should trigger
this section when state law declares that the debtor holds the proceeds in trust for the creditor. Here, as elsewhere, what should matter is not whether state law calls it a fiduciary duty, but whether it
bears the attributes of a fiduciary duty, such as an obligation to maintain separate accounts. The debtor who commits willful and mali-
cious torts, including willful conversions of property, cannot discharge them in Chapter 7, nor can debtors discharge obligations that
arise from drunken driving. Certain fines and penalties payable to the
government are also not dischargeable.

The list of nondischargeable debts appears to be growing over
time. When Congress is presented with the narrow question whether
a particular kind of obligation should be nondischargeable, it may

seem that it should be. But it is unwise to focus on one type of obligation isolated from all others. For example, obligations arising from drunken driving are excepted from discharge while those arising from many other tortious acts are not. Chapter 13, as originally acted, provided a superdischarge that made only a few debts nondischargeable. The same dynamic, however, has played out there, and the two lists now increasingly resemble each other.

A debtor may wish that the scope of the fresh start were narrower than the one the Bankruptcy Code gives. A debtor may find that the discharge of a particular debt is not desirable. For example, if a debt is discharged, the creditor may try to collect the debt from a friend or a relative who acted as a guarantor of the initial obligation. Alternatively, the debtor may want to keep a car in which an automobile dealer has a security interest. The discharge will free the debtor from the obligation to pay the dealer, but, under *Long v. Bullard*, the discharge will not affect the dealer's right to repossess the car after the debtor's default as soon as the bankruptcy is over. The creditor may be willing to forgo calling the guarantee or to let the debtor keep the car only if the debtor *reaffirms* the debt. A debtor is always free to repay a debt that has been discharged in bankruptcy. The question of reaffirmation concerns whether debtors can legally bind themselves to repay a debt once it has been discharged.

Under the 1898 Act, reaffirmation was left to the realm of general contract law. One of the innovations of the 1978 Bankruptcy Code was to place bankruptcy restrictions on reaffirmations. The rules governing reaffirmations, codified in §524(c) and (d), set forth a two-step inquiry. First, the reaffirmation must be effective under non-bankruptcy law. Second, if it is, the reaffirmation must meet certain requirements. A reaffirmation, to be effective, must be made before the debtor has formally been granted a discharge. In addition, the reaffirmation must come, in the case of an individual, after the debtor has appeared before the bankruptcy court for a discharge hearing. At this time, the debtor will be told that no discharged debt need be reaffirmed. In addition, the consequences of reaffirmation will be set out. This procedure is the bankruptcy equivalent of a *Miranda* warning.

If the debtor is represented by an attorney, the attorney must file an affidavit stating that the reaffirmation agreement is voluntary and does not impose undue hardship on the debtor. In the absence of an attorney, the court must conclude that the agreement will not impose undue hardship on the debtor and is in the debtor's best interest. Courts are generally reluctant to find reaffirmation in the debtor's best interest when the debtor wants to reaffirm in order to keep driving a luxury car. They are similarly reluctant when a debtor wishes to reaffirm in order to keep a creditor from calling on a guarantee that a relative or friend executed in the debtor's favor. Even if all of these requirements have been satisfied, the debtor still gets a sixty-day cooling-off period, during which the debtor is free to rescind the reaffirmation.

Wage-Earner Plans Under Chapter 13

Chapter 7 forces individuals to give up existing assets but allows them to keep future earnings. Chapter 13 reverses things. In a Chapter 13 case, the debtor keeps all assets except a portion of future wages. The portion of the wages that the debtor does not keep is turned over to the trustee for distribution to the prepetition creditors. A debtor who completes performance under the plan is then granted a discharge from all debts provided for by the plan under §1328.

Fewer debts are nondischargeable in Chapter 13 than in Chapter 7, but, as mentioned earlier, the number has been increasing over time. In recent years, Congress has excepted drunken driving debts, educational loans, and criminal restitution obligations from discharge in Chapter 13. After a Chapter 13 discharge, one can use Chapter 7 or Chapter 11 within six years if the Chapter 13 discharge was granted on at least a 70 percent payout plan. §727(a)(9). Thus, the main advantages of Chapter 13 are that one can keep existing assets and that one may be able to discharge a greater number of debts.

Over the last decade, Chapter 13 has proved increasingly important for individual debtors in financial trouble. Each year, hundreds of thousands of Chapter 13 petitions are filed and billions of dollars are paid out under Chapter 13 plans. Those who file Chapter 13 petitions often face problems quite different from those who file under Chapter 7. For example, Chapter 13 is sometimes used not only because a debtor needs to sort out its obligations to general creditors but also because the debtor has fallen behind in payments to the bank that holds a mortgage on the debtor's home. Chapter 13 allows the debtor to take advantage of the automatic stay without at the same time giving up nonexempt assets.

Many have argued that Chapter 13 should be the primary avenue of relief for those with substantial incomes who have the ability to repay a significant amount of their debt. Under this view, Chapter 7 relief should be available only to those who lack the means to repay their debts. The wisdom of making means testing a part of the Bankruptcy Code, however, cannot rest on the notion that Chapter 13 under current conditions is an unequivocal success. Not only are those who use it quite different from those while file under Chapter 7, but only one-third of those who file under Chapter 13 complete their plans.

In contrast to Chapter 7, not every individual debtor is eligible for Chapter 13. Under §109, those whose debts exceed set amounts—a little more than a quarter of a million and three-quarters of million dollars for unsecured and secured debt, respectively—may not file for Chapter 13 relief. Chapter 13 is designed for working individual debtors or couples with limited financial affairs, typically consumers or proprietors of small businesses. Individuals with more at stake cannot use it.

As in Chapter 7, a trustee is appointed in every Chapter 13 case. See §1302. The debtor herself, however, is charged with moving the process forward. Under §1321 she must file a plan with the court that sets out the way in which her future income will be used to pay creditors. The plan, which may modify or reduce the debtor's obligations, see §1322(b), must oblige the debtor to pay her creditors from some or all of her future income. Under §1322(a)(1) and (d), plan payments are generally limited to three years but may be extended to five years on a showing of cause.

The plan must also satisfy a series of important payment conditions. First, the plan must provide for the full satisfaction, in deferred cash payments, of all allowed claims (and administrative expenses) entitled to priority under §507 unless the holder of such a priority claim (or expense) agrees to some other treatment. See §1322. Second, a plan must provide for the satisfaction of all allowed unsecured claims with property (including promises) of a value, as of the effective date of the plan, at least equal to the amount that the creditors would receive from a Chapter 7 liquidation on that date. See §1325(a)(4). In theory, these provisions together ensure that creditors are no worse off than they would be if the debtor filed under Chapter 7, while priority claims may receive even more.

The requirements imposed on Chapter 13 plans protect unsecured creditors in one more way. Under §1325(b)(1) the trustee (or a creditor who is not being paid in full) may insist that the plan require the debtor to pay out all projected disposable income for three years. Disposable income is defined as income "not reasonably necessary to be expended for the maintenance or support of the debtor or a dependent of the debtor." To counter this, the debtor may under §1307 convert the case to Chapter 7 or dismiss the case altogether at any time. This power usually prevents creditors from pressing too hard, but only when the creditors believe the debtor is willing or able to convert. If the debtor has nonexempt assets that have a high subjective value, she may be willing to pay a creditor out of future income an amount even greater than what these assets are worth in the creditors' hands. Alternatively, the debtor may have a debt that is dischargeable in Chapter 13 but not in Chapter 7. Finally, a debtor may have already tried to use Chapter 7 but had her case dismissed under §707(b).

Under any of these circumstances, the disposable-income test can become the central focus of a Chapter 13 case. The standard that has emerged from the cases defies easy categorization, but common sense is a useful guide to understanding what kinds of expenses are reasonably necessary for the maintenance and support of the debtor and the debtor's dependents. They typically stop short of the standard of living that the bankruptcy judge enjoys. The debtor cannot expect to keep a car that is fancier than the one the judge drives.[38] The reasonably necessary standard of §1325(b)(2), however, lacks clear contours. A number of courts, for example, have come to different conclusions about whether private schooling is reasonably necessary.[39] Rigid rules may make even less sense, given how dramatically each debtor's circumstances can differ. Of course, if Congress imposes means testing on the use of Chapter 7, the dynamics of Chapter 13 will change considerably and the disposable-income test will likely become pivotal in many more cases.

One more important requirement imposed in Chapter 13 plans protects holders of secured claims. If the plan provides that the debtor retain property securing a claim, the plan must provide for full payment of the secured claim unless the creditor consents to less. Recall, however, that under §506(a) claims are bifurcated. A creditor's *secured* claim is limited to the value of the collateral. The balance is the creditor's unsecured claim. Payment on the secured claim may occur over time, if paid with interest, but the debtor's obligation under the plan must be secured by a lien on the original collateral. See §1325(a)(5).

If a plan meets these requirements and otherwise complies with the provisions of Chapter 13—such as the requirements of a plan's good faith, see §1325(a)(3), and feasibility, see §1325(a)(6)—the court must confirm the plan. Keep in mind, however, that even after confirmation, the bankruptcy case still remains open. The debtor's

---

[38] Various tests are set out in cases such as In re Jones, 55 Bankr. 462 (Bankr. D. Minn. 1985), and In re Sutliff, 79 Bankr. 151 (Bankr. N.D.N.Y. 1987).

[39] See, e.g., In re Nicola, 244 Bankr. 795 (N.D. Ill. 2000).

creditors remain stayed from collection by §362 (and an individual co-liable with the debtor generally is protected by §1301). The debtor's postpetition acquisitions and earnings become property of the estate under §1306.

A debtor who successfully completes performance under a Chapter 13 plan holds his property "free and clear of any claim or interest of any creditor provided for under the plan." §1327(c). He also earns a discharge under §1328(a). Moreover, a discharge granted under §1328(a) is not subject to all the exceptions to discharge that are in Chapter 7. (These are set out in §523.) For example, some tax obligations that cannot be discharged in Chapter 7 can be in Chapter 13 even when the plan does not provide for paying them in full. Congress, however, continues to expand the number of nondischargeable debts in Chapter 13, and this difference between the two chapters is likely to become less important over time.

If the debtor cannot meet payments under the plan, he may seek to modify it under §1329 or he may request a discharge if creditors have already received as much as they would have received under Chapter 7. The court might grant such a discharge under §1328(b) only if the plan cannot be modified practically and if the debtor failed for reasons beyond his control. Even in such a case, the discharge extends only to those debts that could have been discharged in Chapter 7. That is, the debtor cannot discharge any debt listed in §523(a). See §1328(c).

Debtors ordinarily choose between using Chapter 7 and Chapter 13. Some debtors try to use the two in sequence. This may happen when a debtor owns commercial real estate that has fallen in value since the debtor subjected the property to a mortgage. By filing in Chapter 7, the debtor discharges her personal obligations, including the obligation to the real estate lender for the difference between the amount of the loan and the value of the collateral. After the Chapter 7 discharge, the debtor still faces a lender with a lien on the real property for the entire amount of the debt. The lender can foreclose unless the debtor pays the entire amount owed on the mortgage loan. The discharge of the lender's unsecured claim prevents the creditor only from seeking a deficiency judgment from the debtor on what it is still owed. The debtor, however, can prevent foreclosure if it now files under Chapter 13 and proposes a plan that provides the lender with a payment stream equal to the present value of its secured claim, a claim worth considerably less than the outstanding amount of the mortgage loan. A debtor who has invested in commercial real estate may initially owe more than the Chapter 13 limit for debt obligations, but Chapter 7 discharges those debts and hence puts the debtor under the limit. These "Chapter 20" cases take advantage of the ability both to insulate future income from creditors under Chapter 7 and to strip down liens in Chapter 13. There is no per se barrier to using them in sequence.[40] A court, however, might refuse to confirm the Chapter 13 plan in a Chapter 20 case on the ground that the plan was filed in bad faith.

A Chapter 13 plan may propose the debtor's retention of collateral for a secured claim and generally "may modify the rights of holders of secured claims." §1322(b). But Chapter 13 protects holders of secured claims from modifications that leave them worse off. The most basic protection is found in §1325(a)(5), which provides that the plan must distribute to the holder of the secured claim property that has a value, as of the effective date of the plan, at least equal to the amount of the claim. Moreover, under the same provision, if the debtor is to retain the collateral, the plan must grant the holder of the secured claim a continuing lien on the collateral until the new obligation is fully paid. Put plainly, a debtor cannot retain collateral unless the plan proposes to pay an amount equal to the value of the collateral, though not necessarily at once. The requirement of a continuing lien supports this full-payment obligation in the event the debtor fails to complete payments under the plan.

Home mortgages often figure centrally in Chapter 13 cases. A debtor who has fallen behind on his mortgage payments is one of those most likely to file under Chapter 13. When a debtor encounters hard times, it may be that outside of bankruptcy he can prevent foreclosure and loss of his home only by paying off a bank's entire loan in full or by reaching a negotiated settlement with the bank. Particularly when the home has fallen in value, the debtor may find the bank uncooperative. The debtor might file for bankruptcy under Chapter 7, but he will find little relief there, as liquidation of the estate will throw the house back to the bank and state law. Chapter 13 offers the debtor breathing room and a last chance to sort things out.

Filing a Chapter 13 petition merely to take advantage of the automatic stay, however, can be found abusive if it is done without any attempt to put in place a plan to restructure debts.[41] One of the most common abuses of Chapter 13 is the serial filing, in which debtors repeatedly file just on the eve of foreclosure, and courts have had to de-

[40] See Johnson v. Home State Bank, 501 U.S. 78 (1991).
[41] See In re Felberman, 196 Bankr. 678, 681 (Bankr. S.D.N.Y. 1995).

vise a number of tools to deter the most flagrant forms of misbehavior.[42]

In addition, Chapter 13 contains a number of special provisions that extend more protection to home mortgage lenders than to other secured creditors. The primary limitation on a debtor's right to affect a home mortgage is the general prohibition on modification of the mortgage. See §1322(b)(2). For other kinds of mortgages, a plan will bifurcate an ordinary undersecured claim under §506(a) into a secured and unsecured claim, then treat each part separately. The plan will provide the holder with two new loan obligations, one on account of the secured claim and one on account of the deficiency. As an unsecured claim, the deficiency may well be paid only a few cents on the dollar. The terms of these loans can differ from each other and from those of the original loan. These new obligations replace the old claim, which may be discharged even if the terms of the original loan are never fully satisfied. Under §1322(b)(2), however, the debtor's ability to modify the rights of holders of secured claims does not extend to rights associated with "a claim secured only by a security interest in real property that is the debtor's principal residence." Section 1322(b)(2) prevents a plan from altering *any* of the terms of the original loan, even if they are not strictly speaking part of the secured claim. An example of such a term would be one that gives the creditor an action against the debtor for the difference between the value of the collateral and the amount of the debt.[43]

Chapter 13 does, however, provide some relief to debtors for their home mortgages. Under §1322(b)(5), a Chapter 13 debtor may cure some defaults on a long-term home mortgage. The cure must occur within a reasonable time and must reinstate the mortgage on its original terms. The exception does not apply if the last mortgage payment becomes due before the final payment under the Chapter 13 plan. In short, Chapter 13 gives debtors a way to keep their homes after a default, even a default that would give the lender a right to foreclose under state law. But during the Chapter 13 plan period and afterward, debtors must continue to pay off the mortgage in full, even if the value of the home has fallen far below the outstanding amount of the debt. The ability to cure only returns debtors to the situation they were in before they defaulted. Unless there has been a change in

---

[42] See Casse v. Key Bank National Association, 198 F.3d 327 (2d Cir. 1999).

[43] Nobelman v. American Savings Bank, 508 U.S. 324, 329 (1993).

their circumstances, debtors can quickly find themselves unable to meet these same obligations once again.

When creditors pursue their nonbankruptcy remedies, sooner or later they must have gone so far in the foreclosure process that a debtor can no longer file for bankruptcy and cure outstanding defaults. Chapter 13 did not deal with this point until 1994, when §1322(c)(1) was added. This section specifies that a debtor loses the right to cure defaults once the residence is sold at a foreclosure sale that is conducted in accordance with applicable nonbankruptcy law.

Home mortgages can run for twenty years or longer. In most cases, the term of the mortgage is longer than the term of the plan and the rule of modification or cure just described will apply. In 1994, however, Congress amended Chapter 13 to provide for the case in which the remaining term of the home mortgage is less than the length of the Chapter 13 plan. In such a case, "the plan may provide for the payment of the claim as modified pursuant to §1325(a)(5)," notwithstanding the §1322(b)(2) anti-modification clause. §1322(c)(2). Chapter 13 thus gives the debtor some maneuvering room with home mortgages that are near the end of their term.

In addition to Chapter 13, there is a special chapter of the Bankruptcy Code that protects farmers. Chapter 12 balances two competing concerns. First, it tries to give family farmers the ability to keep their farms even when they owe a secured creditor more than their farms are worth. Second, it tries to ensure that the property interests of the secured creditors are respected and that these creditors receive the value of their secured claim. These two goals might seem incompatible. If the farm is worth less than what the secured creditor is owed, then giving the secured creditor less than the entire farm seems undercompensatory. The residual interest that the farmer holds has *some* value. To the extent that the interest the farmer keeps has value, the secured creditor would seem to receive less than the full amount of its secured claim. Chapter 12, however, is premised on the notion that a reorganization plan that leaves a farm 100 percent leveraged is permissible.

The interplay of farmers and bankruptcy law has a long history. The politics of the 1841 bankruptcy statute were tied to the farm crisis that existed at the time. Similarly, the Frazier–Lemke Act protected farmers in the 1930s. A characteristic of much farm relief legislation has been that it remains in effect for only a finite number of years and then must be reenacted. Congress has regularly reenacted Chapter 12 for more than a decade now, but whether it continues to do so will depend greatly on the condition of the economy and the financial circumstances in which farmers find themselves at that time.

Chapter Three

Corporate Reorganizations and the Absolute Priority Rule

Introduction

We saw in chapter 2 that the animating principle of bankruptcy law for individual debtors is the fresh start, the right to discharge past debts and free future income and other exempt property from the claims of creditors. In this chapter we see that a different principle—the absolute priority rule—animates the law of corporate reorganizations. The absolute priority rule is so central to Chapter 11 and the negotiations surrounding it that we shall spend the bulk of this chapter trying to understand its origins as well as its shape today.

A corporation in Chapter 11, like an individual in Chapter 7, receives a discharge at the end of the bankruptcy proceeding, but the discharge has radically different consequences in the two cases. In the case of the individual debtor, the discharge works in conjunction with other parts of the Bankruptcy Code to ensure a fresh start. Discharging old debt does not itself keep creditors from reaching the debtor's future income. What matters in the case of an individual is not simply that debts are discharged under §727, but also that future earnings do not become property of the estate under §541. In contrast, a corporation's future earnings *do* become property of the estate. For this reason, the discharge itself does not put future income beyond the reach of those who held rights against it before the petition was filed. The discharge of corporate debt provided for in §1141 must serve a purpose altogether different from the discharge of individual debt in §727.

A limited liability corporation is not a flesh-and-blood individual, but rather a juridical being that owns assets against which many individuals have rights. We must focus on shareholders and creditors and others and ask what happens to their rights in the wake of the discharge. In the case of an individual in Chapter 7, we have to look at the exclusion of an individual debtor's future income provided by §541 to understand the effect of §727's discharge. Similarly, in the case of a corporation in Chapter 11, we have to look to the other parts of the Code that allocate rights to the corporation's future earnings to understand the effect of §1141's discharge. Section 1141 does not tell us how the earnings of the reorganized firm are split among the old creditors and shareholders. Instead, it is the absolute priority rule, as codified in §1129 and other parts of Chapter 11, that determines how those who held rights against the old firm will enjoy rights in the reorganized firm.

Before we look at the absolute priority rule, it is important to understand the purpose of Chapter 11 for corporate debtors. In the case of the individual debtor, Chapter 7 is meant to provide a substantive right: it allows an individual to enjoy a new life free of the burdens of unmanageable debt. A corporation is different. We may care about the workers or the shareholders or the creditors, but the corporation itself is merely a legal fiction. It is not a sentient being, and there is no virtue in preserving a corporate charter for its own sake.

Moreover, Chapter 11 cannot remedy the problems of an unsound business venture. Suppose an entrepreneur decides to open a new restaurant in a remote strip-mall in southern California. The restaurant specializes in Chicago dim sum. Customers eat in sequence small plates of food that provide a sample of every ethnic neighborhood in the city. The typical meal begins with a miniature bratwurst. Next is a small deep-dish pizza, followed by mu shu pork, and then a small portion of barbeque ribs, and then a piece of Baklava from Greektown for dessert. As it happens, aging, calorie-conscious baby-boomers in California have little interest either in going to this strip-mall or in sampling this kind of cuisine. Chapter 11 can do nothing to make this restaurant or Chicago dim sum a success. It does not matter whether the restaurant has no creditors or dozens of them. No one wants to dine at this restaurant, and bankruptcy law can do nothing to change this. The assets of the restaurant are best put to another use.

Some firms that cannot pay their debts may nevertheless be enterprises that are worth keeping intact. The archetypal case is a railroad. (As we shall see shortly, reorganizations of railroads in the late nineteenth century are the progenitor of modern Chapter 11.) The assets of a railroad—rights-of-way over narrow strips of land, hundreds or thousands of miles of iron rails, millions of wooden ties, and assorted bridges across the country—have relatively little scrap value. For this reason, a railroad may be worth keeping intact even if it does not carry enough traffic to pay back its construction costs. Building the railroad may have been a mistake, but, once built, the best use of the assets may still be as a railroad. Unlike a restaurant in a bad location that serves bad food, the railroad's assets may have no better use.

Nevertheless, everyone has to confront the fact that the firm cannot pay off its creditors. There needs to be a forum in which the rights of creditors and shareholders are sorted out.

If creditors of the railroad had the right to invoke the rules of various states governing debt collection, any given creditor would have a chance of being paid in full. It could grab the nearest assets of the railroad and sell them for scrap. But a remedy premised on each creditor's pursuit of its own interests could lead to the dismemberment of the railroad. The creditors are better off if the railroad is kept in one piece. They need to enforce their claims against the railroad in a way that preserves the railroad's value as a going concern. The struggle to sort out competing claims to the assets should not keep the assets from being put to their best use.

Ensuring assets are put to their best use requires recognizing that some parties are not going to be paid in full, and a coherent bankruptcy law has to identify them. The basic distributional rule of Chapter 11—the one as central to it as the fresh start policy is to individuals—is the absolute priority rule. The substantive idea behind the absolute priority rule can be put simply: senior creditors are paid before junior creditors, and creditors are paid before shareholders. The procedures that Chapter 11 uses to implement this substantive idea are quite complicated, and the easiest way to understand them is to see where they came from. Hence, we need to look to history.

Equity Receiverships and the Origins of Chapter 11

We can trace the roots of Chapter 11 back to the problems attending the rise of the great railroads in the late nineteenth century. These were the first giant corporations. They connected all parts of the United States and revolutionized the way people lived. The railroad, for example, brought fresh milk to city dwellers. Before the railroads, milk would spoil long before it reached the urban marketplace. By 1860, however, private investment in railroads exceeded one billion dollars, and investment bankers such as J. P. Morgan, August Belmont, and Kidder Peabody had to turn to large commercial centers of Europe for the capital to finance the transcontinental railroads that were to be built over the next three decades. These investment bankers sat on the boards of the various railroads and represented the interests of their European investors.[1] Because they counted on re-

---

[1] See Alfred D. Chandler Jr., The Visible Hand: The Managerial Revolution in American Business 146 (1977).

peated dealings with these investors, they had the incentive to represent them well.

The period between 1865 and 1890 was one of enormous growth for railroads. The period also saw the consolidation of different lines in haphazard and unpredictable ways. More than 75,000 miles of track were laid down in the 1880s alone. This was a time of both increasing competition and increasing government regulation. Competition among the different lines intensified; cartels came into existence and then fell apart. At the same time, the early 1890s brought on one of the United States's worst economic downturns. All these factors created an industry that by the mid-1890s was insolvent. Most of the railroads that had been built could not meet their fixed obligations. More than half the railroads in the United States went through reorganization during this period, some more than once.[2]

The typical railroad needing reorganization had few general creditors. There were different classes of bonds, each widely held by diverse investors, many of whom were in Europe. One bond was secured by track between points A and B, another by track between B and C, a third between C and D, and so on. Points B through Y were in the middle of nowhere, and the terminals at points A and Z connected to solvent railroads owned by the shareholders. The collateral of individual creditors added value to the ongoing railroad. This value, however, could not be realized by foreclosing on the collateral; only through the active participation of all parties could the value of the constituent parts be maximized.

Bringing about a successful reorganization was difficult. The value of the railroad had to be estimated against a background of rapid technological and regulatory change. The claim of the many different kinds of bondholders turned on how much their collateral contributed to the earnings of the railroad as a whole. Moreover, many of the investors lived abroad and could not actively participate in the reorganization. They had to rely on their investment bankers and their lawyers to represent them. Although Congress had the power to enact federal bankruptcy law, none was in place in this period. Faced with dispersed interests with uncertain value and no statutory guidance, the lawyers used the equity receivership to reorganize the railroads.

Because the railroads were the first experiments in large aggregations of capital from diverse investors, many of the terms of the in-

---

[2] For a history of railroad reorganizations of the 1890s, see Stuart Daggett, Railroad Reorganization (1908).

vestment contracts were left blank or imported mechanically from real estate transactions. The law of equity receiverships had to supply the missing terms, and these had to respond to the distinct problems that arose when the firm needed a new capital structure. What emerged in the end were the basic features of Chapter 11.

Consider a railroad that owes $100 million to several dozen different kinds of bondholders, each of whom has a security interest in different assets of the railroad. In the aggregate, these bonds cover all the hard assets of the railroad. The railroad also owes a diverse group of general creditors $1 million. The railroad cannot meet payments on the $101 million debt. The bondholders realize that the time has come to restructure the firm. They call on their lawyers and their investment bankers. The lawyers persuade a general creditor to ask a federal court to appoint a receiver for the railroad. The receiver the court appoints is often the group of manager-shareholders that has been running the railroad. In the meantime, lawyers and the investment bankers form committees, each representing the interests of a different group of shareholders or creditors.

Each bondholders committee then tries to persuade those holding its bonds to deposit them with it and give it the power to assert all the rights of the bondholders in the reorganization. Let's assume that in our case, 90 percent of the bondholders give their bonds to their respective committees. Similarly, another committee holds 90 percent of the stock. The various committees then meet and create a new committee, the reorganization committee, on which members of each of the other committees sit and that is empowered to act on behalf of the other committees. The reorganization committee now controls 90 percent of all outstanding securities. It then proceeds to form a plan of reorganization.

Under the plan, each participant in the reorganization who holds a $100 bond in some asset of railroad will give it up in exchange for a $50 bond secured by all the assets of the firm. The participating shareholders are given the option to acquire equity of the reorganized railroad in exchange for their shares in the old firm and $1 million in new cash. Through their representatives on the reorganization committee, all the participating creditors and shareholders consent to this plan.

The reorganization committee then borrows $10 million from a bank on a short-term basis. At this point, the receiver conducts a foreclosure sale in which the assets of the railroad are sold to the highest bidder. At the sale, the reorganization committee is the only bidder. It bids $10 million for the entire railroad and takes over the assets of the railroad after it pays the receiver. The receiver takes the $10 million and distributes it to the bondholders. (Nothing goes to the general creditors, because the sale price is not enough to pay the bondholders in full.) Because the reorganization committee itself owns 90 percent of the bonds, the receiver gives back to the reorganization committee $9 million of the $10 million the committee paid to buy the railroad. The receiver pays the other $1 million to the nonparticipating bondholders who did not give their bonds to their committees.

The old corporation is now a hollow shell and the old shareholders dissolve it under state law. Because the legal entity that was the railroad now no longer exists, all claims against it are worthless. The stockholders who did not turn over their rights to the relevant committee are out of luck, as are the general creditors who did not have any chance to participate at all. At this point, the reorganization committee has the assets of the railroad and the $9 million it received from the receiver. The committee now forms a new corporation and transfers all the assets of the railroad to it. The new corporation creates $45 million in bonds and gives them to the old participating bondholders as promised in the reorganization plan. All the stock in the new firm is given to the old shareholders when they come up with the $1 million in cash they promised in the reorganization plan. With this $1 million and the $9 million the receiver gave it, the committee repays the $10 million bank loan. The reorganization committee now goes out of existence.

If we focus entirely on legal forms, we see a new corporation with a new set of ownership claims against it. In substance, however, the story is quite different. If one collapses the various steps in this elaborate dance, most of the bondholders and shareholders have simply exchanged their old claims against the firm for new ones that take better account of the condition in which the railroad finds itself. We have exactly the same railroad with the same managers and the same investors, but the ownership rights of the investors have been adjusted so that they are in line with the revenue that the railroad actually earns.

Under Chapter 11 of the Bankruptcy Code, we would say that the railroad's old obligations to its creditors have been discharged. As we noted at the start of this discussion, however, "discharge" in this context means something quite different from what it does in the case of the individual who is given a fresh start. The discharge is only one part of the mechanism that allows the firm to acquire a new capital structure.

The debates over the railroad reorganization therefore revolved not around the meaning of a fresh start for corporations but around other issues. First, there was the question of the rights of those who did not participate in the reorganization. In our example, these included 10 percent of the bondholders and the diverse general creditors. The bondholders who did not participate argued that they were given only ten cents on the dollar, while those who did participate were given fifty cents on the dollar. To the response that they could have participated and enjoyed fifty cents on the dollar if they had wanted, these bondholders would argue that the reorganization forced them to choose between the lesser of two evils. Either their claims would be cashed out at ten cents on the dollar at a fictitious foreclosure sale or they would have to submit to whatever terms the reorganization committee dictated. None of the individual bondholders had enough of an investment in the railroad to go through the effort necessary to keep the reorganization committee from doing whatever it pleased. As a result, insiders remained in control of the process and ended up in control of the firm.

The equity receivership thus had to navigate between two dangers: that of insiders taking advantage of the scattered bondholders and that of a few dissident bondholders free riding on the efforts of others to recapitalize the railroad. Under the solution that ultimately emerged in the equity receivership, the judge insisted on an *upset price*, a minimum price that the reorganization committee would have to bid at the foreclosure sale to acquire the assets of the railroad. By ensuring that the upset price was sufficiently high, the minority bondholders would be given an amount commensurate with the value of their nonbankruptcy rights.[3] The defect of this approach in practice was that judges tended to keep the upset price low. They feared that a high upset price would undermine the successful reorganization because it would require the reorganization committee to come up with more cash than it could raise.

The 1978 Bankruptcy Code replaced this way of protecting dissenters in a class of creditors. Congress folded into the corporate reorganization a procedure that had been used in plans under the 1898 Bankruptcy Act. Under the 1898 Act, the debtor would meet with creditors, fill out schedules of assets and liabilities, and subject itself to examination. At this point, the debtor would propose a plan, or *composition*, in which the creditors' claims were scaled back. If the plan was accepted by a majority of the creditors and if the majority

---

[3] See First National Bank of Cincinnati v. Flershem, 290 U.S. 504 (1934).

held more than half of the outstanding debt, the court would approve it if, among other requirements, the plan was in the best interests of the creditors.[4] Courts interpreted "best interests" to mean that those creditors who did not vote in favor of the plan had to receive as much as they would receive in an orderly liquidation of the firm.[5] This method of protecting dissenters in a class of creditors, codified in §1129(a)(7), replaced the use of an upset price in the equity receivership (and its statutory successor in old Chapter x).

More important in the dynamics of modern Chapter 11 are the procedures that emerged in response to the complaints from the general creditors who had no chance to participate in the reorganization at all. It might seem that the general creditors have nothing to complain about. The railroad is worth less than $100 million, the amount the bondholders were owed. Even if the firm were sold for cash at its fair market value, the general creditors would receive nothing. Given the sorry condition of the firm, they are not entitled to anything. This risk is one they should have taken into account when they extended credit to the firm.

Nevertheless, we must at least have in place procedures that ensure that the railroad is indeed worth less than $100 million. We need to be sure that the senior creditors and the shareholders have not restructured the firm in a way that slighted others' rights. To ensure the protection of such rights, courts fashioned over the course of many decades a set of rules, loosely identified as the *fair and equitable principle*. Section 1129(b) codifies this principle. It requires that a plan be fair and equitable before it can be confirmed over the objection of a class of claims. To understand what "fair and equitable" means, one must know the sequence of cases from which the principle emerged. The most important of these is *Northern Pacific Railway Company v. Boyd*.[6]

In 1886 a man named Spaulding had supplied $25,000 worth of materials and labor to the Coeur D'Alene Railroad for which he was never paid. The assets of the Coeur D'Alene, after several restructurings, ultimately became part of the Northern Pacific Railroad. Spaulding believed he could hold the Northern Pacific Railroad liable for this debt. Before he acquired a judgment against it, however, the Northern Pacific Railroad became insolvent and went through

---

[4] Act of July 1, 1898, ch. 541, §12b, 30 Stat. 541, 549.

[5] See Fleischmann & Devine Inc. v. Saul Wolfson Dry Goods Co., 299 F. 15 (5th Cir. 1924).

[6] 228 U.S. 482 (1913).

an equity receivership, out of which emerged a new entity called the Northern Pacific Railway.

Spaulding's successor, a man named Boyd, did not participate in the reorganization of the Northern Pacific Railroad and instead sued the new entity. The dispute finally reached the United States Supreme Court in 1913. The Court found first that the old Northern Pacific had indeed been responsible for the obligations of Coeur D'Alene. The Court then had to ask whether the new Northern Pacific was responsible for the debts of the old.

Boyd argued that the court-supervised sale could not extinguish his rights because the old shareholders remained the shareholders of the new entity. He invoked the common law rule, based on fraudulent conveyance doctrine, that a landowner who purchases back his property at a foreclosure sale takes subject to the claims of junior creditors, even though a third party buying at arm's length would not. Boyd had not participated in the reorganization or relinquished his claims. Thus he could hold the Northern Pacific Railway answerable for the obligations of the Northern Pacific Railroad.

Lawyers for the Northern Pacific Railway argued that the sale had to be respected. The real estate analogy was inapt, they asserted. The Railway was an entity that was distinct from the Railroad. One should respect the formal differences, even though the shareholders of the two were the same. The judicial sale was regular in form and free from fraud. The assets had been sold for a fair price and that price was for less than what the secured creditors were owed. Had Boyd participated in the reorganization, he would have received nothing. Recharacterizing the transaction would only foster strike suits and make reorganizations of insolvent railroads impracticable. The Northern Pacific Railway lost below and appealed to the Supreme Court.

In *Boyd*, a divided Court found that the common law principle limiting the effect of debtor purchases at a foreclosure sale existed in the law of corporate reorganizations as well:

> As against creditors, [the sale] was a mere form. Though the Northern Pacific Railroad was divested of the legal title, the old stockholders were still owners of the same railroad, encumbered by the same debts. The circumlocution did not better their title against Boyd as a nonassenting creditor. They had changed the name but not the relation.[7]

---

[7] Id. at 506–07.

Nor did it matter that the assets were worth less than what creditors senior to Boyd were owed:

> [T]he question must be decided according to a fixed principle, not leaving the rights of the creditors to depend upon the balancing of evidence as to whether, on the day of sale the property was insufficient to pay prior encumbrances.[8]

The Court did not go so far as to say that all of real estate foreclosure law should be mechanically transplanted to the law of corporate reorganizations. The Court held only that a complete freezeout of an intervening creditor was not permitted. Indeed, the Court itself was quick to note that its holding was narrow:

> [We do not] require the impossible and make it necessary to pay an unsecured creditor in cash as a condition of stockholders retaining an interest in the reorganized company. His interest can be preserved by the issuance, on equitable terms, of income bonds or preferred stock. If he declines a fair offer he is left to protect himself as any other creditor of a judgment debtor, and, having refused to come into a just reorganization, could not thereafter be heard in a court of equity to attack it.[9]

In contrast to real estate foreclosures, a plan of reorganization could include shareholders if the creditor were given a fair offer in a just reorganization. Exactly what these terms meant, the Court did not explain. Lower courts had to identify on their own the contours of the "fixed principle" that should be at work and out of this emerged a set of ideas of what constituted a fair and equitable plan.

After *Boyd*, a plan could not bypass junior creditors unless such creditors consented or had their day in court. Ex post assertions of fairness by a coalition of senior creditors and shareholders would not suffice. The question remained, however, whether or under what conditions a nonconsensual bypass of junior creditors was permissible *even given* their day in court. The Court ultimately confronted this question in *Case v. Los Angeles Lumber Products*.[10]

In *Case*, the debtor was a holding company whose principal asset was the Los Angeles Shipbuilding & Drydock Corporation. This corporation had built ships for the navy during World War I but languished during the 1920s and 1930s. It sought to reorganize itself in

[8] Id. at 507–08.

[9] Id. at 508.

[10] 308 U.S. 106 (1939).

1937. The only creditors were holders of twenty-year bonds due in 1944. Holders of more than 90 percent of the face amount of the bonds voted in favor of the plan. The plan gave 23 percent of the stock in the new corporation to the old shareholders. These shareholders planned to continue to play a managerial role in operating the business, but they were not contributing any new cash.

The district court had held that the plan was fair and equitable. It noted that only two bondholders had objected to the plan, and the court did not want to give a couple of dissenters the ability to hold up a reorganization approved by a substantial majority of the bondholders. The court justified the continued participation of the old equityholders on the grounds that the shareholders were willing to assume managerial responsibilities in the company and that they were "the only persons who [were] familiar with the company's operations and who [had] experience in shipbuilding." In addition, the court noted,

> [m]ost of the present bondholders are widely scattered with small holdings, and their position would be benefited by being associated with old stockholders of financial influence and stability who might be able to assist in proper financing.[11]

The reorganization was brought about, it seems, from the need for additional capital, not by the threat of foreclosure by existing creditors. Because of a previous workout, interest payments were owed only if earned, and the creditors lacked the power to foreclose until 1944.

When *Case* reached the Supreme Court on appeal, the Court had a vehicle to confront the different interpretations of the "fair and equitable" principle that had been debated in the wake of *Boyd*. Under one view, the approval of the plan by 90 percent of the creditors was enough. Requiring unanimity was unreasonable, and the old shareholders had to be given some of the going-concern value or they would not cooperate in reorganizing the firm. A court should confirm a plan if a class of diverse investors approved the plan, if each investor received what it would receive in a liquidation, and if the overall process was regular.

The competing view was altogether different. Under this view, allowing the old equity to continue was a source of mischief. Rather than making it possible to obtain their help after the reorganization,

---

[11] In re Los Angeles Lumber Products Co., 24 F. Supp. 501, 513 (S.D. Cal. 1938), aff'd, 100 F.2d 963 (9th Cir.), rev'd, 308 U.S. 106 (1939).

it gave old shareholders an opportunity to hold up other investors. In a firm such as a shipyard, shareholders do not control the day-to-day operations. Professionals can be brought in to do the job. Only in the narrowest of circumstances should old equity be permitted to continue in the face of any dissent.

Speaking through Justice William O. Douglas, the *Case* Court sided squarely with the second view. The Court first rejected the idea that dissenters are entitled only to their share of a debtor's liquidation value, leaving others to decide how any surplus would be divided. The Court held instead that the fair and equitable standard afforded each creditor its "full right of priority" in the firm as a going concern. *Case* thus forged a link between the phrases "fair and equitable" and "absolute priority," a link that lawyers, judges, and Congress have accepted ever since.

Once Justice Douglas established this link, he was led to cut back sharply on the shareholders' ability to participate in the reorganization of an insolvent firm over a creditor's objection. The absolute priority rule allowed shareholders to participate in the new venture only if they paid fair value for their continuing interest in a reorganized debtor. Moreover, to ensure that the shareholders paid fair value, the Court required that such payments be easy to value. If a creditor objected to an insolvent debtor's plan of reorganization, the plan could not include a distribution to old equity unless each stockholder's participation was based "on a contribution in money or in money's worth, reasonably equivalent in view of all the circumstances to the participation of the stockholder."[12]

Under pre-Code law, a single dissenting creditor could insist that a plan be fair and equitable. This gave one creditor considerable holdup power. Indeed, in *Case* itself, one of the dissenting creditors had a long history of buying claims at a deep discount and holding up reorganizations until he was paid in full. Under the Bankruptcy Code, the "full right" of absolute priority Justice Douglas identified now comes into play only if a class as a whole opposes the plan.

The "fair and equitable" language in §1129(b) embodies the absolute priority rule, and it has two essential components. First, those with rights against the assets of a firm under nonbankruptcy law receive interests in the new firm according to the priority they enjoyed under nonbankruptcy law. A creditor who is entitled to be paid before another creditor outside of bankruptcy (by virtue, let us say, of a security interest) is entitled to be paid first in bankruptcy as well.

[12] 308 U.S. at 122.

Similarly, general creditors are entitled to be paid before share-holders. The effect of the discharge, in other words, is almost the opposite of what we see in the case of the flesh-and-blood individual debtor. In the case of an individual, the discharge (coupled with the exclusion of future income from property of the estate) allows individuals to preserve their right to future earnings in the face of creditors' claims. In the case of a corporation, discharge (coupled with the absolute priority rule) allows creditors to extinguish the shareholders' right to future earnings when the assets are not worth enough to pay the creditors off in full. We will look more closely at the mechanics of §1129 in the next section.

Chapter 11 and the Absolute Priority Rule

Section 1129(b) is invoked when a reorganization plan fails to garner the acceptance of all adversely affected (or *impaired*) classes of claims and interests and thus fails to satisfy §1129(a)(8). Section 1129(b)'s requirement that a plan not "discriminate unfairly" is relatively straightforward. If two classes contain claims or interests of identical priority, absent some special circumstance that would justify subordination of one class, a plan cannot provide less to one class on a pro rata basis unless that class consents. The requirement stops short of mandating identical treatment for classes at the same priority level. A plan does not discriminate unfairly merely because it gives cash to one class of general creditors and long-term notes to another. The plan will pass muster if there is a reason for the different treatment and if the cash payments and the notes give claims in each class the same pro rata share of the debtor's assets. A tort victim who needs surgery, for example, might be paid in cash, while an institutional lender might receive a note, as it has no similar need for payment in cash.

Section 1129(b) implements the absolute priority rule first by requiring that each class that rejects the plan be treated in a way that is fair and equitable. The section then goes on to add specific requirements for secured claims, unsecured claims, and equity interests included within the concept of fair and equitable. These requirements have the effect of ensuring that the core ideas of the judicially created fair and equitable doctrine remain fixed even if the edges of the doctrine continue to evolve.

With respect to a class of allowed secured claims, the fair and equitable principle requires, at a minimum, that each holder of a secured claim receive a stream of payments with a discounted present value equal to the value of the collateral. See §1129(b)(2)(A). Moreover, this stream of payments must be secured by a lien on the creditor's collateral. If the collateral is sold, the creditor's lien attaches to the proceeds. Alternatively, the plan could propose a different treatment that provides for the realization of the *indubitable equivalent* of the secured claim. This language is taken from Learned Hand's opinion in *In re Murel Holding*.[13] The test, however, is sufficiently stringent that it is likely to be of use to the debtor only under narrow circumstances.

A reorganization plan must meet an additional requirement to be confirmed over the objection of a class of secured claims. The plan must also provide a stream of payments equal to the face amount of the secured claim. In most cases, this requirement is redundant. In a world in which discount rates are positive, a stream of payments over time equal in value to a given amount must total more than the face amount owed. Hence, this requirement matters only if the secured claim is for more than the value of the collateral despite the operation of §506(a), which generally equates the two. A mismatch can occur if a secured creditor makes what is called the §1111(b)(2) election. Under this provision, a secured creditor can elect to have its entire claim treated as secured regardless of the collateral's value. As a result, the stream of a plan's payments must not only be equal in value to the collateral, as determined by the judge, but the face amount of the stream of payments in the aggregate must equal the total amount of the claim that the collateral supports. The election is a way in which the secured creditor gives up its deficiency claim and in return limits the extent to which its lien can be stripped down as a result of judicial undervaluation of the collateral.

Section 1129(b)(2)(B) fleshes out the fair and equitable standard for a class of unsecured claims that rejects the plan. If the plan awards any property to old equity (or to a junior class of claims) on account of the old equity interest (or junior claim), the plan must provide each holder of an unsecured claim with property that is at least equal in value to the amount of the claim. In other words, unless the plan proposes to pay unsecured claims in full, those junior to them must be wiped out if the plan is to be crammed down over objection by the holders of unsecured claims. This provision seems straightforward enough. But complications arise when holders of old equity wish to remain and are contributing new value. They can argue that they receive new equity on account of the new capital, not "on account of" their old interests. Hence, holders of old equity argue, notwith-

---

[13] 75 F.2d 941 (2d Cir. 1935).

standing §1129(b), the plan does not have to pay the unsecured claims in full.

If the equityholders enjoy the exclusive right to buy the equity, however, they have an option, which is itself a form of property. In the last chapter of this book we shall return to the question of equity participation when a class of claimholders votes against the plan. For the moment, it is worth noting that in the continuing evolution of the fair and equitable principle, courts have further protected creditors by insisting that market benchmarks be used to ensure that equity is paying top dollar. A judge might, for example, lift exclusivity and entertain other plans as soon as the debtor proposes a plan in which the old equity participates and a class of claimholders objects.[14]

Section §1129(b)(2)(c) applies to a class of preferred stock interests. Under corporate law, preferred stock, though classified as equity and thus as an interest, is a hybrid between debt and equity, inferior to the former but superior to the latter. The "preference" is typically a right to insist that neither dividends nor any other payments go to the firm's common shares unless and until the firm pays the preferred shareholders specified amounts analogous to interest and principal on a debt. The fair and equitable standard requires that a reorganization plan honor these preferences—called *liquidation preferences* or sometimes *redemption prices*—with provision of full payment, though not necessarily in cash. If the plan fails to do this, then the holders of more junior interests, those who hold common stock, may not receive any property on account of their old interests.

For its part, common equity also is protected by the fair and equitable standard of §1129(b)(2)(c), though in a more limited way befitting common equity's status of lowest priority. A plan is not fair and equitable to a class of common equity interests unless the plan provides property of a value at least equal to the value of those interests. This is simply a requirement that creditors not capture the entire value of a solvent debtor. Thus, this requirement is only as important as solvent debtors in bankruptcy are common.

As you consider these provisions, keep in mind that the fair and equitable standard is a *class-based* right. The holder of an individual claim or interest can demand at least what it would have received in a Chapter 7 liquidation. If, however, a class votes to make a sacrifice of

---

[14] Bank of America v. 203 North LaSalle Street Partnership, 526 U.S. 434 (1999).

its priority, a dissenter within the approving class cannot block the plan on the basis of that sacrifice.

The absolute priority rule sets the ground rules for Chapter 11, but it does not identify all the effects of filing a Chapter 11 petition. For example, a secured creditor may worry that if it works too closely with the debtor in crafting a nonbankruptcy workout, it will be charged with being an insider or be subject to labor laws or environmental laws.[15] A nonbankruptcy restructuring of the debt may also bring unfavorable tax consequences for the secured creditor that can be avoided in bankruptcy. If the secured creditor continues to finance a firm, it may be better off doing it under the umbrella of Chapter 11 as a debtor-in-possession (commonly abbreviated as a "dip") financer. Finally, the secured creditor has to face the possibility that a nonbankruptcy workout will only postpone the inevitable. If the secured creditor makes compromises in the workout, it may be worse off in a subsequent Chapter 11 case relative to those who refused to compromise. A long-term secured creditor may be better off in Chapter 11 than it would be if it had to wait and watch while the debtor paid off short-term obligations that were junior to the one owed it.

The ambition of every lawyer whose client files a Chapter 11 petition is to persuade each group of creditors to consent to a plan of reorganization. Whether a group consents depends on its rights under the plan versus the rights it would have if it refused to go along with the plan. The absolute priority rule is central to the law of corporate reorganizations because it is the source of the substantive rights as well as the procedural protections that each participant in a reorganization enjoys. Parties can insist that the priority rights they enjoyed outside of bankruptcy be respected inside. Nevertheless, every junior party, including the shareholders, can invoke elaborate procedures before their rights are compromised. The absolute priority rule allows the senior parties to insist on full payment, but it also grants all junior parties those procedural protections necessary for a "just reorganization." Resolving this tension between substantive and procedural rights that began with *Boyd* remains central to answering the hard questions that arise under Chapter 11.

The law and practice of Chapter 11 establishes a framework for negotiations. The dynamics of any negotiation are defined by what there is to bargain over and the place of each of the parties in the pecking order. Before a plan of reorganization can take place, we

[15] See United States v. Fleet Factors Corp., 901 F.2d 1550 (11th Cir. 1990).

must find out what assets the debtor has and we must know the relative positions of each of the parties. In the next few chapters, we step back from the dynamics of reorganization practice per se and explore how we go about establishing the stakes the parties are fighting over and their rights vis-à-vis one another. Once we understand these, we will return to the reorganization process itself and explore it in greater detail.

Chapter Four

Claims Against the Estate

We now turn to the way bankruptcy law establishes the debtor's *liabilities* and *assets*—what the debtor's obligations are and what assets exist to meet them. We must determine who gets what. Figuring out the "who" is the problem of claims, which we examine in this chapter. Figuring out the "what" is the problem of assets, which we focus on in the next chapter. In both cases our starting point is nonbankruptcy law. The *Butner* principle is perhaps most powerful when we look at the subject of claims in bankruptcy. As the Supreme Court noted in that case, "[c]reditors' entitlements in bankruptcy arise in the first instance from the underlying substantive law creating the debtor's obligation."[1] Another Supreme Court case—*Chicago Board of Trade v. Johnson*[2]—tells us to use the nonbankruptcy baseline to identify the debtor's assets.

Establishing a Claim Against the Estate

A creditor often first learns of a bankruptcy filing when it receives notice of it from the bankruptcy clerk. Rule 2002. When a debtor files for bankruptcy, it must fill out schedules that list its liabilities and the names and addresses of its creditors. If you are a creditor and are included on this list, you will be sent notice of the bankruptcy and you will be given a chance to take the appropriate procedural steps to vindicate your rights. Your first step would be to file a form known as a proof of claim. Once that is filed, the claim is "allowed" in the absence of objection. The consequences of failing to file a proof of claim depend on whether your debtor is an individual or a corporation, whether your debtor is in Chapter 7 or Chapter 11, and whether you are listed on the debtor's schedules.

Take first the case of an individual debtor who files a Chapter 7 petition and fails to list your claim. If you do not file a proof of claim, you will not share in the distribution of assets. But if you do not know about the bankruptcy, §523(a)(3) prevents your claim against the

[1] Raleigh v. Illinois Department of Revenue, 530 U.S. •••, ••• (2000).
[2] 264 U.S. 1 (1924).

79

debtor from being discharged.[3] You can pursue the debtor after the bankruptcy is over.

Your rights against a corporation in Chapter 7 are different, however, because a corporation has no life after bankruptcy. If a corporation files a Chapter 7 petition, you must file a proof of claim to share in the distribution of the debtor's assets regardless of whether your claim is listed or whether you learn of the bankruptcy. To be sure, no corporate debts are discharged in Chapter 7.[4] The discharge, however, is irrelevant because the corporation distributes all of its assets in Chapter 7 and then dissolves. At the end of the Chapter 7 case, all the assets are gone and there is nothing left to satisfy your claim.

There is a procedural difference in Chapter 11. A creditor must file a proof of claim only if its claim is not listed in the schedules or is disputed, contingent, or unliquidated. §1111(a); Rule 3003(c). The substantive outcome, however, is the same for a creditor whose claim is not listed or whose claim is contingent. Even though the corporation has a continuing life after bankruptcy, all the debts of the corporation are discharged in Chapter 11, even if they are not scheduled. A creditor who is not listed on the schedules is obliged to file a proof of claim and is left out of the distribution if it fails to do so.[5]

Ordinarily, the treatment of claims is straightforward. The amount each creditor is owed is listed on the schedules and is not disputed. All one has to do is figure out how to divide whatever assets there are among the various claimants. Suppose there are 100 creditors, and all are listed and properly notified. The debtor owes them $10,000. The average claim is $100, but some are owed $10 and one is owed more than $1,000. All the debtor's assets are sold for a total of $1,000.[6] Only 10 cents in assets is available for every dollar of liability. How do we divide the pie, as small as it is? Since at least the sixteenth century the rule has been one of pro rata distribution: in this case, then, each creditor receives 10 cents for every dollar it is owed. A creditor that is owed $1,000 gets $100. A creditor that is owed $50 gets $5. Rule 3010 provides that no dividend of less than $5 is paid since it costs that much just to cut the check.

---

[3] As we discussed in chapter 2, an exception may exist in the no-asset case. See p. 51 *supra*.

[4] Under §727, only individuals enjoy a discharge in Chapter 7.

[5] The creditor's only recourse is to argue that the bankruptcy process itself failed to satisfy the basic requirements of due process. See p. 203 *infra*.

[6] Unless specified otherwise, figures exclude the costs of bankruptcy.

The rule of pro rata distribution provides a way to approximate the rights of each of the general creditors. We should bear in mind, however, that it is only an approximation. We do not know what the nonbankruptcy right would be for each creditor because bankruptcy has put a halt to the race among them. We know that without the automatic stay, some of them would have been paid in full and others would have received nothing, but it is not worth the effort to figure out who would have come first. There are other complications. Smaller creditors might have been more likely to be paid in full because they would not have had to seize much to satisfy their claims. For this reason, some might argue that we should give them more than their pro rata share. Large creditors, however, have more to lose and therefore might spend more time and effort monitoring the debtor. One could also argue that they should receive more than their pro rata share. In the end, we have the pro rata sharing rule because trying to answer arguments like these is more trouble than it is worth. The kinds of distributions in these cases are in the neighborhood of 10 cents on the dollar for general creditors.

Now let us flesh out the story somewhat. Suppose that a fully perfected secured creditor is owed $500. It has a fully and properly perfected security interest on every asset that the debtor has. In this case, the secured creditor gets 100 cents on the dollar, or $500, out of the $1,000 pie. From the remaining $500 we subtract the fees that the trustee gets (and, more important, the fees of the lawyer for the trustee, who is frequently a lawyer at the trustee's firm). Whatever is left is divided among the general creditors pro rata. If the remainder is $150 and the general creditors are still owed $10,000, then the distribution is at the rate of 1.5 cents on the dollar. If you are owed $1,000, you get $15. If you are owed $600, you get $9.

We also need to put a value on disputed claims, such as a lawsuit against the debtor that is in litigation. To see how the Bankruptcy Code handles these claims, it is useful to look at a straightforward example. Let us assume that a software producer is suing the debtor for unfair competition. If the debtor owes anything, it will owe $12,000. But the debtor argues that all it did was engage in some hardball competition. The liability is an all-or-nothing affair. The software producer's chances of winning in state court are roughly one in three. The trial is still many years away.

Under §101, the software producer is viewed as a creditor who holds a claim against the debtor. The claim, however, is both disputed and unliquidated. After the producer files its proof of claim and the debtor files its objection, the bankruptcy judge may conduct a streamlined trial and decide the merits of the dispute. §502(b). The shortened process makes sense. Even if the producer wins, it is not going to be paid in full. In most Chapter 11 bankruptcies, general creditors are lucky to receive more than 20 cents on the dollar. In deciding the merits of the producer's claim, the bankruptcy judge follows nonbankruptcy substantive rules and bankruptcy's procedural rules. The judge turns to state law to find out what conduct constitutes unfair competition, but the judge may decide factual questions rather than leaving them to a jury. A bankruptcy court is entitled to use chancery methods in putting a value on a claim.

A bankruptcy judge is not, however, required to *fix* a value on the claim. Under §502(c) the judge can estimate the value for the purposes of the bankruptcy proceeding and allow the creditor to reappear if it gets a judgment for a different amount. In the meantime, the creditor participates as if its claim is equal to the estimate. There can even be a distribution according to the estimate, perhaps with some way (such as the issuance of new equity) to increase the distribution after the case is over.

Estimating the producer's claim is not easy. It is a $12,000 lawsuit, but it has only one chance in three of succeeding. Let us assume that other general creditors are owed $3,000 and that the assets are worth $1,000. If we value the producer's claim at its present probability of success, it would have a claim for $4,000. The producer's claim, even discounted, makes it the largest unsecured creditor. The producer would dominate the bankruptcy proceeding even though in the end its lawsuit would probably not succeed and the debtor would owe it nothing.

Giving the producer a voice according to its present probability of success therefore seems unattractive, but there may be no better alternatives. If the producer prevailed in the end, it would be entitled to 80 percent of the debtor's assets and would virtually be able to dictate the plan of reorganization. Valuing the producer's claim at its present probability of success would be undervaluing it if the producer ultimately wins. By the same measure , we would be overvaluing it if it turns out that the producer loses. Discounting the producer's claim by its present probability of success would give the producer too large a role in some instances and too small a role in others.

It might be useful to view the estimation of claims as a coerced settlement. Outside of bankruptcy, most civil cases are settled. Every settlement reflects an estimate by both parties of their chances of success on the merits. Disregarding concerns about reputation and other complications, the settlement value of the producer's claim against the debtor is about $4,000. It might make sense for a bank-ruptcy judge to estimate a claim according to its present probability of success. Even though this amount will necessarily be different from the outcome of any litigation, it may match the settlement that we would have seen in the absence of bankruptcy.

There is, however, a good reason to estimate the value of the pro-ducer's suit at zero for purposes of determining the kind of role that the producer plays in drawing up the plan of reorganization. The producer should not be allowed to force a settlement on terms more favorable than would be possible outside of bankruptcy. What may be crucial is not that the producer's present probability of success is less than 50 percent, but that it is less than 100 percent. Even though creditors in some sense always deal at arm's length with their debtor, in bankruptcy they are acting as equityholders. They are the residual claimants. Giving the producer a voice in the reorganization is analo-gous to allowing a shareholder to sue the corporation. Estimating the producer's claim at zero makes the most sense when the producer would be able to pursue the claim, unaffected by the bankruptcy process. Courts are most likely to take this approach when the claim is large and the probability of success low.[7]

A person with a personal injury or wrongful death claim has a pro-cedural right in bankruptcy that a contract creditor does not. Unlike a contract creditor, a tort victim has the same right to a jury trial in bankruptcy as would exist under nonbankruptcy law. 28 U.S.C. §1411. As elsewhere in bankruptcy, this additional procedural right may generate substantive consequences. In mass tort cases involving A.H. Robins and Manville, however, the courts limited the scope of the trial right. The courts used §502(c) to estimate the total liability to tort victims. These courts then allowed a fund of this amount to be established that would serve as the victims' sole source of compen-sation. They confined the scope of the jury trial right to the adjudica-tion of individual claims against the fund.

Apart from these differences, a tort creditor occupies the same po-sition as a contract creditor. Tort victims enjoy no special priority outside of bankruptcy and hence none in. They are simply general creditors with disputed claims. One can argue that as a matter of nonbankruptcy law this is a bad idea. The purpose of tort law is to make firms internalize the costs of hazardous activities. If creditors through loan covenants or some other kind of monitoring can

[7] See Bittner v. Borne Chemical Co., 691 F.2d 134 (3d Cir. 1982).

influence a firm's behavior, giving tort victims a priority right may have the effect of reducing the number of torts the firm commits. Other creditors might complain that there is nothing they can do to make the firm more careful, but the risk of having another creditor take priority over them gives them an incentive to think twice about whether there is in fact anything they can force the firm to do. If a victim of an accident involving a truck takes priority over a creditor with a security interest in the truck, that creditor will have an incentive to make sure that the truck is properly maintained, that the driver is well qualified, and that the debtor carries insurance. As Samuel Johnson might note, the prospect of being beaten out by another creditor, like the prospect of being hanged in a fortnight, concentrates the mind wonderfully. But existing law does not work this way. Inside of bankruptcy and out, tort victims are general creditors.

Some debtors may have committed some act before the petition that will injure some as yet unidentified person long after the bankruptcy case is over. The technical question is whether the victim has a claim arising before the filing of the petition for purposes of §101. An aircraft manufacturer has made thousands of planes that are still flying. Some will crash in the future and expose the manufacturer to liability. These as yet unknown victims may not have a prepetition connection with the debtor sufficient to give rise to a claim within the meaning of §101.[8]

The effect of finding that future victims possess claims depends on the kind of case involved. First is the mass tort case in which a firm is liquidating in Chapter 7. If future victims do not have prepetition claims within the meaning of the Bankruptcy Code, they will receive nothing in Chapter 7 even though they would receive something if the firm dissolved under nonbankruptcy law. In a nonbankruptcy dissolution of a corporation, a fund usually must be set up to cover any liabilities that appear on the corporation's books. So long as the accountants have recognized the obligation (as they should if matters have deteriorated sufficiently), the tort victim will be able to recover from this fund even though the victim does not know about the injury until after the firm goes out of existence.

Second is the case in which the firm is in Chapter 11 and will have a postbankruptcy life. Here, tort victims may be better off if they do not have a prepetition claim. To be sure, if tort victims lack a prepe-

---

[8] See Epstein v. Official Committee of Unsecured Creditors, 58 F.3d 1573 (11th Cir. 1995); Hexcel Corp. v. Stepan Co., 239 Bankr. 564 (N.D. Cal. 1999).

tition claim, they will be unable to share in the distribution in bankruptcy, but they will be able to pursue the firm in its postbankruptcy incarnation. Remember that only "claims" are discharged under §1141. Such victims may be able to recover more than they would have received had they participated in the bankruptcy case.

In the wake of the Manville bankruptcy, §523(g) of the Bankruptcy Code was amended to allow the bankruptcy court to enjoin subsequent actions against reorganized firms and even third parties such as insurers, but this provision by its terms applies only to mass torts involving asbestos. In other cases, the law is less settled.[9] Courts are especially unsympathetic to plans that release nondebtors from liability as part of a reorganization.[10] Moreover, even when a debtor attempts to sell assets free and clear of claims against it, the bankruptcy court cannot insulate buyers from potential successor liability under state law.[11]

Several technical complications arise when we try to put a dollar value on each creditor's claim. The best way to understand how the process works is to imagine that the filing of a bankruptcy petition is a presumptive event of default that accelerates all the debtor's obligations.[12] As part of this process, we must decide two basic issues: how interest affects the calculation of claims, and what caps are placed on some types of claims.

Suppose I borrowed $100 from First Bank last year when interest rates were 7 percent. This year I borrowed $100 from Second Bank at 12 percent. Although I am not in default on either loan, I file a bankruptcy petition. My assets are worth $150. Who gets what? Should the two banks receive the same amount? In the absence of a bankruptcy filing, First Bank is in a worse position than Second Bank. Other things being equal, it would rather have my promise to repay $100 at 12 percent than at 7 percent. In Chapter 7 of the Bankruptcy Code, however, we ignore these differences. Section 502(b)(2) does not allow claims for unaccrued interest. Both banks would have claims of $100. Because the assets are worth $150, each bank would get 75 cents on the dollar. Treating the two lenders equally makes

[9] See Alan N. Resnick, Bankruptcy as a Vehicle for Resolving Enterprise-Threatening Mass Tort Liability, 148 U. Pa. L. Rev. 2045 (2000).

[10] See, e.g., Gillman v. Continental Airlines, 203 F.3d 203 (3d Cir. 2000).

[11] Western Auto Supply Co. v. Savage Arms, Inc., 43 F.3d 714 (1st Cir. 1994); Zerand-Bernal Group, Inc. v. Cox, 23 F.3d 159 (7th Cir. 1994).

[12] As we shall see in the last chapter of the book, §1124 gives debtors the right to de-accelerate loans in Chapter 11.

sense. If the debtor defaulted outside of bankruptcy, the obligation to pay back the principal of both loans would be accelerated. At this point, both lenders would be in the same position. Both would have the right to recover $100 immediately. When it ignores differences in the interest rates, all that bankruptcy is doing is treating the filing of a petition as a default. This seems a sensible off-the-rack rule that most lenders would include in their loan agreements.

We can think of a Chapter 7 bankruptcy liquidation as financial death. We call in all the loans, gather the assets, and have a general day of reckoning. Sometimes it will not be easy to distinguish principal from unaccrued interest. The simplest case arises when there is a zero-coupon note. I borrow $900 and I promise to pay you $1,000 in a year's time. On the face of it, the principal amount of the loan is $1,000 and the interest rate is 0 percent. We can be confident, however, that the principal is in fact $900 and the interest rate is 11 percent. In the case of zero-coupon notes, only the principal and interest already owed is accelerated. If I default immediately, you have a claim for $900. If I default in six months, you have a claim for $950. More complicated cases arise when the interest rate is not 0 percent but is still substantially below market, and when the note is issued not for cash but in exchange for other securities.[13] Also less clear are cases in which a consumer buys on the installment plan and the interest-rate component is hard to identify.

The second issue that arises when putting a dollar value on creditors' claims concerns the caps that the Bankruptcy Code places on damages for two classes of creditors. Sections 502(b)(6) and (7) limit what both landlords and employees can recover if the debtor rejects a long-term contract with them in bankruptcy. Suppose you lease land to a debtor for $5 a year for a term of years. A year or so later, the bottom drops out of the real estate market. The land falls in value, and now you could rent it out at only $1 a year. The debtor files a bankruptcy petition. Your damages by the ordinary contract rule (the contract–market differential) are $4 for each year remaining on the lease. The Bankruptcy Code, however, limits your recovery. The limit depends on how long the lease lasts. Your cap will never be less than one year's rent ($5). If 15 percent of all the payments remaining turn out to be greater than one year's rent, you get 15 percent of all the payments remaining. But in no event can the amount you get exceed

---

[13] See Thrifty Oil Co. v. Bank of America National Trust & Savings Association, 249 Bankr. 537 (S.D. Cal. 2000); Brown v. Sayyah (In re ICH Corp.), 230 Bankr. 88 (N.D. Tex. 1999).

three years' rent. When the rental payments under the lease are constant, your damages are the lesser of (1) actual damages according to the contract–market differential or (2) one year's rent if fewer than 6.7 years are left on the lease, 15 percent of the remaining payments if between 6.7 and 20 years are left, and three years' rent if more than 20 years are left.

The usual justification for capping a landlord's damages is that they are hard to measure, but this assertion is not sound. Section 502(b)(6) does not free you from estimating damages. Moreover, it assumes that judges are apt to think damages are too high, but not too low. If there is a ceiling on damages, it would seem that there should also be a floor. There may, however, be a better justification for such limits in the case of employees under §502(b)(7). The employees most likely to be affected by the breach of long-term employment contracts are employees with golden parachutes, and they frequently are insider-shareholders. When these contracts are unusually favorable, there may be a significant chance of self-dealing that violates the rights of creditors as a group. The cap in the case of an employee under a long-term contract may be a means of policing misbehavior that cannot be controlled directly. In considering the merits of capping landlord and employee damage claims, you should bear in mind that this limitation applies only to damages flowing from termination of the agreement. It does not limit the damages landlords or employees might be able to get from other causes, such as the damages that arise if the debtor damaged the premises before filing or terminated an employee without justification.

As mentioned in the beginning of this section, assessing claims against the estate involves asking who is owed what and whether someone has a priority. The most common kind of privileged party is a creditor with a perfected security interest. Some priority rights are established in the Bankruptcy Code itself, in §507(a). Workers, for example, enjoy a priority with respect to $2,000 in back wages. The tax collector has a special priority as well. Special priority rules are hard to defend as a matter of first principle and are often the product of special interest lobbying. Among those that enjoy a special priority in bankruptcy, tax claims are by far the most important.

Secured Claims

Secured credit, put simply, is a loan supported by a contingent property interest. Outside of bankruptcy, default on the loan satisfies the contingency and triggers the creditor's right to take the property the debtor has pledged as collateral. The creditor then conducts a foreclosure sale. If the proceeds from the sale are greater than the outstanding loan, the creditor remits the excess. If the proceeds from the sale are less than the outstanding loan, the creditor maintains a claim against the debtor for the deficiency. Section 554 allows the bankruptcy trustee to abandon collateral and permit a secured creditor to take the assets and then foreclose under state law. The secured creditor still participates in the bankruptcy process on account of its deficiency claim. Unless the secured creditor agrees otherwise at the time of the loan, that creditor possesses all the rights of an unsecured creditor. Collateral gives a creditor extra rights. Thus, to the extent its collateral falls short of repaying the loan in full, the secured creditor participates in the bankruptcy process as the holder of an unsecured claim.

A trustee may not wish to abandon collateral, however. She may instead intend the debtor to keep the property as part of a reorganization or adjustment of the debtor's obligations. When the debtor is to retain, rather than abandon, collateral, bankruptcy law provides a procedure that takes the place of a foreclosure sale's valuation of property. Section 506(a) of the Code instructs the bankruptcy court to value a creditor's interest in property of the estate and to designate the creditor's claim a "secured claim to the extent of the value of such creditor's interest." Any remaining claim amount is designated as an unsecured claim. The same process separates into secured and unsecured portions any claim held by someone who enjoys a setoff right. In the most common case, the debtor maintains a deposit account at a bank from which it has borrowed money. The bank has the ability under nonbankruptcy law to "set off" against the loan whatever is in the account. The Bankruptcy Code treats the portion of claim subject to a setoff right as a secured claim and the balance as an unsecured claim. If, for example, the bank had lent the debtor $300 and the debtor has $100 in its account, the Bankruptcy Code gives the bank a secured claim for $100 and an unsecured claim for $200.

In broad strokes, the bifurcation process of §506(a) mimics nonbankruptcy law. The secured creditor receives the full value of her collateral and shares in the debtor's other assets to the extent that the collateral value is less than the creditor's claim. Sometimes, however, the picture is not so clearly defined. Assume that collateral valuation and thus bifurcation of an allowed secured claim occurs at the outset of the bankruptcy process, at the same time the claim itself is allowed. A court must decide how to value the collateral. This is not a simple task. The secured creditor will argue for a high valuation (and thus a larger secured claim), while the debtor's other creditors, represented by the trustee, will argue for a low valuation. If the judge does not allow the sale of the collateral, he must settle this conflict and estimate the value.

The bankruptcy judge needs an objective benchmark when she goes about valuing collateral. The judge might start with the amount that the secured creditor would realize in a foreclosure sale under nonbankruptcy law. This amount, however, might be too low. The debtor is keeping the asset and may value it more than anyone else. The halfway point between the amount that could be realized on foreclosure and the value of the property to the debtor might be a better place to start. This may better track the nonbankruptcy outcome in which the secured creditor and the debtor might compromise and agree to split the difference between the foreclosure price and its value to the debtor.[14] In *Associates Commercial Corporation v. Rash*, the Supreme Court proposed a third alternative. The starting point is the replacement value of the asset. This amount, however, must be adjusted downward. The price a third party would charge for the replacement property would include costs associated with an actual sale, and these should not be counted in determining the secured creditor's rights. For example, the price a dealer would charge if the debtor sought to replace the property would include its costs of shipping and storing the property and any costs associated with warranties it provided. The judge must deduct such costs from the replacement value.

It is essential to distinguish between the rights that a secured creditor enjoys against the debtor by virtue of its claim and the rights that such a creditor enjoys against particular assets by virtue of its lien—its property interest—in those assets. In a simple Chapter 7 liquidation, the lien that the creditor enjoys is unaffected: it passes through bankruptcy. The doctrine of lien pass-through was first set out in *Long v. Bullard*.[15] Recall the example in chapter 1 above. A bank lends a debtor $100 and takes a security interest in a piece of real property that the debtor owns. A recession hits and the property drops in value and is now worth only $25. The debtor files a Chapter 7 petition. The trustee abandons the property, giving it back to the debtor. The Bankruptcy Code provides that the debtor's personal liability to the bank and all other creditors is discharged. The bank

[14] See In re Hoskins, 102 F.3d 311 (7th Cir. 1996).
[15] 117 U.S. 617 (1886).

remains free to foreclose on the land once it is in the debtor's hands because the lien survives, or passes through, bankruptcy.

Although the question whether liens pass through bankruptcy is straightforward, the extent to which they do is controversial. Return to our example. Assume that immediately after bankruptcy, the debtor is able to raise $25 from friends to pay off the bank. Can the bank insist that even though its claim has been discharged, the lien survives at its original amount of $100? The debtor will argue that the lien was stripped down as it passed through bankruptcy. On the face of it, the debtor might seem right. Section 506(d) of the Bankruptcy Code permits lien strip-down of a claim bifurcated by §506(a): "To the extent that a lien secures a claim against the debtor that is not an allowed secured claim, such lien is void." This language seems to provide that the bank's lien is void to the extent that it exceeds the amount of its secured claim. The debtor originally owed the bank $100, but the bank's secured claim is for only $25. Hence, the lien is void to the extent it exceeds $25. The debtor could pay the bank $25 and remove the lien on the property.

The bank, however, can argue that §506(d) was not aimed at lien strip-down at all. Rather, the provision was designed to prevent liens from surviving bankruptcy if the underlying claim was disallowed. Consider the following example. A lawyer provides legal services at an exorbitant fee and secures it with a lien on the debtor's property. Another section of the Bankruptcy Code disallows the lawyer's claim, but only §506(d) voids the lawyer's lien. Under this view, the purpose of §506(d) was not to strip down liens but rather to make sure that a creditor's lien fares no better than her claim. Section 506(d) ensures that the lawyer is both denied a pro rata share of the debtor's assets in bankruptcy and prevented from seizing collateral after the bankruptcy is over. The language, aimed at this specific kind of abuse, was never intended to deal with a valid creditor's lien and should not be read to do so.

Stripping down a lien in bankruptcy has the effect after the fact of benefiting debtors at the expense of creditors. If the bankruptcy judge places too high a value on the land, the debtor can surrender the land to the secured creditor. If the bankruptcy judge errs on the low side, the debtor can pay the bank this amount and keep the land. In other words, debtors can systematically take advantage of judicial valuations that are too low but not be stuck with valuations that are too high. Lien stripping runs contrary to established practice in bankruptcy before the 1978 Bankruptcy Act. It also runs contrary to the notion in real estate law that when a debtor defaults, the value of the land is set through a foreclosure sale rather than through a judicial valuation.

The Court accepted the bank's argument against lien strip-down in *Dewsnup v. Timm*.[16] The majority's opinion noted that had it simply looked at §506 "on a clean slate," it would have agreed with the debtor and stripped down the lien to the value of the property. But in light of the historical practice against lien strip-down and a plausible argument that the provision was aimed at an altogether different problem, the majority concluded that strip-down was not allowed.

Because of the special treatment accorded liens in Chapters 11 and 13, *Dewsnup* has limited impact. Nevertheless, it sparked a major debate over statutory interpretation. In a strong dissent, Justice Antonin Scalia rejected the bank's interpretation of §506(d). To have the effect that the bank claimed, Justice Scalia wrote, the provision should have been phrased this way: "To the extent that a lien secures a claim against the debtor that is not an allowed claim, such lien is void." In Justice Scalia's view, we should not treat the allowed *secured* claims of creditors like the bank as if they were the same as "allowed claims." The result here may be contrary to preexisting practice, undesirable for creditors, and unsound as a matter of bankruptcy policy, but that should not be enough to deny the statutory language the meaning that both makes sense on its own and is consistent with the way the language is used elsewhere in the Code. Justice Scalia noted that the concept of the allowed secured claim is unique to the 1978 Act and has no statutory or case-law antecedents. These words are carefully defined and repeatedly and consistently used in other parts of the 1978 Act. Courts should assume that drafters knew what they were doing, Justice Scalia argued. Competent drafters are unlikely to make such mistakes with stylized terms of art that are a fundamental part of the architecture of the statute. Although Justice Scalia failed to command a majority in *Dewsnup*, his concerns frequently surface both in majority opinions of the Court and in the bankruptcy courts. As a result, as a matter of good advocacy, one should avoid relying on legislative history as well as on pre-Code law in the absence of an invitation embedded in the statutory text itself.

[16] 502 U.S. 410 (1992).

Chapter Five

Property of the Estate and the
Strong-Arm Powers

After establishing what claims creditors have, we need to know what assets are available to satisfy them. Outside of bankruptcy, creditors rely on assets that the debtor itself owns. Bankruptcy law ensures that creditors can look to these assets in bankruptcy as well. Through §541(a), creditors are able to enjoy whatever the debtor itself could enjoy, and all these assets become property of the estate. If we are dealing with a limited liability corporation, the creditors are entitled to whatever the debtor has, including future income. Section 541 lets the trustee sell the debtor's equipment, collect money owed the debtor, and bring the lawsuits the debtor has against third parties for the benefit of the general creditors. If we are dealing with a flesh-and-blood individual debtor, matters are slightly more complicated. The fresh start policy requires that we exclude future income from property of the estate and that we allow the debtor to share in property of the estate that is exempt. Section 541 is otherwise quite straightforward. The principal difficulty is ensuring that the bankruptcy process does not expand or contract the property rights the debtor enjoyed outside of bankruptcy.

Creditors outside of bankruptcy sometimes can reach assets that the debtor has attempted to transfer in whole or in part to someone else. Under the Bankruptcy Code, the trustee has analogous powers he can exercise on behalf of the creditors. The trustee can *avoid*—that is, nullify or undo—transfers that the debtor makes with the intent to delay, hinder, or defraud creditors. Similarly, the trustee can void security interests in assets that have not been properly perfected. These assets become part of the bankruptcy estate by virtue of the trustee's *strong-arm power*. This power is based on a sensible sharing rule in which an unperfected secured creditor is treated the same as a general creditor who has not yet reduced its claim to judgment. The operation of the strong-arm power in §§544 and 545 is quite straightforward, as is its relationship with §541(a)(1). Whenever there is an asset that the creditors want, we ask first whether the asset is one that the debtor could enjoy outside of bankruptcy. If the answer is yes, the asset becomes property of the estate under §541(a)(1). If the answer is no, we ask next whether the trustee can bring the asset into the estate by virtue of the strong-arm powers. By remember-

92

ing that the strong-arm power always works to supplement property of the estate, we avoid the dangers of relying too much on §541(a)(1) and of forcing it to do the work that is properly the domain of §§544 and 545.

Property of the Estate and the Scope of §541

Section 541(a)(1) ensures that in the case of the corporate debtor, creditors are able to reach all of the debtor's property in bankruptcy that they would be able to reach outside of bankruptcy. If a corporate debtor could enjoy a particular right outside of bankruptcy, the trustee enjoys it inside of bankruptcy. It is useful to see how §541 handles the easy cases. Suppose you take some clothes to the dry cleaner. Your dry cleaner also sells used clothing. The dry cleaner, much to your surprise, shuts down and files a Chapter 7 bankruptcy petition. It has thousands of creditors. You are not one of them. The debtor promised to clean your clothes for $5, the market price for cleaning them, due upon completion. The debtor has broken its promise, but if you have suffered no damages, you have no claim against it under nonbankruptcy law. Let us assume you have no immediate need for the clothes and you can easily find someone else to clean them for the same price. You go to the debtor and try to pick up your clothes and take them someplace else. The trustee tells you that you cannot have the clothes back.

Can the trustee wave §541 at you and say that your clothes are now property of the dry cleaner's bankruptcy estate? Section 541(a)(1) gives the trustee "all legal or equitable interests of the debtor in property as of the commencement of the case." Does the debtor have a right to your clothes that amounts to an interest in property? What are the debtor's rights with respect to the clothes? Under the Uniform Commercial Code, the debtor has the *power* (though not the *right*) to give good title to the clothes to a buyer in ordinary course of business. U.C.C. §2-403(2). The debtor is a merchant who deals in used clothes and you have entrusted your clothes to it.

Under §541(a)(1), we worry about only the debtor's rights. For purposes of this section, we focus on whether it is able to keep the clothes in the face of your assertion of ownership. If the dry cleaner has actually cleaned the clothes, it may have a mechanic's lien on the clothes that would give it a property interest in the clothes. The mechanic's lien would allow the trustee to keep the clothes until you paid for the cleaning, but let us assume the trustee has shut down operations and that the clothes have not been and will not be cleaned. In this case, the debtor cannot keep you from taking the clothes back outside of bankruptcy. Hence, the clothes do not become property of the estate under §541(a)(1). Because the debtor has no right to the clothes, the creditors do not have any rights to the clothes under §541(a)(1), either. The rights of the debtor define the outer limits of what the trustee can claim under §541(a)(1).

Cases can arise in which the debtor's ownership of a right is not clear. Consider, for example, an insurance policy. The policy itself belongs to the debtor and is property of the estate. The debtor, however, may not be entitled to the proceeds of the policy outside of bankruptcy. The policy, for example, may provide that the insurance company's obligation runs to the victim of an accident, not to the debtor. The debtor may have no ability to reach these proceeds under nonbankruptcy law. In this event, the proceeds of the insurance are not property of the estate. The victim of the accident, in addition to being a general creditor, may be entitled to pursue the insurance company during or after bankruptcy and to keep the proceeds of the policy rather than sharing them with the other creditors of the debtor.[1]

Section 541(a)(1) gives the creditors only those rights that the debtor itself enjoyed outside of bankruptcy. If a debtor owns a one-half interest in an oil well and files for bankruptcy, only the one-half interest becomes part of the estate, not the entire oil well. This rule is perfectly sensible. Suppose two firms each have a one-half interest in the same well and both file bankruptcy petitions. We could not allow the trustees of both debtors to be entitled to the entire well.

Chicago Board of Trade v. Johnson is the old case that sets out this basic principle.[2] A man named Henderson owned a seat on the Chicago Board of Trade. At the time, a seat on the Board of Trade could be sold so long as the Board members were paid immediately what they were owed for the seat. Henderson went into bankruptcy owing money to lots of people, including members of the Board of Trade. Those members argued that the seat was not property of the estate and that the trustee in bankruptcy could not touch it. Henderson could sell the seat, but the Board members had the right to the pro-

---

[1] See Houston v. Edgeworth, 993 F.2d 51 (5th Cir. 1993); First Fidelity Bank v. McAteer, 985 F.2d 114 (3d Cir. 1993). Because the insurance policy (as opposed to the proceeds of the policy) is property of the estate, the accident victim should seek relief from the automatic stay to reach the policy proceeds during the bankruptcy. As we shall see in chapter 9 below, when the victim's right to the proceeds is clear, relief from the stay is routinely granted.

[2] 264 U.S. 1 (1924).

ceeds. The trustee argued that the seat was property of the estate, and that the proceeds should be divided pro rata among all the creditors.

The Supreme Court rejected both arguments. It held that the seat was property of the estate, but that the creditors in bankruptcy could enjoy only what the debtor had the right to enjoy. The general creditors derived their rights from the debtor. If the debtor had the right to the proceeds only after the Board members were paid, then the general creditors had the right to the proceeds only after the Board members were paid. They could not do any better outside of bankruptcy, so they should not be able to do any better inside of bankruptcy. It was not relevant whether state law called the seat "property." (The Illinois Supreme Court had already held that state law did not.) What mattered were the relevant attributes under state law, and under state law the creditors had no right to reach the proceeds of the sale until the claims of Henderson's fellow Board members had been satisfied. *Chicago Board of Trade* remains good law, both for its narrow point about the treatment of seats on exchanges in bankruptcy and for the broad principle it embraces.[3]

In *Chicago Board of Trade*, the trustee won the battle but lost the war. The seat came into the estate, but it came into the estate subject to the claims of the other Board members. Suppose Henderson chose not to sell the seat. Would it still have become property of the estate? Under state law, creditors could not levy on the seat or force an individual debtor to sell it. If Henderson decided not to sell the seat, then it might not become property of the estate. Consider the case, however, in which a seat is owned by a corporation. In this event, the debtor's *ability* to sell the seat is itself decisive, even if it does not intend to do so. The creditors outside of bankruptcy could have a court appoint a receiver who would take control of the corporation and sell the asset. If anything were left after the claims of the other Board members were satisfied, the creditors would be able to reach it outside of bankruptcy. If creditors can reach property outside of bankruptcy, they should be able to reach it in bankruptcy as well.

Let us take a more difficult case. The debtor is again a corporation, but the rule of the Board of Trade is that these seats cannot be sold at all. To say that the seat cannot be sold means in effect that the

[3] See In re Drexel Burnham Lambert Group Inc., 120 Bankr. 724 (Bankr. S.D.N.Y. 1990).

seat survives only so long as the firm survives as a distinct entity. You cannot sell the seat apart from the other assets of the firm. If, outside of bankruptcy, the seat can be sold only if it is bundled with the name, the goodwill, the desks, and the client lists of the old firm, then it comes into the bankruptcy estate, but it is subject to the same limitation. The trustee does not lose the right to sell the seat, but has no special right to sell it by itself. The most common example of an asset that can be sold only in connection with another is a trademark. It cannot be conveyed apart from the goodwill associated with the mark.[4]

Let us look at one more possibility. Suppose the seat on the Board is freely salable, but the Board's rules provide that the seat is forfeited if the debtor files a bankruptcy petition. Is this rule permissible? Although we generally respect rights as defined outside of bankruptcy, we do not allow anyone to opt out of bankruptcy altogether. Bankruptcy law respects restrictions that apply generally inside of bankruptcy and out, but those that apply only in bankruptcy are ignored. This principle is reflected in §541(c)(1) and in §545 with respect to statutory liens and in §365 with respect to executory contracts. Defining property of the estate in *Chicago Board of Trade* has the effect of setting priorities among creditors. This should not trouble us, however, if the priority is one that exists both inside of bankruptcy and out.

The principle of *Chicago Board of Trade* applies quite broadly. It is useful, for example, when we want to understand the rights that creditors enjoy by virtue of a license that their debtor enjoys. Courts have included in property of the estate everything from casino and racetrack licenses to broadcast licenses.[5] The *Chicago Board of Trade* principle ensures that debtors in bankruptcy enjoy the license on the same terms and subject to the same conditions as they did outside of bankruptcy. Suppose a failing airline files a Chapter 7 petition. It has a right to landing slots at a major airport, and another airline would pay a lot to have them. The airline's landing slots are, of course, property of the estate. The airline, however, needs to shut down its operations for a time, and FAA rules provide that an airline loses its

---

[4] See, e.g., Patterson Laboratories v. Roman Cleanser Co., 802 F.2d 207 (6th Cir. 1986).

[5] See, e.g., Elsinore Shore Associates v. Casino Control Commission, 66 Bankr. 723 (Bankr. D.N.J. 1986); In re National Cattle Congress, Inc., 179 Bankr. 588 (Bankr. N.D. Iowa 1995), remanded on other grounds, 91 F.3d 1113 (8th Cir. 1996); Ramsay v. Dowden, 68 F.3d 213 (8th Cir. 1995).

licenses once it stops using them. This constraint on the right is one that applies outside of bankruptcy and hence inside of bankruptcy as well.[6] A debtor's property does not shrink by happenstance of bankruptcy, but it does not expand, either.

A more troublesome case arises when the issuer of the license is also a creditor. Suppose a town decides to auction off a taxi medallion. To encourage small entrepreneurs, the town agrees to finance much of the purchase price. One company makes a winning bid of $11,000 for the medallion. The company makes a down payment of $1,000 and promises to pay the balance over a number of years. The company borrows an additional $10,000 to pay for a used cab. The company's owner is confident that the taxi can generate enough money to pay back the town and the creditors and still leave the owner with a healthy profit. The local economy suffers a downturn, however, and the cab service is less popular than expected. As a result, the company cannot meet its obligations to the town and to the other creditors. It files a Chapter 11 petition. The company is insolvent: it owes $20,000, but the business is worth only $15,000.

The taxi medallion is property of the estate under §541(a) and comes into the estate. Consistent with *Chicago Board of Trade*, however, it becomes part of the estate subject to all its nonbankruptcy limitations. If the company had no ability to sell the medallion outside of bankruptcy, it has no ability to do so inside.[7] At the same time, under §541(c)(1) the town could not cause the medallion to be forfeited in the event of bankruptcy. This rule vindicates again the principle that bankruptcy itself does not expand or limit a debtor's property rights.

As we shall see when we discuss the reach of the automatic stay in chapter 9 below, it is not always so easy to draw the line between actions that the government takes by virtue of its position as postpetition regulator and those it takes as the holder of a prepetition claim. In the example above, nothing should prevent the license from becoming property of the estate. When the regulator is the federal government, however, the dispute may not even be adjudicated in the bankruptcy forum. Judicial oversight of federal administrative agencies may occur first through administrative tribunals and then through the court of appeals.[8]

[6] See Federal Aviation Administration v. Gull Air, Inc., 890 F.2d 1255, 1261 n.8 (1st Cir. 1989).

[7] See, e.g., In re Tak Communications, Inc., 985 F.2d 916 (7th Cir. 1993).

[8] See In re Federal Communications Commission, 217 F.3d 125 (2d Cir. 2000).

The Strong-Arm Power Under §544(a)

Outside of bankruptcy, a general creditor sometimes has greater rights than its debtor and can levy on assets to which the debtor does not enjoy paramount rights. The most common case arises when a debtor buys a machine from someone who retains a security interest in it but fails to perfect that interest by filing a financing statement. The debtor has no right to keep the machine vis-à-vis its seller if the debtor defaults on its payments. Under nonbankruptcy law, however, a creditor that reduces its claim to judgment can levy on the machine and take priority over the seller. To ensure that creditors can look to the same assets inside a bankruptcy proceeding as outside, the Bankruptcy Code must provide some mechanism to ensure that these assets become part of the estate as well. Section 544(a) serves this function.

Section 544(a) gives the trustee the right to that which the general creditors could have reached under nonbankruptcy law. The trustee has, in the case of personal property, the rights of a hypothetical lien creditor who comes into being and levies at the moment the petition is filed. In the case of real property, the trustee has the rights of a hypothetical bona fide purchaser for value. Section 544(b) enables the trustee to assert the rights that actual creditors would have had under state law, even if a creditor who came into being only at the time of the petition would have arrived too late to have a cause of action. Among the most important of these rights is the right of creditors to set aside transfers that a debtor makes, while insolvent, for less than reasonably equivalent value as well as any transfers that delay, hinder, or defraud creditors. These transfers, known as fraudulent conveyances, are examined in chapter 7 below. Here we will focus on the general structure of §544 itself.

Section 544(a) gives us a measuring rod to determine who prevails in a contest between the trustee and adverse claimants: if an imaginary lien creditor (or bona fide purchaser) as defined in §544(a) would prevail against the adverse interest, the trustee wins. The person whose interest is avoided is reduced to the status of a general creditor. The property itself becomes property of the estate, and all the general creditors (including the erstwhile property claimant) share in it pro rata. There are two important points to keep in mind here: first, the trustee's rights are being measured by those of a *third party*, and second, this particular third party is a *hypothetical* one.

In the case of personal property, the trustee enjoys the powers of a lien creditor. The effect of granting the trustee this power is to preserve the relative positions of unperfected secured creditors and general creditors outside of bankruptcy. Article 9 of the Uniform Commercial Code provides that a secured creditor will win against a general creditor if the secured creditor perfects its interest, either by filing a financing statement or by seizing the collateral before the general creditor acquires a lien on it. If a general creditor brings a lawsuit against the debtor outside of bankruptcy, reduces its claim to judgment, and levies on the property before the unperfected secured creditor asserts its rights, the secured creditor will lose. Every general creditor is a potential lien creditor.

Article 9 embraces the principle that the unperfected secured creditor claims an interest in property that is invisible to third parties. Anglo-American law generally does not recognize such ownership interests vis-à-vis third parties unless public notice is given or some other step is taken to cure the ostensible ownership problem that arises from the separation of ownership and possession. Between two competing creditors, the one who is first to cure the ostensible ownership problem is typically the one who takes priority. A general creditor acquires its property interest and cures the ostensible ownership problem in one fell swoop, by levying on the property—by having it physically seized. Hence, outside of bankruptcy the general creditor prevails over the secured creditor if it levies before the secured creditor perfects, but not otherwise.

In short, outside of bankruptcy the unperfected secured creditor and the general creditor are in a race with each other. The outcome of this race is uncertain. The effect of giving the trustee the power to avoid the unperfected secured creditor's interest is to declare a tie. In bankruptcy, the trustee represents the interests of all the general creditors, and an unperfected secured creditor whose lien is avoided becomes a general creditor. (You are never worse off trying to get a security interest and failing than you would have been if you had never tried at all.) To say that the trustee wins is to say that all creditors share equally. The bankruptcy rule, in other words, preserves the nonbankruptcy rule in the sense that in the presence of uncertainty, the creditors share equally.

In the case of real property, the trustee has the rights of a bona fide purchaser for value, not only the rights of a lien creditor. This expanded power may be premised on the notion that the trustee should always win if the competing property owner (typically a mortgagee) has not done everything that it could have done to cure the ostensible ownership problem. Under some state laws, only a bona fide purchaser, not a lien creditor, prevails against unperfected secured creditors. But giving the trustee this right is not inconsistent with the idea

that the trustee is simply vindicating the rights of the general creditors. Even though lien creditors may not be able to defeat unrecorded
real property interests directly, they may be able to do so indirectly.
(A purchaser at the sheriff's sale may take good title and the lien
creditors may be able to keep the proceeds.)

Suppose a debtor borrows $100,000 from a finance company on
January 1 and grants the company a security interest. The finance
company fails to file the financing statement in the proper office. Under Revised Article 9, the proper office for most types of collateral is
the secretary of state's office in the jurisdiction in which the debtor
resides. When the debtor is a corporation, it is deemed to reside in
the state in which it was incorporated. Under the previous enact-
ment of Article 9, the proper place to file was determined by the location of the collateral.

The first responsibility of a lawyer representing a lender with a security interest is to ensure that the client has properly perfected its
security interest. If bankruptcy is already on the horizon, it may be
too late, but often it is not. Moreover, mistakes are all too common,
and lenders' interests can be unperfected for a number of reasons.
Lenders might misspell the debtor's name and thus make the financing statement inaccessible. They could file in the wrong place, something that is easy to do when states have different versions of Article 9
on their books. Moreover, Article 9 does not completely occupy the
field. Federal law sometimes preempts Article 9. A prudent creditor
who takes a security interest in a copyright, for example, will file both
in the appropriate secretary of state's office and with the registrar of
copyrights.[9]

Assume that the debtor mentioned above files for bankruptcy on
March 1. Under nonbankruptcy law, lien creditors prevail over (or, as
many lawyers would say, *prime*) secured creditors if their lien arises
before the security interest is perfected. To perfect its interest, the
finance company must file a financing statement in the proper office.
Because the company failed to do that, it will lose to a lien creditor
on March 1, the date the debtor files for bankruptcy. The trustee has
the powers of a lien creditor, so the finance company will lose to the
trustee in bankruptcy. There is, however, a small hitch in the literal
language of §544. Section 544(a) seems to require that the secured
creditor have an interest that is "voidable" by a lien creditor. Under

[9] See National Peregrine, Inc. v. Capitol Federal Savings & Loan Association (In
re Peregrine Entertainment, Ltd.), 116 Bankr. 194 (C.D. Cal. 1990) (Circuit Judge
Kozinski, sitting by designation).

nonbankruptcy law, however, a lien creditor can only make the secured creditor's interest "subordinate" to its own.

Suppose instead that the finance company does file its interest the day before the debtor files for bankruptcy. Under Article 9, the finance company's security interest is perfected on the date it filed. On March 1, could a lien creditor defeat the finance company's interest? The answer is no, it could not. A lien creditor needs to become a lien creditor *before* the security interest is perfected. Because a creditor cannot win if it levies after the security interest is perfected, the trustee cannot win under §544(a). So long as no other part of the Bankruptcy Code allows the trustee to set aside the finance company's property interest, the finance company's security interest will be respected in bankruptcy and it will be paid ahead any of the general creditors.

The finance company's last-minute grab is suspicious, but this kind of conduct is not something to which §544(a) is directed, just as §541(a)(1) is not directed at reaching assets that the debtor could not enjoy outside of bankruptcy. As we will see in chapter 8 below, the trustee will probably be able to avoid the finance company's interest as a preference under §547. Given that these sections work cumulatively, it is important to resist the temptation to assess the Bankruptcy Code's results prematurely.

The Trustee as Successor to Creditor Claims

Section 544(b) is quite different from §544(a). To use §544(b), the trustee must find a real, live creditor with an *allowable* and *unsecured* claim. Thus, the trustee must find an actual unsecured creditor of the debtor who, on the date of bankruptcy, is able to assert an interest in property that the debtor has transferred to a third party. If this creditor can reach that asset outside of bankruptcy notwithstanding the transfer (or, to use the language of the Bankruptcy Code, can avoid the debtor's transfer of that asset), the trustee can use §544(b) to step into the shoes of that creditor. The trustee recovers the asset from the third party. The trustee does not then turn over the asset to the creditor who would have reached it outside of bankruptcy. Instead, the asset is placed in the pile of assets that is divided pro rata among all the general creditors. This part of §544(b) is difficult to justify. One must explain why the creditor who had this right outside of bankruptcy must share it with other creditors inside bankruptcy.

The best justification for it is an entirely pragmatic one. Often when the trustee uses §544(b), nearly all of the creditors have the right to avoid the transfer. To exclude from the distribution the creditors who would not have shared in the recovery under nonbankruptcy law may impose substantial administrative costs and have only a small effect on the distribution of the assets. Imagine, for example, that the debtor made a bulk sale of its inventory and did not follow the procedures set out in Article 6 of the Uniform Commercial Code. Article 6 allows only creditors of the debtor at the time of the bulk sale to avoid it.[10] There may be few creditors at the time of the petition who were not also creditors at the time of the bulk sale. Nevertheless, the trustee cannot set aside the transfer under §544(a). Under that section, the trustee asserts the rights of a hypothetical lien creditor who came into being only at the time of the filing of the bankruptcy petition. Section 544(b) is therefore needed to allow the creditors to act collectively. Because identifying the few creditors who were not creditors at the time of the bulk sale is difficult, distributing the recovery to everyone may sensibly approximate the nonbankruptcy regime.

A second feature of §544(b) is more troubling. Section 544(b) gives the trustee the power to avoid a transfer in its entirety, even if the party into whose shoes the trustee steps could have avoided only part of it. Consider a firm that goes through a leveraged buyout. If the leveraged buyout leaves the firm insolvent, the buyout is a fraudulent conveyance.[11] Under state nonbankruptcy law, only creditors who had lent money to the firm before the buyout would be able to bring a fraudulent conveyance action. The overwhelming majority of the creditors, however, appeared on the scene after the leveraged buyout, having lent with full knowledge of the leveraged buyout. Under state law, then, neither these creditors nor a hypothetical lien creditor who came into being at the time of the petition could bring a fraudulent conveyance action. Only one creditor was owed money at the time of the buyout and is still unpaid at the time of the petition. That creditor is a consumer who bought an oven under warranty and who now has a $1 claim because the oven's light bulb has burned out. This consumer is a creditor within the meaning of state fraudulent con-

---

[10] As we discover in the next section, the revised version of Article 6 introduces a complication, ignored here, by characterizing the rights against buyers as damage actions rather than avoidance actions.

[11] This problem arose a number of times in the late 1980s and early 1990s. See Kupetz v. Wolf, 845 F.2d 842 (9th Cir. 1988). We examine the way fraudulent conveyances affect leveraged buyouts and other corporate transactions in greater detail in chapter 7 below.

veyance law both at the time of the petition and at the time of the buyout.[12] Under nonbankruptcy law, this creditor could bring a fraudulent conveyance action at the time the bankruptcy petition is filed. Section 544(b) allows the trustee to step into the shoes of this single creditor. Under nonbankruptcy law, this creditor could never recover more than $1. The trustee, however, faces no such cap. The trustee can set aside a billion dollar transfer on the basis of a single creditor's $1 claim. All that matters is the existence of a single creditor at the time of the petition who has the power to bring an avoidance action against someone. The amount of that creditor's claim places no limit on the extent of the trustee's power to avoid the transfer. This strange rule originated in *Moore v. Bay*.[13]

The Limits of the Trustee's Avoiding Power

Assume that many general creditors lend money to a firm. The firm's shareholders are so casual about maintaining the corporate form and separating their own assets from those of the corporation that the general creditors, under nonbankruptcy law, will be able to *pierce the corporate veil* that shields shareholders from the obligations of the corporation. When they are able to pierce the veil, creditors can sue the shareholders directly and recover what the creditors lent the corporation. If the firm files for bankruptcy, should the trustee be able to bring the veil-piercing action on behalf of the general creditors? If the corporation itself has the power under nonbankruptcy law to sue its own shareholders and recover from them, the cause of action would be property of the estate under §541. The trustee would be able to assert it for the benefit of the creditors, just as the trustee can bring a contract or tort action that the debtor could have brought outside of bankruptcy. One never reaches the question whether the trustee could bring the action by using one of the avoiding powers.

But if the debtor could not itself bring the action, the trustee likely cannot bring it, either. In *Caplin v. Marine Midland Grace Trust Company*, the Supreme Court examined the trustee's ability to bring dam-

---

[12] It does not matter whether the creditor's claim is matured or unmatured, liquidated or unliquidated, fixed or contingent, disputed or undisputed. See Unif. Fraudulent Transfer Act §1(3).

[13] 284 U.S. 4 (1931). The opinion itself is opaque. For an analysis of it under the Bankruptcy Code, see Lippe v. Bairnco Corp., 225 Bankr. 846 (S.D.N.Y. 1998).

age actions that the debtor itself could not have brought.[14] In that case, the Supreme Court held under the old Bankruptcy Act that the trustee could not bring a damage action on behalf of bondholders against the agent charged with representing their interests.[15] The agent may have failed to monitor the debtor as it was charged to do, but the action the bondholders had against their agent was of no concern to the debtor's other creditors. The fiduciary duty breached in *Caplin* was owed to the bondholders, not to the debtor. A creditor of a debtor ordinarily cannot complain when a third party violates a duty owed to another creditor.

Section 544(b) allows the trustee only to avoid *transfers* that the debtor made or obligations the debtor incurred. It does not give the trustee the right to bring *damage actions*; rather, the trustee can bring damage actions only if the debtor itself would have been able to bring the action outside of bankruptcy. As noted, this issue commonly arises when the debtor has so disregarded its corporate form that its shareholders are liable for its obligations. Veil-piercing actions are in many respects identical to the avoiding actions that the trustee undoubtedly enjoys under §544(a). It is difficult to explain why the trustee should be able to avoid transfers of property that the creditors could have avoided, but not bring damage actions. The purpose of the trustee's strong-arm powers under §544 is to vindicate the rights of creditors as a group. Why the trustee may bring a fraudulent conveyance action against shareholders when the firm transfers assets to them while it is insolvent, yet not bring a veil-piercing action when the shareholders fail to capitalize the firm adequately initially, is a mystery. Nevertheless, as §544 has generally been interpreted, the trustee does not possess the power to bring such damage actions in her own right. She can bring them only if the debtor itself could.[16]

Some federal courts have found that the debtor can bring veil-piercing actions against its own shareholders, and hence the trustee can as well because of §541.[17] State law authority for this proposi-

---

[14] 406 U.S. 416 (1972).

[15] The agent is usually called the *indenture trustee.*

[16] See, e.g., Mediators, Inc. v. Manney, 105 F.3d 822 (2d Cir. 1997); Steinberg v. Buczynski, 40 F.3d 890 (7th Cir. 1994); Schertz-Cibolo-Universal City Independent School District v. Wright, 25 F.3d 1281 (5th Cir. 1994); Williams v. California First Bank, 859 F.2d 664 (9th Cir. 1988).

[17] See, e.g., St. Paul Fire & Marine Insurance Co. v. Pepsico, Inc., 884 F.2d 688 (2d Cir. 1989); Steyr-Daimler-Puch of America Corp. v. Pappas, 852 F.2d 132 (4th Cir. 1988); S.I. Acquisition, Inc. v. Eastern Delivery Service, 817 F.2d 1142 (5th Cir.

tion, however, is not easy to find. Indeed, the gravamen of the action—that the firm and the shareholders are one and the same—is inconsistent with the idea that the firm can sue the shareholders. At least one state supreme court has repudiated a federal circuit court's opinion that the debtor did possess such a cause of action against its shareholders.[18]

Because the debtor in possession has the same powers as the trustee, allowing the trustee to bring a veil-piercing action creates a conflict of interest in the typical Chapter 11 case. The debtor in possession is ordinarily the group of managers running the firm; often the managers are substantial shareholders and thus unlikely to bring an action against themselves. In such cases, an individual creditor or the creditors committee can ask the court for leave to bring the action for and in the name of the debtor in possession.[19] To obtain permission to bring the action, a creditor or the creditors committee must establish both that the trustee or debtor in possession has unjustifiably refused a demand to pursue the action and that the cause of action is worth pursuing.[20] Alternatively, either can ask for the appointment of an examiner to bring the action.

There is another justification for limiting the trustee's ability to bring damage actions, quite apart from the conflict of interest that arises when we are in Chapter 11 and there is a debtor in possession. Recall the rule of *Moore v. Bay*. It requires the trustee to turn over any avoided transfer or damage recovery to creditors as a group, not those creditors who would have been able to avoid it under nonbankruptcy law. Given the rule in *Moore v. Bay*, *Caplin* serves to prevent general creditors from sharing in a recovery that only a few creditors would enjoy under nonbankruptcy law.

Whenever such anomalies exist, we should expect related areas of the law to be affected as well. The sharp distinction that *Caplin* and its progeny have drawn between creditor avoidance actions and creditor damage actions led the drafters of Revised Article 6 of the Uniform Commercial Code to recharacterize as a damage action the right creditors have against a buyer who runs afoul of the bulk sales

---

1987). See also Koch Refining v. Farmers Union Central Exchange, 831 F.2d 1339, 1347 n.11 (7th Cir. 1987).

[18] See In re Rehabilitation of Centaur Insurance Co., 632 N.E.2d 1015 (Ill. 1994).

[19] See Louisiana World Exposition v. Federal Insurance Co., 858 F.2d 233 (5th Cir. 1988).

[20] See In re Perkins, 902 F.2d 1254 (7th Cir. 1990).

act. This change from prior law was made to take advantage of *Caplin* and limit the trustee's rights in bankruptcy.[21]

Statutory Liens and Constructive Trusts

The different roles that §§541 and 544 play becomes especially important when confronting cases involving statutory liens and constructive trusts. Take first the case in which some creditors benefit from a special state statute. Many states, for example, have statutes that protect special interests, such as those of liquor wholesalers. The state statute entitles these creditors to be paid in full before any of the general creditors.[22] Constructive trust cases involve victims of some egregious fraud. The debtor is still holding the money or other property it purloined from the victims, and the victims insist that they are entitled to it before any of the general creditors. The victims argue that the money or other property is held by the debtor in constructive trust.[23] We look at each situation in turn.

The case of the liquor wholesaler is the easier one. As already mentioned, a state statute that applies only when the debtor is in bankruptcy (or that is geared to the financial condition of the debtor) should not be respected. States can establish generally applicable priorities, but they cannot dictate federal bankruptcy policy. The Bankruptcy Code tells us this explicitly in §§541(c)(1) and in 545(1). Let us assume, then, that the state statute in our case applies inside of bankruptcy and out. The assets that the trustee gathers under §541(a)(1) are subject to this priority claim, but this does not end the inquiry. To say that property of the estate under §541(a)(1) is subject to the claims of the liquor wholesalers is not to say that the liquor wholesalers prime the general creditors. The trustee, in addition to asserting the rights of the debtor vis-à-vis the wholesalers under §541(a)(1), also asserts the rights of the general creditors. Section 545 follows the same principle as §544(a). We need to ask how the liquor wholesalers would fare against the hypothetical person into whose shoes the trustee steps.

We saw in §544(a) that, against secured creditors and other transferees, the trustee asserts the rights of a hypothetical person, acting in good faith, who either levied on the property or purchased

---

[21] See U.C.C. §6-107 (1988), Official Comment 2.

[22] See California v. Farmers Markets, Inc., 792 F.2d 1400 (9th Cir. 1986); Max Sobel Wholesale Liquors v. Nolden, 520 F.2d 761 (9th Cir. 1975).

[23] See Heyman v. Kemp (In re Teltronics, Ltd.), 649 F.2d 1236 (7th Cir. 1981).

at the time of the petition. Section 545 tells us that against the holders of statutory liens, as against those with security interests in real property, the trustee exercises the rights of a bona fide purchaser for value. Hence, one must ask whether the debtor could have sold the liquor free of the claims of the wholesalers. The case law has invented distinctions between such things as "statutory liens" and illegitimate "statutory priorities." In the end, however, these distinctions do not focus on the two-step inquiry the Bankruptcy Code sets out. What matters is whether the wholesaler's priority right is good inside bankruptcy and out and whether that right gives the wholesaler priority under nonbankruptcy law over a bona fide purchaser for value.

The constructive trust cases are less clear. They typically arise when a general partner buys real property for the partnership. The property is recorded in the name of the general partner, not in the name of the partnership.[24] Under state law, the general partner is not the beneficial owner of the property and is deemed to hold it in constructive trust for the partnership. Nevertheless, a dishonest general partner can convey the property to a bona fide purchaser for value free of the interests of the limited partners. Because the debtor holds the property in constructive trust, the property does not become property of the estate under §541(a)(1). The question is whether the trustee can bring it into the estate by using §544(a). Remember that in the case of real property, the trustee has the rights of a hypothetical bona fide purchaser for value. We need to establish whether the limited partners' property interest takes priority over the bona fide purchaser whom the trustee represents. Can a bona fide purchaser reach and take the property free of the claims of the fraud victims? Outside of bankruptcy, the bona fide purchaser can indeed take the property free of such claims. Hence, even when state law treats the land as held in constructive trust, the trustee can pull all of it back into the estate for the benefit of all the creditors. These, of course, include (but are not limited to) the defrauded partners.[25]

This is a sensible result. Under state law, the general creditors of the debtor could sue, reduce their claim to judgment, force a judicial sale to a bona fide purchaser for value, and enjoy the proceeds free of the claims of the partnership. Similarly, the partnership could record its interest and prevail over a bona fide purchaser (and hence the trus-

---

[24] Belisle v. Plunkett, 877 F.2d 512 (7th Cir. 1989); City National Bank v. General Coffee Corp., 828 F.2d 699 (11th Cir. 1987).

[25] See Mullins v. Burtch, 249 Bankr. 360 (D. Del. 2000). But see Vineyard v. McKenzie, 752 F.2d 1009 (5th Cir. 1985).

tee as well). Rather than guess who would have won this race outside of bankruptcy, §544(a) treats the partnership and the general creditors in the same manner. They share what there is pro rata.

In the case of personal property, the analysis applies except that we use the benchmark of the hypothetical lien creditor. We ask whether the fraud victims could prevail over a creditor who tried to levy on the property at the time of the bankruptcy petition. The case law here is unclear. Some courts hold that bankruptcy judges should not find that a constructive trust exists at all under these circumstances.[26] Under nonbankruptcy law, a constructive trust exists when fraud victims can trace the funds that the debtor took from them. Bankruptcy courts often rely on this test to conclude that when tracing is possible, the assets do not come into the estate under §541. Too often, however, these courts stop with their analysis of §541 and fail to continue the inquiry. They do not ask whether the trustee can nevertheless bring the assets into the estate using her strong-arm powers.[27] The victims should prevail only if beneficiaries of a constructive trust could prevent lien creditors from reaching assets outside of bankruptcy.

The relationship between property of the estate under §541 and the strong-arm powers of §§544 and 545 is one of the most important and least appreciated in all of bankruptcy law. The trustee enjoys the rights of the debtor under §541. In addition, the trustee can assert the rights that the creditors could assert against the debtor's property outside of bankruptcy under §§544 and 545. The most common trap lawyers face in confronting these questions is to focus exclusively on §541 in analyzing these problems and forget that much of the work is done by §§544 and §545.

In this chapter and the one before it, we have seen how the Bankruptcy Code sensibly translates the rights and obligations of a debtor to the bankruptcy forum. In the next chapter, we examine how the Bankruptcy Code handles situations in which the rights and obligations are fused together. These issues—those associated with executory contracts—present a special set of challenges.

---

[26] See XL/Datacomp, Inc. v. Wilson, 16 F.3d 1443 (6th Cir. 1994).

[27] See, e.g., First American Title Insurance Co. v. Lett, 238 Bankr. 167 (Bankr. W.D. Mo. 1999).

Chapter Six

Executory Contracts

General Nature of Executory Contracts

Thus far it has been easy to distinguish assets of the estate from claims against the estate. A tort action that a third party has against the debtor is a claim; a tort action that the debtor has against someone else is an asset. An executory contract is something that is both an asset and a liability simultaneously. When a contract is executory, the debtor is obliged to a party and that party is obliged to the debtor. The Bankruptcy Code itself does not define the term *executory contract*. The best-known and most widely accepted definition is Vern Countryman's. In his view, an executory contract is [a contract under which the obligation of both the [debtor] and the other party to the contract are so far unperformed that the failure of either to complete performance would constitute a material breach excusing the performance of the other."]

An executory contract is a good thing for the debtor if the debtor's obligation is less than what the other party owes the debtor in return. Section 365 ensures that the creditors (through the trustee) can enjoy the benefits of an executory contract that is favorable to the debtor. It also ensures that if the contract is unfavorable, the third party stands in the same position it would have been in had the debtor defaulted on a contract outside of bankruptcy.

Let's start with the following case. I am Debtor Corporation. I pay you $5 and you agree to give me a bushel of wheat in a week. In the interim I file a bankruptcy petition. My trustee looks at this situation. The $5 I have paid out is gone forever. But the trustee does have a right to get a bushel of wheat from you. If you do not deliver, the trustee is going to sue you. What the trustee has is an asset under §541. All the creditors of the estate are better off with your promise to deliver a bushel of wheat than they would be without it.

Let's take a different case. You give me a bushel of wheat and I promise to pay you in a week. In the interim I file a bankruptcy petition. What does the trustee find? You are one of the many people

---

[1] Vern Countryman, Executory Contracts in Bankruptcy (Part I), 57 Minn. L. Rev. 439 (1973).

knocking on the door. You are a creditor. Your right to get $5 from me is a garden-variety claim.

Let's combine the first two cases. You and I enter into a contract. You promise to give me a bushel of wheat in a week, and I promise to pay you $5 for it. Here there is both a liability (I have to pay you $5 in a week's time) and an asset (I have a right to get a bushel of wheat from you). We give the name *executory contract* to this kind of arrangement. It is one in which the debtor has an obligation to a third party and the third party owes the debtor an obligation in return. What matters, of course, is how we treat such a beast, not what we call it.

We first want to ask what basic problems arise in cases like this. How does the trustee feel about this deal in which at the end of the week, the debtor is supposed to fork over $5 and get a bushel of wheat in return? It all depends on what has happened to the market price of wheat. Assume that the market price of wheat has gone way up. A bushel of wheat now costs $10. In this case, the trustee is thrilled. This executory contract is a winner. The trustee can use $5 and get something in return that is worth $10 (the bushel of wheat). This is a good deal. Should the trustee be able to go through with this deal? Why not? Why should you not be held to your bargain? You asked for $5, you will get $5. It is a losing deal, but it would have been a losing deal even if no bankruptcy petition had been filed. There is nothing about bankruptcy that should let you off the hook.

The trustee is simply new management.[2] There is nothing about the deal that we entered into that conditioned your obligation to give me a bushel of wheat in exchange for $5 upon the management's staying the same. We want to have a rule that says simply this: If the debtor has a good deal that new managers would have been able to enjoy outside of bankruptcy, the trustee should be able to take advantage of it inside of bankruptcy. At first cut, §365 does exactly this. As in the nonbankruptcy world, of course, the trustee has to keep the other side of the bargain. The trustee cannot get the wheat without parting with the $5. The formal process by which the trustee takes advantage of the favorable contract (and lives up to the debtor's obligations under the contract) is called *assumption*. When the trustee assumes the contract and brings it into the bankruptcy estate, the estate enjoys all the benefits of the contract, but bears all of its burdens as well.

[2] See Commodity Futures Trading Commission v. Weintraub, 471 U.S. 343 (1985).

But let us take the opposite case. Suppose the price of wheat plummets. You can now go out and buy wheat for $1. Any wheat you have you will be able to sell for only $1. The deal does not look so great. I promised to pay $5 for something that is now worth only $1. It is making deals like this that drove me into bankruptcy. Ridding one-self of a burdensome contract and exposing oneself to a damage action is a power that everyone enjoys. We live in a Holmesian world.[3] The new managers of a corporation can break a contract that the old managers entered into, provided they are liable for damages. The trustee is new management and can breach a contract if it is in the interests of the estate. The ability of the trustee to breach an execu-tory contract (and trigger the third party's claim for damages) is, in the language of the Bankruptcy Code, the ability to *reject*. Rejection of an executory contract is not quite the same as a breach of a con-tract outside of bankruptcy. Rejecting an unfavorable executory con-tract is akin to abandoning an asset.[4] Little of consequence turns on this, however, and this subtlety is one that we do not pursue further.

It is important to give the trustee the ability to breach to ensure equal treatment among those who are similarly situated. As far as their legal rights are concerned, a party who has a contract with the debtor is in the same situation as someone who has lent the debtor money. Both have the right to sue for damages if the debtor does not do what was promised. An insolvent debtor cannot keep all its promises. Rather than favor one group over another, the general rule of bankruptcy is one of pro rata sharing. Allowing the trustee to re-ject the debtor's contracts ensures that all those with damage actions against the debtor are treated the same way. At the end of the day, they all have a claim against the debtor and they all share pro rata in the bankruptcy estate.

This, as a very rough approximation, tells you what is at stake in §365. Painted with very broad strokes, it makes good sense. The par-ticular details of §365, however, are harder to reconcile with one an-other. What we want to do now is look at the more complicated cases. The problems we face under this section fall into two catego-ries. One is the problem that arises when the contract is a bad one and the trustee wants to breach. This is the problem of *rejection*. The

---

[3] See Oliver Wendell Holmes, The Path of the Law, 10 Harv. L. Rev. 457, 462 (1897) ("The duty to keep a contract at common law means a prediction that you must pay damages if you do not keep it—and nothing else.").

[4] See Brown v. O'Keefe, 300 U.S. 598 (1937); Sparhawk v. Yerkes, 142 U.S. 1 (1891).

other arises when the contract is terrific and the trustee wants to keep a good thing going. This is the problem of *assumption*.

Rejection

Much of the difficulty in reconciling the case law on the rejection of executory contracts stems from the failure of a number of courts to distinguish the power of rejection from the consequences that flow from rejection. Some courts, for example, have held that the rejection of an executory contract not only triggers a prepetition claim for damages but also deprives the other party of any benefits of the contract. This result is unsound if the other party would have been entitled to these benefits had the breach occurred outside of bankruptcy. There is no bankruptcy policy in favor of "executoriness."[5] Section 365 is not an avoiding power designed to expand the assets of the estate and give creditors inside of bankruptcy something they would not have had outside. Several examples illustrate this point.

A firm promises to sell you the Van Gogh that has been in the lobby of its headquarters for $1 million. Before payment or delivery, the price of works by Van Gogh goes through the ceiling. The firm goes broke in the meantime and it files a bankruptcy petition. Its assets (apart from the Van Gogh) are worth $1 million. The firm owes its creditors (not counting you) $5 million. The managers of the firm have been spending too much time buying art and not enough time managing the business.

The trustee wants out of this bad deal because the Van Gogh can now be sold for $2 million. The trustee reasons that breaching the contract is in the interests of the general creditors because if the firm performs on the contract and sells you the Van Gogh, there will be $2 million in assets ($1 million in other assets and the $1 million you fork over) and $5 million in claims. The general creditors will get 40 cents on the dollar. But if the trustee backs out of the deal, the Van Gogh can be sold for $2 million. Then the assets of the firm are $3 million ($1 million from other assets and $2 million from the sale of the painting). The liabilities are $6 million ($5 million in other claims and $1 million from you for damages for the breach of contract). The damages from the breach of contract is the $1 million difference between the current market price and the amount set in the contract

---

[5] See Michael Andrew, Executory Contracts in Bankruptcy: Understanding "Rejection," 59 U. Colo. L. Rev. 845 (1988); Jay Lawrence Westbrook, A Functional Analysis of Executory Contracts, 74 Minn. L. Rev. 227 (1989).

($2 million minus $1 million). Creditors will get 50 cents on the dollar.

To understand whether the trustee can in fact reject this contract and face only a damage action from you, we need to ask what would have happened if the firm's managers had refused to turn over the Van Gogh outside of bankruptcy. You would be able to bring a specific performance action. Vis-à-vis the firm, you have the right to the painting. Because the Van Gogh is unique, you do not simply get money damages. You get the painting. But you are in a race with the firm's general creditors. You also need to ask whether you would be able to take the Van Gogh in the face of their claims.

We must go through the same process we went through in chapter 5 when we looked at rights that the creditors enjoyed by virtue of §541(a)(1) and those they enjoyed by virtue of the trustee's strong-arm power under §§544 and 545. To measure your rights in bankruptcy, you have to worry about how well you would fare not only against the debtor but also against creditors of the debtor who reduced their claims to judgment and levied on the painting. If a lien creditor could prime your right to the painting outside of bankruptcy, you should not be able to insist on getting the painting when the firm is in bankruptcy. Nonbankruptcy law generally gives priority to the lien creditor. Under U.C.C. §2-402, the property is subject to creditor levy so long as the seller retains possession. You might have a special buyer's lien on these goods if you had already paid for them, but you have not. The rule we have is that your rights to the picture are superior to those of firm's creditors only after you cure the ostensible ownership problem. For this reason, you should have only a damage claim in the firm's bankruptcy if you have not taken possession of the picture. Section 365 provides for this result.

Section 365 also applies to leases. Let's take some simple cases. Suppose I have rented a store on Rodeo Drive from you. I am paying $10,000 a month in rent, and I am bound to pay you this amount each year for five years, for a total of $600,000. The market for stores on Rodeo Drive collapses. The rental value of the store is now much lower. I file a bankruptcy petition. My trustee can break this lease, just as I was free to break the lease outside of bankruptcy. Outside of bankruptcy, you would have an action for the damages you have suffered as a result of my breach. In bankruptcy, the trustee can reject the lease and you are left with an action for damages.[6]

---

[6] Recall, however, that there is a cap on damages from the breach of a lease under §502(b)(6).

Let's look at the other side of this transaction. I own a piece of real property that you rent from me. You agreed to pay me $5,000 a month for six years. The lease obliges me to heat and cool the building, which costs me $2,000 a month. A year into the lease we find ourselves in the midst of a real estate boom. If you were to lease the property from me now, you would have to pay me $10,000 a month. I file a bankruptcy petition. What can my trustee do? More specifically, is there any way that the trustee can take advantage of the dramatic increase in the rental value of the property?

Outside of bankruptcy, I could cut off the heating and cooling of the building. In most jurisdictions, you could respond by either leaving the property and suing me for damages or by remaining in possession of the property and paying for the heating and cooling by deducting it from the rent. If we raise these questions in bankruptcy, we find much the same answers. The trustee can reject the lease and cease heating and cooling the building. Just as you could outside of bankruptcy, you can call off the whole deal and sue for damages. Alternatively, you can exercise your right to pay for heating and cooling out of the rental payments that would otherwise be owing. Your right to stay in possession and offset such costs is given explicitly in §365(h). The trustee's rejection of my obligations under the lease, however, does nothing to dispossess you of the property. You have a right to stay in possession of the property. You have a leasehold interest. This property interest gives you a right to the asset that primes that of any of my creditors. Not even a bona fide purchaser of the property from the debtor can take it free of your right to enjoy the property for the remainder of the lease term. Although the general rule of *Chicago Board of Trade* would itself be sufficient to give us this result, §365(h) makes the point explicitly.

The drafters of the Bankruptcy Code created problems by providing such an explicit rule for real property but not for personal property. Should one infer that, notwithstanding *Chicago Board of Trade*, personal property is to be treated differently? Suppose I lease you a fancy computer. You pay $5,000 a month in rent. This computer now leases for $10,000 a month. I file a bankruptcy petition. The trustee can reject this lease, but what does it mean to reject it? Under nonbankruptcy law, I cannot force you to give the computer back by declaring that I am in breach. I have conveyed a property interest to you. It is a done deal. You are in possession. I can yell "I breach!" all I want, but I cannot force you to give me the computer back. In bankruptcy, the trustee can convert any service obligations I owed you into a general claim you have against my bankruptcy estate.

It is just like the heating and cooling obligation in the case of real property. But does rejection mean anything more than that? Does it mean that the trustee can get the computer back? There is no §365(h) to which we can turn. There is nothing to say that you can keep the computer in the face of the rejection.

We could infer that the absence of an analog to §365(h) means, in our case, that when my trustee breaks a lease of personal property, you cannot remain in possession. Under the maxim of statutory interpretation of *expressio unius*, one infers from the inclusion of one thing the exclusion of another. One can infer that Congress, by providing explicitly that lessees of real property could remain in possession after rejection, implicitly found that lessees of personal property could not. One can also reach the opposite conclusion, however. An equally plausible view begins with the observation that few cases arise in which the trustee wants to reject a personal property lease. Rejection becomes attractive only when the property increases in value. This is unlikely to happen in the case of personal property. When Congress enacted §365(h), it merely confronted the case that was most likely to arise. Congress may have decided not to trust courts to rely on the principle of *Chicago Board of Trade* in the case of real property, but not have thought about the analogous case of personal property at all. Setting out the rule explicitly in the case of real property does not require the inference that Congress was repudiating the general principle elsewhere. Indeed, why would Congress repudiate so important a doctrine by indirection?

There is an important lesson here. It is one thing to say that the trustee can reject and free the estate from ongoing obligations with respect to a lease or an executory contract. It is quite another thing to identify the consequences that flow in the wake of such a rejection. Rejection does not necessarily return the parties to the position they were in before they entered into the deal. A trustee can reject a lease of property, but that does not mean that the leasehold is extinguished and that the estate regains ownership of the property. Nothing about the nature of "rejection" requires that the trustee be able to undo (or "avoid") what is tantamount to a consummated property transfer. We need to keep this lesson in mind as we look at the rejection of technology licensing agreements, covenants not to compete, and the like.

Let's look at the following problem. A firm develops a new soft drink. Your client acquires the exclusive right to sell it in Kalamazoo, paying $10,000 up front and agreeing to pay an additional $1 for each case it sells. (Your client has the formula, and it does all the manufacturing of the drink itself. The firm, however, promises to run various local and national advertising campaigns.) The soft drink is a big hit in Kalamazoo, but it is a bust in the rest of the country. The firm files a Chapter II petition. The firm's trustee wants to take away your client's exclusive right to distribute the soft drink in Kalamazoo. If the trustee could do this, the trustee could then enter into a new licensing agreement with your client at a much higher fee. Alternatively, the trustee could sell the right to market the soft drink in Kalamazoo to someone else. The trustee argues that the exclusive distribution right is an executory contract. Moreover, the trustee contends that your client loses the right to sell the drink as soon as the contract is rejected and the firm gains the ability to license others to sell it in Kalamazoo. Under the franchising arrangement, each party has obligations remaining that would, if breached under nonbankruptcy law, allow the other to call off the deal. The firm has the obligation to provide some marketing support and to pay for some advertising. Your client, of course, has obligations because it has to pay the royalty of $1 per case.

One may be able to argue these obligations do not necessarily make the right to manufacture the soft drink in Kalamazoo part of an executory contract. Take the following example. A firm sells you a machine and promises to service it. You promise to pay for the service. The trustee could not bundle this whole package together, call it an executory contract, take the machine back and sell it to someone else on that ground. This transaction may be no different. Your client bargained for the exclusive right to sell this soft drink in Kalamazoo. Your client already has this right. The firm should no more be able to get this right back in its bankruptcy than it should be able to get back a machine it sold to you. The right to sell the soft drink in Kalamazoo does not belong to the firm anymore. One can argue that it is not the paradigm case in which I promise to sell you wheat and you promise to pay for it, but rather the quite different case in which I have already sold the wheat. Once I have sold the wheat, it is not mine anymore.

But let's assume this is wrong. Assume that what we have in the Kalamazoo case is an executory contract. Even if the distribution right is an executory contract, we still need to identify the consequences of the rejection. The trustee refuses to go ahead with the firm's obligations under the contract and to advertise the product. But that does not trouble your client much. The soft drink is so popular that no advertising is needed. In any event, your client has a claim for the value of the ads that the firm promised and this claim can be offset against any royalties that are owed. But can your client keep on selling the soft drink? This seems to parallel the ability of a lessee to remain in possession. Under nonbankruptcy law, the firm would not be able to stop your client from selling the soft drink. The firm is the breaching party. It cannot go to court and get your client to stop, just as a lessor of real property on Rodeo Drive cannot file a bankruptcy petition, reject the lease, and evict its tenant. Your client is a licensee who is "in possession." Why should rejection under §365 give the trustee the right to dispossess your client?

What about the firm's desire to give someone else the right to make and sell the drink in Kalamazoo? Outside of bankruptcy, if the firm said it was breaking its contract and started giving others the right to sell the soft drink in Kalamazoo, you could get a negative injunction in a hurry. More to the point, the general creditors of the firm cannot have a receiver appointed and assign to others your right to sell the soft drink in Kalamazoo. This case is crucially different from your right of specific performance when the trustee breached and refused to give you the Van Gogh. In that case, you had no right to the painting vis-à-vis a lien creditor. In this case, your rights are paramount. No matter how broadly we define the trustee's strong-arm powers under §544(a), they would not enable the trustee to defeat your client's right to market the soft drink. Outside of bankruptcy, neither the firm nor its creditors would have the ability to stop your client from making the soft drink. Moreover, your client would be able to enjoin the firm from marketing the drink. In addition, your client would also be able to enjoin any third party who acquired rights from the firm, such as a buyer of the business or its assets. Before we conclude that your client should prevail, however, we need to ask whether any other bankruptcy policy enters into the picture. The principal question focuses on how the firm's discharge will affect your client's rights.

Suppose a store sells you a computer with a warranty and you promise to pay for the computer in thirty days. The store delivers the computer. The store files a bankruptcy petition and rejects its contract with you. The computer is in short supply, and the store would like to reclaim it from you and sell it to someone else. If the trustee rejects the store's executory contract with you, you will have a claim against the store for breach of the warranty obligations. The store's discharge will extinguish your claim, but it will not change your right to keep the computer.

The strong-arm power does the trustee no good here. Using the strong-arm power, the trustee could reach the computer only if the store or a party claiming through the store could reach it. To be sure, nonbankruptcy law calls the rights you have in the machine a "property interest," but what matters is whether the trustee can assert a superior claim to it using §544(a), not whether the right is "property" under nonbankruptcy law. You have a "property interest" in the machine under nonbankruptcy law as soon as the computer is identified to the contract, but your paramount right to it does not arise until later. Given the trustee's strong-arm power, the "property interest" that arises on the identification of the goods to the contract does you no good if you have not paid for the computer and are not in possession of it.

The discharge does not affect your rights, either. Your claim against the store is discharged, but you still retain the computer and the ability to bring actions against the store to enforce the right. (The store could not seize the computer and resist your replevin action on the ground that bankruptcy had discharged your claim.) Discharge affects only general claims that third parties have against the store. Other rights that third parties enjoy pass through bankruptcy.

Similarly, in the case of the soft drink firm, discharge affects your client's ability to reach the assets of the firm after the bankruptcy is over. It does not give creditors the ability to control a valuable asset (like the right to sell the soft drink in Kalamazoo) that they could not have reached outside of bankruptcy. It should not matter whether the transaction involved a traditional property interest or an intangible right such as a right to distribute a soft drink. We should treat rights like those of the soft drink distributor in Kalamazoo in the same way we treat traditional property interests. So long as neither the debtor nor any hypothetical party claiming through the debtor can upset those rights under nonbankruptcy law, bankruptcy should leave them unaffected.[7]

The law in this area is clear when a traditional property right is in issue. Assume that Debtor sold Blackacre to Buyer. If Debtor later tries to move back onto Blackacre and then files a bankruptcy petition, everyone understands that Buyer's trespass action is a claim and that this claim is discharged. Everyone also understands that the discharge has no effect on Buyer's continuing ownership of Blackacre or on Buyer's ability to bring trespass actions in the future if Debtor tries to move back again. Buyer prevails because Debtor's creditors cannot bring Blackacre into the bankruptcy estate through the use of one of the avoiding powers. Discharge is itself irrelevant.

---

[7] See In re Printronics, Inc., 189 Bankr. 995 (Bankr. N.D. Fla. 1995).

The case law, however, is less clear when the right is something like a covenant not to compete and the debtor is an individual. In such cases, some courts have found that the power to reject in §365 serves to protect the flesh-and-blood individual's right to a fresh start.[8] The debate over the effect of such a covenant on an individual, however, is better located in the doctrines that have grown around the fresh start policy and §541(a)(6). Discharge alone does not extinguish encumbrances or liens on the debtor's property or otherwise affect the rights that the debtor has conveyed to a third party. The fresh start for individuals, however, includes more than a simple discharge. As we discussed in chapter 2 above, the principle of *Local Loan Company v. Hunt* gives individual debtors the right to free themselves from encumbrances on their future earnings.[9] Whether this principle should allow individual debtors to rid themselves of covenants not to compete is an interesting question, but it has nothing to do with §365. Grafting a fresh start policy onto §365 by insisting that rejection is something more than the ability to breach is inherently problematic, as §365 applies equally to corporations and to individuals.

Congress confronted the consequences that flow from rejection in the case of technology licenses, when the licensor is the debtor and it seeks to recapture a license it has already issued.[10] In the main, Congress embraced the idea that rejection itself should not allow the trustee to recapture rights that the debtor has already conveyed away. The specific rules governing technology licenses in §365(n) are analogous to the specific rules governing real property in §365(h). The effect of §365(n) on intellectual property it does not specifically cover (such as trademarks and franchise agreements) remains unclear.[11] Courts may apply the maxim of *expressio unius*. Congress's decision to deny debtors the ability to recapture rights they have already conveyed in the case of technology licenses might be used to justify granting debtors this right in analogous cases that are not explicitly covered. There is no evidence, however, that Congress con-

---

[8] See, e.g., Cloyd v. GRP Records, 238 Bank. 328 (Bankr. E.D. Mich. 1999).

[9] 292 U.S. 234 (1934).

[10] Congress acted in the wake of Lubrizol Enterprises v. Richmond Metal Finishers, 756 F.2d 1043 (4th Cir. 1985), an opinion that interpreted too expansively the power to reject.

[11] Compare Blackstone Potato Chip Co. v. Mr. Popper, Inc., 109 Bankr. 557 (Bankr. D.R.I. 1990), with In re Ron Matusalem & Matusa of Florida, Inc., 158 Bankr. 514 (Bankr. S.D. Fla. 1993).

sidered other kinds of rights when it thought about technology licenses.

Arguments that justify giving the trustee the power to recapture rights that could never be taken from a third party outside of bankruptcy should not, in principle, rest on the idea that there is a bankruptcy policy in favor of rehabilitating the debtor. The trustee's power to reject executory contracts under §365 is the same in Chapter 7 as in Chapter 11. Nothing in the Bankruptcy Code or its antecedents suggests that the power to reject turns on whether the debtor is liquidating or reorganizing. If it does not, then the debtor's chances of reorganizing successfully should play no role in deciding the contours of §365. The firm's ability to regain control of the soft drink franchise should be independent of whether it needs the money to stay in business or whether the trustee is simply distributing the proceeds to the general creditors.

Assumption and Limitations on the Power to Assume

We now turn to the less bleak subject of *assumption* of an executory contract. We have been looking at bad deals of several types, but life is not always so grim. Now we turn to look at deals that the debtor has made that are good. Let's recall what our basic problem is. There are some things that a debtor has that are mixed assets and liabilities. I can live in this apartment, which is great, but I have to pay rent, which is not so great. I have your promise to give me wheat next week, which is great. But I have to pay you $5 for it, which is not so great. We have been looking at cases in which the burdens outweigh the benefits. Now we want to look at those cases in which the burdens are light and the benefits substantial. Can you keep this good deal even though you have filed a bankruptcy petition?

Section 541 tells us that states cannot dictate distributions in bankruptcy. Any priority scheme they create has to be one that applies generally inside of bankruptcy and out. The same principle applies to contracts that the debtor makes with others. A third party may ask for an *ipso facto clause*, which allows it to terminate the contract in the event that a bankruptcy petition is filed. The debtor may be quite willing to grant such a clause. Outside of bankruptcy, those who act on behalf of the debtor worry principally about the interests of the shareholders. The shareholders are the ones who ultimately hire and fire the managers of a firm. Shareholders may have little incentive to resist clauses that will prove costly only when they are no longer in the picture, as is typically the case when the firm is insolvent. For this reason, §365 makes ipso facto clauses unenforceable.

As in the case of §541, this prohibition extends beyond termination clauses tied to the start of a bankruptcy case and applies to clauses tied to the insolvency or financial condition of the debtor as well. The net must be cast wide enough so that parties cannot do indirectly what they are forbidden from doing directly.

Parties are not made worse off by having unenforceable clauses in their contracts. Moreover, such clauses were enforceable under the 1898 Bankruptcy Act, even though case law watered them down to some extent.[12] For both these reasons, ipso facto clauses still abound in form books and preprinted contracts. Their pervasiveness should not lead you, however, to draw the inference that they are enforceable. They survive because no one has an incentive to remove them. (Indeed, they may give some contracting parties a false belief that they will not have to deal with their contracting opposite if it ever files a bankruptcy petition.) Nevertheless, the trustee's ability to assume executory contracts still presumes that the contract has not been terminated before the filing of the bankruptcy petition.[13]

Many of the issues involving the assumption of executory contracts could be handled easily if §365 did not exist at all. Courts would treat a favorable executory contract as property of the estate under §541 and apply the general principle of *Chicago Board of Trade v. Johnson*. Let's go through some examples. You run a Holiday Inn in Camden, New Jersey. You pay Holiday Inn a certain amount of money every month and you are obliged to run your hotel in a certain way. You must have ice machines on every floor. Outside of bankruptcy, your ability to keep the franchise will depend on whether you comply with these conditions. Courts will not second-guess their wisdom or purpose. (This may be a good thing. Judges make for poor hoteliers, and there is always the risk they will regard as unnecessary requirements that are in fact forward-looking. Holiday Inn, for example, insisted on wheel chair accessibility long before others did.)

The benefits of being a Holiday Inn are quite substantial. You have the benefit of the company's computerized reservation system; you get a discount on credit card fees. (Credit card companies charge those who accept credit cards for reimbursing them.) You also get extra business from people who have never heard of your hotel before they came to Camden because they know what to expect. If you had exactly the same hotel, but did not have the Holiday Inn sign, your hotel would be worth much less.

[12] See Queens Blvd. Wine & Liquor Corp. v. Blum, 503 F.2d 202 (2d Cir. 1974).
[13] Nemko, Inc. v. Motorola, Inc., 163 Bankr. 927 (Bankr. E.D.N.Y. 1994).

Notwithstanding the Holiday Inn franchise, however, your hotel is a complete bust. The idea of a Holiday Inn in Camden seemed like a good one at the time, but not that many people who come to Camden want to spend the night there. You can get more money for the assets if you blow up the building and use the property as a parking lot rather than as a hotel. Let's assume that you have been religious in complying with the rules. You have never let an ice machine run out of ice. When you close up shop, can you sell your franchise to someone else? We have already talked about this question. The answer should hinge entirely on whether the right you have acquired can be transferred. Whether the franchise can be transferred, like the question that arose in *Chicago Board of Trade* over whether a seat could be sold, should turn on applicable nonbankruptcy rules.

Let's assume that each franchise is tied to a particular location. You are allowed to sell the franchise, only if you sell the hotel as a going concern. Note that any bankruptcy policy that justifies a different outcome has nothing to do with giving you a fresh start. You are out of the hotel business. The hotel itself is being converted into a parking lot. Your general creditors would like to sell the Holiday Inn franchise to some third party who operates a hotel at a different location. If they were able to do this, your creditors are better off and Holiday Inn is worse off. Your creditors would have the proceeds from the sale of the franchise instead of Holiday Inn. In addition, Holiday Inn would lose the ability to choose the new location and its operator. (For example, the new owner might not conform to Holiday Inn's efforts to make each Holiday Inn be like every other and thereby ensure that its guests will not face any unwelcome surprises in a strange place.) The general creditors, however, should not be able to sell a franchise by itself inside of bankruptcy if they cannot sell it by itself outside of bankruptcy. There is no bankruptcy policy that suggests that we should deprive the Holiday Inns of this world of the revenue from the sale of franchises or control over their franchisees in order to put money into the hands of the general creditors. Giving general creditors more and third parties less, of course, has utterly no bearing on an individual's fresh start.

But consider a different case. Suppose you want to stay in the hotel business. The idea may have been bad, but given the investment you have already made, you are better off using the building as a hotel. Everyone would lose even more if the building were torn down and the land used as a parking lot. The hotel is generating a positive cash flow and cannot generate more in a different configuration. You decide to stay in the hotel business but restructure the debt by filing for Chapter II. In this case, you should be able to continue to call yourself a Holiday Inn. At most, the filing of a bankruptcy petition brings about a change in management, but because you continue as the debtor in possession, even this change is small. The financial structure of the firm changes when it is in Chapter II, but its operations need not. Unless the guests of the hotel hang around bankruptcy court, they will not notice the slightest change. As far as the franchise is concerned, the bankruptcy case should not make any difference. If, in the course of the bankruptcy case, substantive changes are made, then the consequences should follow inside bankruptcy that would follow outside. Assume, for example, that you are an incompetent manager and the creditors want to replace you with someone else. The control that Holiday Inn would have over the selection of the new manager should be no different from the kind of control they could exert outside of bankruptcy.

We cannot, however, rely on §541 and the principle of *Chicago Board of Trade* to resolve these questions, as the Bankruptcy Code deals with them explicitly in §365. Unfortunately, §365 makes it difficult to deal with these issues consistently. The trouble begins with §365(c), which limits the kinds of contracts that may be assumed:

> The trustee may not assume ... any executory contract ... whether or not such contract ... prohibits or restricts assignment of rights or delegation of duties, if ... applicable law excuses a party, other than the debtor, to such contract ... from accepting performance from or rendering performance to an entity other than the debtor or the debtor in possession.

This limitation is inconsistent with §541(c)(1). The trustee should be able to assert control over the debtor's assets and ensure that the creditors can enjoy whatever assets they could enjoy outside of bankruptcy.

With respect to individuals in Chapter 7, §365(c) might seem to bring about a sensible result. An opera singer has a contract to sing with an opera house next year. The singer is slightly past his prime, and the opera house would not engage this singer if it were making the decision now. The singer is deeply in debt and files a Chapter 7 petition. The singer wants to be able to sing at the opera house and enjoy the promised fee. The opera company would like the engagement cancelled. The creditors of the opera singer want to be able reach the lucrative fee to recover some of what they are owed. As a matter of first principle, however, the singer should be able to take advantage of the contract as it is part of his future earnings and therefore his fresh start. The creditors should not be able to reach the fee for the same reason. *Butner* tells us that the opera house should not be excused from an unfavorable contract by the happenstance of the singer's financial problems.

It might seem that §365(c) exists to ensure that we reach this result. Under it, a trustee cannot assume such a contract, a contract that an individual debtor could not have delegated to anyone else outside of bankruptcy. Applying §365(c) to the opera singer's contract, however, does not mean that the opera singer can take advantage of the contract. Once one assumes that the singer's deal with the opera company is an executory contract that falls within the ambit of §365, the inability of the trustee to assume the contract means that it is rejected and §365(g) deems rejection a breach of the contract. The singer's bankruptcy filing released the opera house from an unfavorable contract. To avoid this outcome, a court might rule that the singer's contract with the opera house is personal to him, thus not subject to the trustee's assumption or rejection. Holding that §365(c) never applies in the case of an individual, however, takes away the only plausible justification for having the provision in the first place. To make §365 consistent with §541(c)(1) and the *Butner* principle, it would have to take on a radically different form. Contracts for future services by individual debtors should be beyond its reach altogether. Moreover, it would need to allow the trustee to assume every contract of a corporate debtor. The law here remains in flux. The most important cases have involved patent licenses. Some courts have found ways to read the statute in a way that allows the debtor in possession to continue to use patent licenses even though nonbankruptcy law provides that they are not assumable. Other courts, invoking Supreme Court opinions that mandate fidelity to statutory text in bankruptcy, have refused to do so.[14]

While §365(c) inappropriately limits the trustee's ability to assume contracts, §365(f)(1) inappropriately expands the trustee's ability to assign whatever contracts the trustee can assume. On its face, it seems to allow the trustee to assign any contract that can be assumed. The power to assume and the power to assign, however, are quite different from each other. If the debtor is to remain intact as a going concern and if the effect of the bankruptcy proceeding is simply to rearrange its capital structure, the trustee's power to assume

[14] Compare Institut Pasteur v. Cambridge Biotech Corp., 104 F.3d 489 (1st Cir. 1997), with Perlman v. Catapult Entertainment, Inc., 165 F.3d 747 (9th Cir. 1999).

should not be limited in any way. A state law limitation on transfer should not matter because the appointment of a trustee is in substance merely the substitution of one manager for another. Section 541(c)(1) makes it clear that, in the case of ordinary assets, a limitation on transfer has no effect on the ability of a trustee to assert the rights of the debtor. In an executory contract, the right in question is linked with an obligation of some kind, but this should not make for a different result. If the debtor had fewer creditors, the debt might have been restructured in a nonbankruptcy workout. There is nothing about the existence of multiple creditors and the need for a collective proceeding to sort out these problems that should change the ability of the firm to enjoy the benefits of whatever contracts into which it has entered.

The power to assign the debtor's rights to some third party, however, is quite different in principle from the power to assume. Under *Chicago Board of Trade*, the trustee should be able to assign a contract to a third party only if it is assignable outside of bankruptcy. Under nonbankruptcy law, the question of assignability is one that is left up to the parties. If the parties specify in their contract that the duty is not delegable, their choice is ordinarily respected, even if the duty would be delegable if they had said nothing.[15] The nonbankruptcy rule presumes that most parties will not allow delegation when performance requires skills that are special or unique, and will allow delegation when they are not,[16] but this is only a presumption.

Section 365(f) neglects the consequences that follow when the nonbankruptcy baseline is merely a presumption. In some environments, such as franchise agreements, parties by contract routinely agree that the franchise is not assignable when the background legal rule provides for the opposite. As with most contract rules, there a few costs when the law provides a default rule provided parties can contract around it easily. There may be some cases in which the legislature restricts freedom of contract, but in such cases the nonbankruptcy law is again written against a background of freedom of contract. State law, for example, often singles out automobile franchisees for special protection. Regardless of what the contract provides, franchisees are protected and they are able to transfer their franchisees provided specified conditions are met.

When applied in bankruptcy, however, the state law protecting automobile franchisees takes on a different meaning. All other fran-

---

[15] See, e.g., U.C.C. §2-210.
[16] Taylor v. Palmer, 31 Cal. 240, 247–48 (1866).

chisees are able to transfer their franchises freely because state law is silent and the contractual limits are made irrelevant. Automobile franchisees—the ones who were the most able to transfer their franchises out of bankruptcy—are not so lucky. The nonbankruptcy law that gave them the ability to transfer provided certain conditions were made is transformed in bankruptcy into a law that deprives them of the ability to make the transfer unless these conditions are met. The automobile dealers are more able to transfer their franchises outside of bankruptcy, but are less able inside. This shift in relative rights cannot be defended. More importantly, it shows how §365 lacks an internal coherence that we see in other parts of the Bankruptcy Code. We should not be surprised that some parts of the Bankruptcy Code do not make perfect sense. It is important, however, to know where a search for internal coherence will not be successful.

Curing Defaults

Section 365(b) provides that the trustee (or the debtor in possession) can assume a contract even if there have been defaults that would give rise to a right of termination. The trustee cures all past defaults, compensates the third party for all losses from the breaches, and provides adequate assurance of future performance. In many cases, however, the defaults may not be curable. A franchise agreement may give the franchisor the right to terminate if the franchisee has failed to operate the business for some period of time. Sometimes the same condition that ultimately pushed the debtor in Chapter 11 forced the debtor to suspend its operations just before the bankruptcy. Even if the debtor subsequently reopens, its failure to remain open triggers a default under the "going-dark" clause that is inherently incapable of being cured. Section 365(b)(2)(D) excuses compliance with "any penalty rate or provision relating to a default arising from any failure by the debtor to perform nonmonetary obligations." This provision, however, may do the debtor no good. The clause the word "penalty" may modify both "rates" and "provisions." The debtor is not as a general matter excused from curing nonmonetary defaults, only those that are penalties.[17]

If the debtor assumes an executory contract, it must assume the entire contract with all of its burdens. It cannot pick and choose

---

[17] See Worthington v. General Motors Corp. (In re Claremont Acquisition Corp.), 113 F.3d 1029 (9th Cir. 1997).

those parts that are to its liking.[18] Adequate assurance of future performance, however, is a term of art. In *In re U.L. Radio*, the court authorized the assignment of a lease of a television sales and service store to someone who wanted to convert it into a bistro on a budget of $50,000 notwithstanding a use restriction in the lease.[19] The court observed that the primary focus of adequate assurance is the assignee's ability to satisfy financial obligations under the lease. In another case, the court authorized a debtor, whose lease limited it to selling paint and hardware, to assign its lease to a store that sold woman's clothing, even though the landlord had promised another lessee not to let another woman's clothing store operate in the building. The court again found that the landlord was not worse off financially and the bankruptcy proceeding itself insulated the landlord from contractual liability to the other tenant because of the doctrine of impossibility.[20] One may doubt whether $50,000 is in fact enough to convert an appliance store into a bistro in New York City or whether the doctrine of impossibility protects the lessor from actions from a third party. More importantly, however, one needs to ask again what bankruptcy policy justifies ignoring use restrictions in a lease.

Timing of the Decision to Assume or Reject

Upon assumption, the obligation becomes one of the estate, and the debtor is required to perform. Any subsequent breach will no longer be a prepetition breach. §365(g). Damages will be entitled to administrative expense priority (if it occurs during bankruptcy), or to ordinary damage rules if breached subsequent to the termination of the bankruptcy proceeding. By contrast, upon rejection, the resulting damage action (if any) is treated as a prepetition claim. The debtor, however, does not make the decision to assume or reject immediately and in most cases the debtor continues to enjoy the benefits of the contract or lease. If the debtor ultimately assumes, it presumably has to pay all of its obligations at the contract rate, as well as cure any defaults. On the other hand, if the debtor ultimately rejects, the outcome is less clear. Section 365(d) requires ongoing performance of obligations before assumption or rejection for leases of nonresidential real property and provides more limited protection

---

[18] See In re Crippin, 877 F.2d 594 (7th Cir. 1989).

[19] 19 Bankr. 537 (Bankr. S.D.N.Y. 1982).

[20] See In re Martin Paint Stores, 199 Bankr. 258 (Bankr. S.D.N.Y. 1996), aff'd, 207 Bankr. 57 (S.D.N.Y. 1997) .

for personal property lessors as well. The case law suggests that with respect to executory contracts and other leases, the third party is entitled to administrative expense priority, not under the terms of the lease or contract, but "under an objective worth standard that measures the fair and reasonable value" of the contract or lease.[21]

If the benefits the debtor receives correspond to the costs the other party incurs, this rule would seem to make sense. The trustee would have a chance to assess the situation and the third party would not bear the costs of the delay. The existing rule, however, does not necessarily make the third party whole. Paying for benefits received is not the same as compensating the third party for all the costs it incurs between the filing of the petition and the rejection. The starkest case arises when the third party is supplying insurance. Assume that debtor fails to make payments on its fire insurance for the first six months of the bankruptcy. It then decides to reject the contract. What is the benefit that the debtor has received? Can the debtor argue that, given that its building did not burn down, it did not receive any benefit? One would not think so, but exactly this problem can arise in more subtle guises. Assume a software producer has agreed to write the operating system for a new computer Debtor is developing. The operating system is due on July 1 and the computer cannot work without it. Debtor files a bankruptcy petition on January 1. In order to finish the program on time, the software producer must spend $10,000 each month. The trustee rejects the contract on June 1 after deciding that the new computer is not worth developing. The software producer seeks $50,000 in damages for all it spent on the program between the filing of the petition and the time of the rejection. The trustee will argue that because the debtor never used the program (and indeed the program was never finished), the debtor never received any benefit and hence does not owe any damages that deserve administrative priority under §503(b).

There is a second and much more common limitation on the protection that third parties receive before assumption or rejection. Many firms in bankruptcy have a single secured creditor with a security interest in the debtor's assets. The trustee is entitled to incur expenses and charge them against the secured creditor's secured claim. Third parties, however, cannot do this.[22] For this reason, those in the position of the software producer or the insurer should negotiate

[21] See, e.g., In re Thompson, 788 F.2d 560, 563 (9th Cir. 1986); In re Patient Education Media, Inc., 221 Bankr. 97 (Bankr. S.D.N.Y. 1998).

[22] See Hartford Underwriters Insurance v. Union Planters Bank, 530 U.S. ••• (2000).

with the secured party at the start of the case to ensure that they are paid. It should immediately ask the court to give the trustee a deadline. §365(d).

A negative implication of §365's decision to give the trustee the power to assume is that the third party cannot terminate the contract on the ground of the debtor's breach, as it would typically be able to do outside of bankruptcy. An effort to terminate is simply a non-event.[23] Section 362 stays everyone from "any act . . . to exercise control over property of the estate." An attempt to terminate might be seen as not merely as a breach, but as an effort to exercise control over property of the debtor (the "property" being the right of the debtor to the performance of the third party) that violates the automatic stay and may expose the producer to sanctions from the court.[24] When one is in doubt, one should always petition the court for a declaratory order that the proposed action does not violate the automatic stay. If the automatic stay applies, one can ask for relief from it or, in the alternative, one can ask for adequate protection. §362(d).

---

[23] See Douglas W. Bordewieck, The Postpetition, Pre-Rejection, Pre-Assumption Status of an Executory Contract, 59 Am. Bankr. L.J. 197, 211–15 (1985).

[24] See Computer Communications v. Codex Corp., 824 F.2d 725 (9th Cir. 1987) (holding an effort to terminate violated the automatic stay, the court awarded $4,750,000 in general damages and $250,000 in punitive damages).

Chapter Seven

Fraudulent Conveyances and Related Doctrines

In this chapter, we examine the protections enjoyed by creditors both inside and outside of bankruptcy. These protections, embodied in fraudulent conveyance law and related doctrines, are best understood as protections that most creditors would bargain for when making their loans.[1] In chapter 8, we look at voidable preferences. This bankruptcy-specific policy ensures that when bankruptcy is on the horizon, no creditor engages in gun-jumping.

Fraudulent Conveyance Law and Its Domain

Fraudulent conveyance law is a feature of state law that the trustee can use by invoking §544(b). A few states have their own versions of fraudulent conveyance law that can be traced back ultimately to the first fraudulent conveyance statute enacted in the sixteenth century. Most states, however, have adopted one of two uniform acts. The Uniform Fraudulent Conveyance Act has been around for a number of decades. Its successor, the Uniform Fraudulent Transfer Act, was drafted in the 1980s and tracks, in many respects, the language of §548 of the Bankruptcy Code. Section 548 can be understood as a provision that allows the trustee to invoke nonbankruptcy law at low cost. When transactions span a number of different jurisdictions, the trustee is able to invoke bankruptcy's fraudulent conveyance rules without having to identify which state's fraudulent conveyance law governs and without having to show that a particular transaction would be voidable under that law. In most situations, §548 is more likely to resemble any given state's fraudulent conveyance law than any given state's law resembles that of another state.

Fraudulent conveyance law first took statutory form in 1571. Transfers made and obligations incurred with the intent to delay, hinder, or defraud creditors are fraudulent and void as against creditors. Although written in general terms, the statute was originally aimed at a very simple transaction. Debtor, hounded by creditors, transfers everything to Sibling for a trivial sum. Debtor hopes to

---

[1] See Robert Charles Clark, The Duties of the Corporate Debtor to its Creditors, 90 Harv. L. Rev. 505 (1977).

shield assets from creditors. When the creditors come to enforce their claims, Debtor will assert that there are no assets on which they can levy. Sibling asserts that the assets belong to her and she is not liable for the debts. By invoking fraudulent conveyance law, the creditors can pierce through form and go to substance. The transfer between Debtor and Sibling is a sham, and the creditors can ignore the transfer and levy on the goods in Sibling's hands as if the transfer never took place.

This core of fraudulent conveyance law has remained essentially unchanged for more than four hundred years, but its reach has expanded over time. It first underwent a dramatic expansion just a few years after it was enacted. In 1600 or thereabouts a Hampshire farmer named Pierce conveyed his sheep to a man named Twyne. Twyne allowed Pierce to remain in possession of the sheep, to shear them, and to mark them as his own. A creditor of Pierce's reduced his claim to judgment and had the sheriff try to levy on the sheep that were still in Pierce's hands even though they had been sold to Twyne. What happened next is unclear. A fight of some kind ensued, and Edward Coke, then the Queen's attorney general, brought a criminal action against Twyne, the buyer of the sheep, in the Star Chamber.[2] The Star Chamber was a court largely reserved for treason trials and other crimes against the state. The Elizabethan fraudulent conveyance statute provided that a share of any assets recovered went to the Crown. The Crown had always enjoyed substantial revenue from those convicted of treason and felony, and fraudulent conveyance law was a useful tool in preventing traitors and felons from putting their property beyond its reach. These concerns may explain why a case involving a creditor levying on sheep was litigated here.[3]

The court in *Twyne's Case* found the transfer of the sheep voidable, not because one could prove that Pierce acted with actual fraudulent intent but because *badges of fraud* were associated with the transaction. A transfer of ownership without a simultaneous transfer of possession was inherently suspect. As the doctrine developed, the badges of fraud ceased to be merely proxies for fraud that was hard to prove and instead captured transactions that, although perhaps not fraudulent, were ones to which creditors would object nevertheless. Included, for example, were transfers the debtor made while insolvent and for which the debtor received nothing, or too little, in return. The paradigm here is a gift. An insolvent debtor gives a birth-

---

[2] Twyne's Case, 3 Coke 80b, 76 Eng. Rep. 809 (Star Chamber 1601).

[3] See Garrard Glenn, Fraudulent Conveyances and Preferences §§61–61e (rev. ed. 1940).

day present to a parent. Under fraudulent conveyance law, the creditors can reach the gift that is now in the parent's hands. This transaction may or may not be part of a scheme to defraud creditors, but making these sorts of transactions voidable may nevertheless make sense. First, it is possible that so many of the transactions in which an insolvent debtor gives away something and receives nothing or too little in return are fraudulent that one is better off voiding all of them rather than engaging in elaborate case-by-case inquiries into fraud. Second, even if most of these transfers are not fraudulent, so many may be transfers that creditors would want banned that we are well off banning all of them.

Fraudulent conveyance law applies to corporations as well as individuals. For example, creditors may be able to recover dividends or the proceeds of a stock repurchase from a corporation's shareholders under fraudulent conveyance law. Like the gift to a relative, these transactions are also ones in which the debtor gives up assets and gets nothing in return. Creditors are entitled to object if the debtor is insolvent or, to use a different rule that has gradually developed, is left with unreasonably small capital.

Let's take the following example. A firm owes its general creditors $2 million. The firm is solvent because its assets, including $900,000 in cash, are easily worth more than the $2 million it owes its creditors. The firm has ten shareholders, each of whom holds ten shares of stock (and therefore holds a 10 percent interest in the firm). The firm decides to repurchase nine shares of stock from each shareholder for $10,000 a share. At the end of the day, the firm is more highly leveraged. The firm still owes its creditors $2 million, but it now has fewer assets. These assets are barely enough to pay the creditors in full. Each of the shareholders now has $90,000 in cash in addition to stock in the firm. To be sure, each shareholder has only one share of the firm's stock rather than ten shares, but this change does not make any of them worse off. Because only ten shares of stock are now outstanding instead of one hundred, each share is worth correspondingly more. Each shareholder still enjoys a 10 percent ownership interest in the firm.

After the fact, the creditors as a group are worse off. Before the transaction, the fortunes of the firm could take a bad turn and the creditors would still be paid in full. Now the smallest reverse will prevent the creditors from recovering the full amount they are owed. The stockholders, to be sure, have a greater chance of being wiped out, but the $900,000 they have received more than compensates them for this additional risk. The stock repurchase is voidable if it left the firm with *unreasonably small capital*. The firm transferred assets to the shareholders but received nothing of value from the shareholders in return when it repurchased the stock. The stock has no value in the firm's hands. Residual rights to the firm are still in the hands of the same people. So far as the balance sheet of the firm is concerned, it is just as if the firm gave the money away. If the stock repurchase left the firm with too little capital, the creditors may reclaim the $900,000 from the shareholders at any time until the relevant statute of limitations runs its course.

Now let's begin to look at the various fraudulent conveyance laws. The Uniform Fraudulent Transfer Act (UFTA), enacted in the 1980s, adopts the same principles as the Uniform Fraudulent Conveyance Act (UFCA), which was enacted in the 1930s. The UFTA tracks §548 of the Bankruptcy Code more closely than does the UFCA. In addition, the UFTA deals explicitly with a few issues on which the UFCA and §548 are silent. The UFTA has been enacted in more than thirty-five jurisdictions, including California, Florida, Illinois, and Texas. The UFCA remains the law in most other jurisdictions. A few states have their own versions of fraudulent conveyance law.

The two basic, substantive sections of the UFCA are §§7 and 4. Under §7, any transfer made or any obligation incurred with the actual intent to hinder, delay, or defraud creditors is considered fraudulent. The parallel provision in the UFTA is §4(a)(1), and the parallel provision in the Bankruptcy Code is §548(a)(1). Most transactions that are voidable under one are voidable under the other, but a few exceptions worth noting. Section 548 reaches back only a year, for example, while its state law counterparts reach back as long as the relevant statute of limitations permits. In fraudulent conveyance law, as in other parts of the Bankruptcy Code, various amendments have been added over time. For example, although gifts by insolvent debtors are typically voidable, §548 excepts most charitable contributions. Unlike financial institutions, religious organizations are thinly capitalized and often use contributions to meet operating costs. They cannot easily return contributions made to them.

Section 4 of the UFCA reflects the idea that a solvent debtor can do what it pleases with its assets, but one who is insolvent (or who becomes insolvent as a result of the transfer) cannot incur obligations or convey assets for less than *fair consideration*. UFTA §5(a) and Bankruptcy Code §548(a)(2) use *reasonably equivalent value* instead of *fair consideration*. How these terms are defined largely determines the scope of fraudulent conveyance laws. Trading one asset for another is an exchange in which there is fair consideration or reasonably equivalent value. Hence, such a transaction is not a fraudulent conveyance, even if the debtor is insolvent. Creditors are stuck with the business decisions its debtor makes so long as the debtor remains in control. Moreover, creditors are powerless to reach assets once they have been placed in the hands of a good faith purchaser for value.

Debtors in financial trouble often try to pay one creditor rather than others. That creditor may be an important supplier or simply a particularly aggressive lender. A transfer to that creditor (called a *preference*) makes the other creditors worse off, but that does not make it a fraudulent conveyance. The UFCA, the UFTA, and §548 ensure this outcome by providing that a transfer on account of an antecedent debt is conclusively presumed to be one for which fair consideration or reasonably equivalent value is given. This result makes sense. Outside of bankruptcy, every creditor must rely on its own efforts to obtain repayment. Obtaining payment on a debt is simply the nature of the game when a collective proceeding is not on the horizon. Such transfers on account of an antecedent debt may affect how assets are distributed among the different creditors, but they do not affect the pool of assets available to the creditors. Creditors as a group are not worse off when one is paid and others are not. A creditor can challenge a payment to another creditor under the fraudulent conveyance laws only if the payment was made with actual fraudulent intent. Such cases most frequently when the creditor is an insider.[4] To challenge a payment to a creditor, one ordinarily must show that it is a preference, a transfer made on the eve of bankruptcy that violates the collective norms of bankruptcy. We will examine preferences at length in chapter 8.

Fraudulent conveyance law must be limited in its domain. Creditors are always worse off when the debtor takes assets whose value is certain (such as cash) and exchanges assets whose value is uncertain. A new machine may or may not make production more efficient. Creditors must choose debtors whom they believe able to make competent decisions about how to run their businesses. The reason you lend the money instead of using it yourself is that you think someone else can do better than you. You do not want your debtors to use the money to buy risk-free securities, like government bonds. You could do that as well as they can. You want your debtors to put their entrepreneurial skills to good use. It is possible that they will not succeed, but you are compensated for that risk. Fraudulent con-

---

[4] See, e.g., Bullard v. Aluminum Co. of America, 468 F.2d 11 (7th Cir. 1972).

veyance law is limited to actions that we are confident most would forbid if they could. For example, all creditors would that the debtor should not hide assets from them when they try to collect. Nor should the debtor be able to give away money when the debtor already lacks the money to pay off creditors in full. The provisions for fair consideration and reasonably equivalent value prevent creditors from using fraudulent conveyance law to second-guess their debtor's business decisions. Creditors who want to stop what they consider misbehavior must bargain for the right to declare a default and then exercise the right.

The provisions for fair consideration and reasonably equivalent value also ensure that fraudulent conveyance law does not extend too far. Without them and a willingness to interpret them sensibly, many transactions would be considered fraudulent conveyances. Suppose a creditor forecloses on property, and that the property is sold at a properly run foreclosure sale. The debtor is insolvent and allows its right to redeem the property to lapse. The debtor's loss of this equity of redemption is itself a transfer of property as defined in §101 of the Bankruptcy Code. If the debtor transferred its equity of redemption while it was insolvent for less than reasonably equivalent value, then the transfer would be considered a fraudulent conveyance. The Supreme Court, however, has found that a regularly conducted, non-collusive foreclosure sale necessarily yields reasonably equivalent value, ensuring that fraudulent conveyance law did not unsettle well-established commercial transactions.[5]

The insolvency test further narrows the scope of the fraudulent conveyance laws. Applying the insolvency test requires us to ask a simple question: Would a solvent buyer be willing to pay a positive price to take on all the debtor's assets and all the debtor's liabilities?[6] Assume that a debtor has guaranteed a $10 million debt of its parent corporation and otherwise has no other obligations. The debtor's assets are worth $1 million. If you were solvent, whether you would pay to acquire the assets and liabilities of this debtor would turn on whether the chance that you will be called upon to honor the guarantee was greater or less than one in ten. No one would agree to take an asset worth $1 million if it came with a 50–50 chance of having to pay $10 million. But a buyer might take the asset if the chance that it would have to pay $10 million were, let us say, only one in twenty.

[5] See BFP v. Resolution Trust Corp., 511 U.S. 531 (1994).
[6] See Covey v. Commercial National Bank, 960 F.2d 657 (7th Cir. 1992).

...ent in the first instance and solvent in the

...is based on the idea that when a firm's assets
...sets, the shareholders are the residual claimants.
...dditional dollar the firm brings in, and they lose
...ollar the firm loses. Because they are the residual
...ernalize the benefit of making the right decisions and
...wrong ones. When a firm is insolvent, the shareholders e.. ..ne of the upside if the firm's fortunes improve enough,
but they bear none of the downside risk. By adding an insolvency requirement, we can ensure that creditors are able to upset only those
transactions where the shareholders do not internalize the costs of
their decisions. Creditors are assumed to trust the shareholders to
make decisions when the shareholders themselves are the first to lose
when they make bad decisions. If they want to limit the shareholders
further, they must bargain for such protections in their loan agreement.

The insolvency requirement, however, is underinclusive. A firm
can be solvent and the shareholders can still have the incentive to engage in transactions that run contrary to the creditors' interest. Assume that a firm owes its creditors $10. One asset is $10 in cash and
the other is a lottery ticket that has a one-in-ten chance of paying
$101. If the firm decides to use the cash to make a dividend of $10, the
firm would still be solvent. Its remaining asset—a lottery ticket
worth a little more than $10—is greater than its $10 in liabilities. But
the dividend would dramatically change the creditors' chances of
being repaid. The insolvency test is not sensitive to lenders' concerns
about both the magnitude of a debtor's assets and liabilities and the
chances that each might change. If a creditor wants to be able to object because the value of the debtor's assets was subject to variance, it
has to bargain for such a right. The off-the-rack protection of
fraudulent conveyance law cannot be carefully fitted to every debtor.

Whether a firm is insolvent at any given moment depends on what
is known at that time, not on what is known in hindsight. Consider
the case in which a firm's sole asset is an oil-drilling venture. Its only
creditor is owed $100. At the time the firm declares a dividend, the
firm is drilling ten wells. There is a 90 percent chance that at least one
of them will strike oil. If any of the wells is successful, the firm will be
worth at least $1,000. There is, however, a 10 percent chance that
none of the wells will produce. In this event, the firm will be worthless. A year passes and all the wells prove to be dry holes. Can the

creditor attack the dividend on the ground that the firm was insolvent at the time of the dividend?

In one sense, the firm was insolvent when it declared the dividend since none of the wells contained oil. Yet this conclusion seems wrong. The determination of insolvency should be tied to what was known at the time the dividend was made. If the insolvency standard permits second-guessing after the fact, fraudulent conveyance law may interfere with ordinary commercial transactions. Much fraudulent conveyance litigation takes place only after things have gone badly. To work effectively, fraudulent conveyance laws must be applied by judges who can put themselves in the position of the parties at the time of the initial transaction.

As we noted in chapter 5, fraudulent conveyance law, working in conjunction with §544(b) and the doctrine of *Moore v. Bay*, is conspicuously defective in one respect. Existing law may not sufficiently distinguish present and future creditors. Suppose a firm issues a huge dividend to its shareholders, and the dividend leaves the firm insolvent. Anyone who was a creditor at the time of the dividend should, of course, have a fraudulent conveyance action against the shareholders. But what about the creditors who came on the scene after the dividend? Unless they lent because they were misled by the past financial health of the firm, they are no different from creditors who lend to a firm that has become insolvent through a market reverse. Ordinarily, those who lend to thinly capitalized firms have no right to reach that firm's shareholders in the event it fails. Such a right typically exists only when the corporate form has been abused. If creditors want shareholders to become liable for the firm's obligations, they must insist on a guarantee, as indeed many do.

The Step-Transaction Doctrine

Perhaps the most difficult part of modern fraudulent conveyance doctrine concerns not whether a fraudulent conveyance exists but rather the person against whom the fraudulent conveyance remedy should apply.[7] Consider the following case. A debtor goes to a jewelry store, gives the store $100, and asks it to give a gold ring to one of his parents. In this case, $100 is transferred from the debtor to the jewelry store and the ring is transferred from the store to the parent. If a creditor tries to recover the ring from the parent, can the parent argue that the creditor has no right to the ring because the debtor never owned it? Under this view, the only transaction that can be

[7] Lippi v. City Bank, 955 F.2d 599 (9th Cir. 1992).

challenged is the one between the debtor and the jeweler. The debtor gave the jeweler $100 and received nothing back. Most of us would reject this argument. In form, there might have been a transfer between the insolvent debtor and the jeweler and then a second transfer between the jeweler and the parent, but the substance of this transaction was quite different: an insolvent debtor bought the ring and then gave it to the parent. A fraudulent conveyance action should lie against the parent but not the jeweler.

Fraudulent conveyance problems involving multiple parties usually arise in corporate transactions, and here it can be much harder to identify the true substance of the transaction. We might begin with each party's knowledge or good faith.[8] This approach may be misguided, however, because it strains the traditional meaning of good faith; ordinarily, the honesty of the lender or any other person against whom the action is brought is not an issue. We need to ask whether, under all the circumstances, the transaction, as a matter of substance and not merely form, was one in which a party gave fair consideration or reasonably equivalent value to another. Answering this question requires determining whether the transaction was at arm's length. We also need to decide the extent to which one creditor should be required to monitor its debtor for the benefit of other creditors. Reducing everything to the procrustean inquiry of whether the party exercised good faith is unlikely to illuminate matters. The alternative standard that some have proposed—asking whether the party had knowledge of the overall transaction—rewards ignorance and stupidity, something that the law should not do.

"Stepping together" discrete transactions often requires an understanding of the policies that fraudulent conveyance law is intended to promote. A simple example involving a leveraged buyout makes this point. Assume that a firm owes $2 million to a group of general creditors and has assets of about $3 million. It has ten shareholders. An entrepreneur buys the shares of one shareholder for $100,000. The firm borrows $900,000 from a lender, and the lender takes a security interest in all the firm's assets. The firm then uses the $900,000 to buy back the shares of the old shareholders. The firm still has assets of about $3 million, but it is now $2.9 million in debt. As the sole remaining shareholder, the entrepreneur now owns the firm. Because the lender took a security interest in all the firm's assets, it is entitled to be paid in full before the general creditors receive anything. The

---

[8] See, e.g., United States v. Tabor Court Realty Corp., 803 F.2d 1288 (3d Cir. 1986).

general creditors' equity cushion has shrunk dramatically or perhaps disappeared altogether. Let us assume that a court would find that the stock repurchase was a fraudulent conveyance because the repurchase gave the firm nothing of value and left it either insolvent or with unreasonably small capital. A fraudulent conveyance exists, but against whom? The entrepreneur? The lender? The old shareholders?

If there is an actual recovery against the entrepreneur or the shareholders, there should be no additional recovery against the lender. But the lender is a more inviting target. The entrepreneur is likely to be judgment-proof, as most of the entrepreneur's wealth is likely to be tied up in the firm, which, by assumption, is now in bankruptcy. Suing each of the shareholders is cumbersome. Moreover, the general creditors need not recover assets from the lender. They need only persuade a court to find that the firm's obligation to repay the lender is void as a fraudulent conveyance and hence the lender is not entitled to share in the estate.

The firm was, from one point of view, far from being insolvent at the end of its transaction with the lender. At the end of *that* transaction (and before the stock repurchase), the firm had $2.9 million in debt and almost $4 million in assets. Before and after the transaction with the lender, there was a million-dollar equity cushion for the other creditors. By this argument, the trustee cannot hold the lender responsible for the firm's decision to use the proceeds of the loan to buy back shares of its stock. Under this view, there are two separate transactions: (1) the deal between the lender and the firm and (2) the deal between the firm and its shareholders.

The question a court faces is whether these two transactions should be collapsed into one. If they are kept separate, the second transaction is a fraudulent conveyance for all the reasons we have already discussed, but the first is not. It is simply a business deal done at arm's length between strangers. The general creditors may have to watch out for such transactions, but the general rule for creditors is that each must watch out for its own interest and cannot rely on someone else to do it for them.

The court, however, may not be willing to separate the loan to the firm from the buyout. The loan from the lender to the firm made the transaction between the firm and the shareholders possible. Collapsing the two transactions may not be unreasonable if we care about substance rather than form. To make the case that there was only one transaction (and thereby reach the lender), one begins by observing that the funds from the lender went into the firm and then out to the old shareholders in the blink of an eye. The lender was in a good position to police against fraudulent conveyances, and we want to encourage it to do that policing. The lender should not be able to pretend that it was giving value to the firm. It was just as if the lender made a loan to shareholders and the firm promised to pay the lender back. To bring a fraudulent conveyance attack against the lender, however, one ultimately has to conclude that, as a matter of sound policy, the lender should be held accountable to some degree for what the firm does with the lender's money. Embracing such a policy, at least when the lender is closely involved with the structuring of the leveraged buyout, may be consistent with the norms that have long been a part of fraudulent conveyance law.

Only a few courts have explicitly recognized the step-transaction doctrine as part of fraudulent conveyance law.[9] Lenders who enter into such transactions are well advised to create a record that shows that the borrowing firm was solvent at the time of the transaction. It is usually easier for the lender to show that the transaction was a sensible deal than that even though it was not, someone else should be held responsible.

Section 550 of the Bankruptcy Code empowers the trustee to recover the value of the transferred property from either the initial transferee or from the entity for whose benefit the transfer was made. The breadth of the phrase "for whose benefit the transfer was made" allows considerable flexibility to reach various parties to this transaction. The absence of any safe harbor for initial transferees may subject them to liability when others are unavailable. Banks or financial intermediaries acting on behalf of clients can argue, however, when they are mere conduits, they are not transferees within the meaning of §550. In other cases, the debtor may be directed to pay a third party. The third party may argue that the person who directed the funds was the transferee and that thus it is entitled to the benefit of the safe harbor for subsequent transferees in §550(b). But courts may be reluctant to insulate them from responsibility.[10]

Intercorporate Guarantees and Fraudulent Conveyances

We now look at transactions involving related corporations, transactions in which one corporation borrows money and the other guarantees the loan and secures the guarantee with collateral. Sup-

---

[9] See, e.g., Orr v. Kinderhill Corp., 991 F.2d 31 (2d Cir. 1993).
[10] See, e.g., Schafer v. Las Vegas Hilton Corp., 127 F.3d 1195 (9th Cir. 1997); Leonard v. First Commercial Mortgage Co., 228 Bankr. 225 (Bankr. D. Minn. 1998).

pose a parent corporation borrows $100,000 from a bank on January 1, and the parent's subsidiary, a wholly owned subsidiary with lots of assets, guarantees the obligation and secures it with a security interest in all the subsidiary's assets. The parent uses the loan to finance a venture that does not involve the subsidiary in any way. On November 1, the parent and subsidiary both file for bankruptcy. If the loan left the subsidiary insolvent at the time of the transfer, the subsidiary's grant of a security interest to the bank is a fraudulent conveyance. The subsidiary does not receive reasonably equivalent value or fair consideration. The loan brought nothing to the subsidiary. One cannot, however, assume that such transactions are fraudulent conveyances merely because the security interest is made by one entity and the loan goes to another. Switch the position of the parent and the subsidiary in our example. The parent guarantees a loan to its subsidiary. Even if the guarantee left the parent insolvent, the parent's trustee may not be able to strike it down for the benefit of the parent's creditors. The guarantee may not be a fraudulent conveyance because the parent remains the ultimate beneficiary of the loan. So long as the subsidiary is solvent at the time of the transaction, the value of the parent's equity interest in the subsidiary increases by a dollar for each dollar that the subsidiary receives from a lender, and the parent's creditors have nothing to complain about. The solvency of the subsidiary, however, is crucial. If the subsidiary is insolvent, the beneficiaries of the loan will be the subsidiary's creditors, not the parent's.[11] In many cases, a loan will be made to a corporate group and the loan will benefit all the related companies, but to a greater or lesser extent. The lender will ask for guarantees for the entire loan from all the subsidiaries. In such a case, the obligation that the subsidiary is assuming may be commensurate with the benefits it will receive from the loan. It is difficult to track down these benefits with precision.[12] Hence, lenders would like to find safe harbors, but these may be elusive.

Return to the case in which the subsidiary guarantees a loan to the parent. The bank can insulate itself from fraudulent conveyance attack by showing that the subsidiary was solvent at the moment that it incurred the obligation to the bank or transferred a security interest to it. Identifying this moment correctly is crucial. Fraudulent conveyance law should focus on the time when the debtor committed itself, not the time when the debtor actually honored the guarantee.

[11] See General Electric Credit Corp. v. Murphy, 895 F.2d 725 (11th Cir. 1990).

[12] For a discussion of how indirect benefits are taken into account, see Leibowitz v. Parkway Bank & Trust Co., 139 F.3d 574 (7th Cir. 1998).

When the guarantee was called on and assets actually left the subsidiary, the debtor was already obliged to make the transfer. That transfer was on account of an antecedent debt and so was presumably supported by fair consideration or reasonably equivalent value.[13] Many intercorporate guarantees, however, secure revolving lines of credit. In these cases, the subsidiary may have the power to call off the loan long after the original guarantee is signed. We may be unable to identify precisely the moment when the subsidiary committed itself.

Another problem arises if solvency is measured at the time the subsidiary signed the guarantee. We need to figure out how great a burden the subsidiary took on by guaranteeing the loan. How the contingent obligation is valued may determine whether the subsidiary was solvent, and the size of the obligation will determine whether the subsidiary received reasonably equivalent value. Some courts have suggested that the obligation be valued at its face amount, but at least two circuit courts have rejected this approach.[14] Valuing these guarantees at their face amount seems out of step with the meaning of a contingent obligation. An insurance company's liabilities are determined by estimating how many policyholders will make claims, not by adding up the policy limits of every person who has bought insurance. An automobile insurance company would be unable to honor its policies if every car it covered were stolen, but of course, not every car is stolen. Similarly, a firm with contingent obligations may be solvent when the face amount of its contingent liabilities exceeds its assets, provided that the contingencies are sufficiently remote and sufficiently independent of one another. The Bankruptcy Code's own definition of insolvency adopts the sensible approach, which is to take account of the possibility that the guarantee will be called on and adjust its value accordingly.

Equitable Subordination and Substantive Consolidation

Sometimes a creditor may acquire a great deal of control over the debtor and may use this control to benefit itself at the expense of other creditors. At some point this creditor may go too far and thereby forfeit its right to take priority over others (if it is secured) or even lose its ability to share with them pro rata. When all the firm's

[13] At least one case does focus on the time the guarantee was called. See Rubin v. Manufacturers Hanover Trust, 661 F.2d 979 (2d Cir. 1981).

[14] See In re Xonics Photochemical, 841 F.2d 198, 199 (7th Cir. 1988); Nordberg v. Arab Banking Corp., 904 F.2d 588 (11th Cir. 1990).

assets go to one secured creditor, the only chance that the general creditors have to recover anything is to find some defect in the claim of the secured creditor. If the secured creditor's interest has been properly perfected and cannot be avoided under the strong-arm powers, the trustee will sometimes examine that creditor's conduct to see whether a claim of *equitable subordination* can be made out.

The origins of the equitable subordination doctrine can be found in *Pepper v. Litton*:

> In the exercise of its equitable jurisdiction the bankruptcy court has the power to sift the circumstances surrounding any claim to see that injustice or unfairness is not done in administration of the bankrupt estate.[15]

In *Pepper v. Litton* the dominant shareholder of a corporation had caused the corporation, before the bankruptcy, to confess judgment on a long-dormant wage claim he had against it. Justice William O. Douglas noted that the dominant shareholder had manipulated the corporation's affairs so that an unsecured creditor would receive nothing. For this reason, he found that the debtor's action failed the test of "whether or not under all the circumstances the transaction carries the earmarks of an arm's length bargain."[16]

There is nothing inherently wrong with insiders or shareholders also being creditors of the firm. Indeed, they are among the ones most likely to be willing to extend credit to the firm, particularly when it is in trouble. But if they want to enjoy the status of creditors or secured creditors, they must cut square corners.[17] A creditor who enjoys the benefit of an insider guarantee or who otherwise is in a position to exercise control over the debtor is also at risk. As the Fifth Circuit noted in *Smith v. Associates Commercial Corporation*, however, creditors acting within the scope of the ordinary powers given to them in their original loan agreements are safe:

> [A] creditor is under no fiduciary obligation to its debtor or to other creditors of the debtor in the collection of its claim. . . . The permissible parameters of a creditor's efforts to seek collection from a debtor are generally those with respect to voidable preferences and fraudulent conveyances proscribed by the Bankruptcy Act; apart from these there is generally no objection to a creditor's using his bargaining position, including his ability to refuse to make fur-

---

[15] 308 U.S. 295, 307–08 (1939).

[16] Id. at 306–07.

[17] See Stoumbos v. Kilimnik, 988 F.2d 949 (9th Cir. 1993).

ther loans needed by the debtor, to improve the status of his existing claims.[18]

Yet the course of this case through the Fifth Circuit illustrates the uncertainty in applying the equitable subordination doctrine. In its first opinion, the same panel unanimously held that the secured creditor's claim should be subordinated. In this opinion, the court emphasized the amount of control that the lender exercised over the debtor's affairs and the way the lender took advantage of this control to ensure that in the end it was paid in full. The trustee used to good advantage the testimony of one of the lender's former employees, who took great delight in explaining how his one goal in life had been to ensure his employer was paid in full "by hook or crook." The panel, however, subsequently reassessed the substance of the employee's testimony, vacated its opinion, and held that the lender's security interest should be respected. The court recognized that every lender "effectively exercises 'control' over its borrower to some degree." It distinguished the ability to control the debtor from "the exercise of such total control over the debtor as to have essentially replaced its decision-making capacity." The Fifth Circuit relied heavily on the fact that the loan agreement itself authorized all the actions that the lender took to enforce its rights.

Asset-based lenders often deal with troubled debtors, and they must walk a fine line. They must keep on top of their debtors while avoiding any action that would trigger equitable subordination. Worse yet, a trustee may bring a lender liability action in which the trustee alleges that the lender broke its duty of good faith or its promises (such as an implied promise not to cut off a credit line without warning). As a result, the lender may be exposed to a substantial damage action. One cannot be sure that exercising only the powers set out in the loan agreement will give lenders a safe harbor, even though some cases suggest as much. Courts possess some leeway in shaping equitable subordination doctrine under §510(c)(1), but they cannot go so far that they effectively alter the priorities that Congress has provided for different kinds of claims.[19] That courts sometimes view their mandate broadly should not obscure the basic lesson of

---

[18] 893 F.2d 693, 702 (5th Cir. 1990), quoting Cosoff v. Rodman, 699 F.2d 599, 609–10 (2d Cir. 1983). See also Sloan v. Zions First National Bank, 990 F.2d 551 (10th Cir. 1993); Kham & Nate's Shoes No. 2 v. First Bank of Whiting, 908 F.2d 1351, 1358 (7th Cir. 1990) ("Although Debtor contends . . . that Bank's termination of advances frustrated Debtor's efforts to secure credit from other sources, and so propelled it down hill, this is legally irrelevant so long as Bank kept its promises.").

[19] United States v. Noland, 517 U.S. 535 (1996).

these cases for creditors: The lender who does more than it was authorized to do in the original loan agreement or who fails to fire the requisite warning shots is asking for trouble.

When the debtor is part of a larger corporate group, the trustee may have an additional place to turn to enhance the bankruptcy estate. The trustee may be able to combine the assets and liabilities of the debtor with those of a related firm. A subsidiary's parent, for example, may have fewer liabilities and more assets than the subsidiary. If the assets and liabilities of both firms were combined, the creditors of the subsidiary would enjoy a larger pro rata share. Putting the assets and liabilities of two related firms into a single pool is known as *substantive consolidation*, but it is rarely used. Substantive consolidation must be distinguished from cases that are jointly administered. Related firms frequently file bankruptcy petitions at the same time, and the different bankruptcy cases can be administered together. Assuming conflicts of interest do not stand in the way, these separate firms can pool their resources and hire the same professionals and the like. Substantive consolidation, however, is quite a different affair. To the extent that the creditors of one firm benefit from substantive consolidation, the creditors of the other are made correspondingly worse off. To justify substantive consolidation, one must not only justify the benefit that one set of creditors receives, but also the harm that other creditors suffer as a result. For this reason, substantive consolidation is typically inappropriate and courts are extremely reluctant to allow it.

The leading discussion of substantive consolidation can be found in *Union Savings Bank v. Augie/Restivo Baking Company, Ltd.*[20] It begins with the idea that creditors of one firm should be able to look to the assets of another only if their nonbankruptcy entitlements permit them to do so. There are only two circumstances under which substantive consolidation should be allowed. First, the affairs of the two firms may be so closely entwined that each lacks a separate existence for all practical purposes. Substantive consolidation in this context is simply the bankruptcy analog for piercing the corporate veil.[21] Sec-

---

[20] 860 F.2d 515, 518–19 (2d Cir. 1988). The D.C. Circuit put forward a slightly different formulation of substantive consolidation in Drabkin v. Midland-Ross Corp. (In re Auto-Train Corp.), 810 F.2d 270 (D.C. Cir. 1987).

[21] For example, the cases of an individual and a firm were substantively consolidated in Alexander v. Compton, 229 F.3d 750 (9th Cir. 2000). Substantive consolidation may be appropriate between other kinds of entities as well, such as between partners and partnerships or even between two individuals. See FDIC v. Colonial Realty, 966 F.2d 57 (2d Cir. 1992).

ond, keeping the firms' affairs separate must be practical. We need to look at the costs of sorting out the affairs of two related firms if they are treated as one entity and if they are treated as two. Even though the firms are sufficiently separate that we would not pierce the corporate veil outside of bankruptcy, the affairs of the two firms may have become so entangled and their assets so meager that unscrambling the mess may simply not be worth the cost. When the administrative costs of sorting out the obligations of the two firms dwarf the benefits to any group of creditors from keeping the firms separate, it is in everyone's interest to consolidate the two.[22]

---

[22] See In re The Leslie Fay Companies, 207 Bankr. 764 (Bankr. S.D.N.Y. 1997).

Chapter Eight

Preferences

Preferences Under §547: The Basic Elements

The descent of a healthy firm into insolvency and then into bankruptcy is a long, slow process. Bankruptcy law has a set of rules to prevent creditors from trying to grab assets when bankruptcy is on the horizon. The rules that prevent creditors from receiving *preferences*—eve-of-bankruptcy transfers to creditors that distort bankruptcy's pro rata sharing rule—are embodied in §547 of the Bankruptcy Code.

A creditor would much rather be paid off in full than work things out with everyone else and ultimately take fewer than 100 cents on the dollar. If we allowed creditors to keep payments they extracted when they knew bankruptcy was imminent, bankruptcy might do more harm than good. The prospect of a bankruptcy proceeding might have the effect of accelerating and exacerbating the creditors' race to the assets. To guard against this prospect, we need a bankruptcy rule that has the effect of turning back the clock and returning people to the positions they were in before bankruptcy was on the horizon. Although its rules are complicated, the basic purpose of preference law is quite straightforward and quite different from the role of fraudulent conveyance law. Recall that a transfer to a creditor on account of an antecedent debt is typically not a fraudulent conveyance since the antecedent debt counts as fair consideration or reasonably equivalent value. Preferences to creditors are themselves unobjectionable so long as a collective proceeding is not in the works. Every creditor is "preferred" when it is paid, and paying a creditor is an ordinary part of commercial life. Section 547 is designed to root out only preferences that are made on the eve of bankruptcy and hence interfere with the collective norms of bankruptcy law.

Section 547(b) defines a transfer as presumptively preferential if it is made by an insolvent debtor to or for the benefit of a creditor on account of an antecedent debt within ninety days of filing a bankruptcy petition, provided the transfer leaves the creditor better off than if the transfer had not been made. Such a transfer is presumptively preferential (and therefore voidable by the trustee) because it is likely to be a "last-minute grab." It is probably the result of opt-out behavior. Because an insider is likely to know more about the debtor and be able to see the prospect of bankruptcy before others, transfers made on account of antecedent debts while the debtor was insolvent are suspect for the entire year before the filing of the petition, provided again that the transfer makes the insider better off.

Like any other bright-line rule, §547(b) is both under- and overinclusive. Some creditors will see bankruptcy coming and act outside the ninety-day preference period; others will be paid within the ninety-day period knowing nothing of the imminent bankruptcy petition. Section 547(c) cuts back on the breadth of the rule by excepting some transfers, but nothing is done to reach deliberate opt-out behavior that takes place outside the ninety-day preference window. As a result, §547 is subject to manipulation. A big creditor can twist the debtor's arm, bleed it dry, and then prop it up for ninety-one days. A review of the case law reveals a large number of filings ninety days after a big transfer to a major creditor. This does not seem a coincidence.

Let's look at how §547(b) plays itself out. The most obvious preference is that of a debtor who pays cash to a creditor a few days before filing a bankruptcy petition. A preference also exists if the debtor gives a general creditor a security interest in its assets just before it files a petition. Even though the trustee cannot strike down the last-minute transfer of a properly perfected security interest using the strong-arm power of §544(a), the trustee can void such a transfer under §547. The security interest gives the creditor priority over other general creditors and, assuming the debtor is insolvent, makes it better off. Section 547, however, covers more than transfers of cash or security interests. For example, assume that a firm buys a season's worth of fuel oil from a supplier and pays in advance. The supplier delivers the fuel on schedule. Spring comes and the supplier files a bankruptcy petition. The supplier's trustee may have a preference attack. The firm became a creditor of the supplier when it paid for the oil in advance. The supplier had an obligation it owed the firm. Each shipment of fuel discharged some of that obligation and was therefore a transfer on account of an antecedent debt owed the firm. So long as the supplier was insolvent at the time it shipped the fuel, each shipment is a preference. There are exceptions to §547(b) in §547(c), but none apply here. There is an exception for payments in ordinary course transactions in §547(c)(2), but here the "transfer" was a shipment of fuel, not a "payment."

There cannot be a preference unless the transfer to or for the benefit of a creditor is made on account of an *antecedent* debt. In every case involving a potential preference, we must ask two questions: When was the debt incurred and when was the transfer made? We do not have a voidable preference unless the first event took place before the second. A lender who makes a loan and simultaneously takes and perfects a security interest in the debtor's property just before the filing of the bankruptcy petition does not receive a preference. The transfer of the security interest to the creditor is on account of a debt, but it is not on account of an *antecedent* debt. Consider another example. You are about to file a bankruptcy petition. You go to a lawyer and ask her to handle your bankruptcy. The lawyer asks for a retainer of $10,000. There are rules in the Bankruptcy Code (such as §329) dealing with compensation of a debtor's lawyer, but is this transaction objectionable so far as preference law is concerned? Isn't the lawyer grabbing assets while bankruptcy is on the horizon? The lawyer is, but this does not matter. Before a lawyer agrees to represent you, the lawyer is not your creditor. When you pay the retainer, you are paying for future services. You are a creditor, not a debtor, in this transaction. You have not made a transfer *on account of an antecedent debt*, the sine qua non of a preference.

If the debtor has enough money to pay everyone in full, there is typically not going to be a race to the assets. All the creditors believe they will be paid in full. Hence §547(b) applies only if the debtor is insolvent at the time of the transfer. Under §547(f), a debtor is presumed insolvent during the ninety days before the filing of the petition. Most debtors are in such bad shape at the time of the petition that they became insolvent well outside the ninety-day period. Bankruptcy petitions are more often filed too late than too early, and insolvency is rarely litigated in preference cases. There is, however, no presumption of insolvency between ninety days and one year before the filing of the petition in the case of an insider. In this situation the trustee carries the burden of showing that the debtor was insolvent at the time of the transfer, and whether the debtor was insolvent a full year before the filing of the petition may not always be evident.

Section 547(b)(5) requires that the transfer make the creditor better off than it would be in a Chapter 7 liquidation. Imagine that you are a fully secured creditor. You have lent Jones $1,000 and you have a fully perfected security interest in Jones's red Porsche. Jones pays you in full ten days before filing for bankruptcy. Is the repayment a voidable preference? Jones was insolvent at the time he paid you, and his payment is a transfer on account of an antecedent debt to you, a creditor, within ninety days of the filing of the bankruptcy petition. The payment, however, does not make you any better off. In bankruptcy, you would, in theory, be paid in full because your security interest in the Porsche would entitle you to priority. We are going to look at this idea more closely later. A secured creditor would much rather be paid in full before the start of the petition than have a fully secured claim in bankruptcy. Nevertheless, the common understanding of §547(b)(5) ensures that transfers to fully secured creditors are not voidable preferences.

The extent to which we apply §547(b)(5) to other transactions is unclear. If the debtor had not made the transfer, the creditor might have behaved differently. For example, it might not have made the debtor another loan or shipped it new supplies. We do not know the extent to which a creditor can make such arguments about what the world would have looked like if the transfer had not been made. The exceptions to the preference power in §547(c) protect the creditor in those cases that matter the most (such as an additional extension of credit after a payment that, in hindsight, turns out to be preferential). Courts, however, may point to these exceptions as a rationale for interpreting §547(b)(5) narrowly.

Let us recap §547(b). The six requirements that must be met before a preference is voidable are that (1) a transfer is made (2) on account of an antecedent debt (3) to or for the benefit of a creditor (4) while the debtor was insolvent (5) within ninety days of the filing of the petition (6) that left the creditor better off than it would have been if the transfer had not been made and it had asserted its claim in a Chapter 7 liquidation. If a transfer is preferential, §550 tells us that the trustee can recover the amount transferred from either the initial transferee or the party for whose benefit the transfer was made. It is worth noting that §547 provides only a weak deterrent against opt-out behavior. The trustee can recover the amount of the transfer and interest on the amount of the transfer, but interest generally runs only from the time that the trustee asks for the transfer back, not from the time of the transfer. The person who receives the transfer enjoys the time value of the transfer from the time it receives the preference until the trustee demands its return. If you see the debtor sinking, why not grab while the grabbing is good? The debtor may survive for ninety days, in which case you are in the clear. Even if the debtor does not survive that long, the trustee may not find you. Even if the trustee does find you, you need only give the property back. You suffer no penalty for having received a preference.

With these basic principles in mind, most preference problems are straightforward. You lend Jones $1,000. The loan is payable on demand. You leave the country for six months. You return, completely unaware that Jones's financial situation has deteriorated substantially. You ask for repayment. Jones obliges you even though Jones is now hopelessly insolvent. A week later Jones files a bankruptcy petition. Is this a voidable preference? Section 547(b) is a per se rule: although it is aimed at opt-out behavior, it does not require us to ask whether there was opt-out behavior in any given case. Hence, the transfer from Jones to you is a voidable preference. It does not matter what your motives were or that you were completely unaware of Jones's financial straits. In making intent irrelevant, the Bankruptcy Code differs from its antecedents. Under the 1898 Act, a transfer was a preference only if the creditor receiving the transfer knew, or had reason to know, of the debtor's insolvency. This intent-based test generated a huge amount of litigation. Under the Bankruptcy Code, some creditors are subjected to a voidable preference attack even though there is no opt-out behavior. It may be better to pick up the few creditors who were genuinely unwitting, however, than to litigate the many cases of creditors who tried to grab assets but deny it after the fact with wide-eyed innocence.

Let's look at a variation on the facts above. You return from your trip and ask for your money back. Jones refuses. You sue, reduce your claim to judgment, and have the sheriff levy on the Porsche. You get your $1,000 back, but only with Jones kicking and screaming all the way. The sheriff seizes and sells the Porsche ten days before the filing of the petition. What do we do about this case? In the past, preferences were thought objectionable because the debtor was picking and choosing among its creditors, and the debtor should not be allowed to favor some creditors over others. From this perspective, the transfer should not be voidable. You simply won the race to the assets fair and square. If another creditor did not like it, it could have joined the race or it could have filed a bankruptcy petition and put a stop to it. Modern preference law, however, focuses on the behavior of creditors and asks whether they were trying to opt out of an impending bankruptcy. It does not matter that the property was taken from the debtor involuntarily. There was still a transfer within the meaning of §101.

Let us focus on another requirement of §547(b), the requirement that there be a transfer of an "interest of the debtor in property." Suppose you take your $1,000 watch to a jeweler to be repaired. You pay the jeweler in advance for the work. Three weeks later, you pick up your watch. The jeweler files a bankruptcy petition a month later. Can the trustee argue that the jeweler's return of the watch was a voidable preference? The jeweler transferred the watch to you within ninety days of the filing of the petition, while insolvent, and on account of an obligation previously incurred. The transfer, however, is a preference only if the watch is property of the debtor within the meaning of §547(b). It might seem obvious that the watch does not belong to the jeweler, but we have to be careful. While in the possession of the watch, the jeweler had the power to convey it to a buyer in ordinary course. To reject the argument that the watch is not the jeweler's, we have to be able to explain why this power is insufficient to make the watch the jeweler's property for purposes of §547.

The answer ultimately lies in the trustee's powers under §§541 and 544(a). We can first ask what would have happened if the jeweler had still possessed the watch at the time of the bankruptcy petition. The watch would not become property of the estate under §541(a)(1) because the jeweler has no right to keep the watch in the face of your claim. Moreover, the trustee could not bring the watch into the estate under §544(a) because a hypothetical lien creditor would have no ability to levy on the watch while it is in the jeweler's hands. That the jeweler could have conveyed good title to a buyer in ordinary course should not matter. The trustee should be able to avoid the transfer only if the transfer took assets out of the reach of creditors.

Other cases can arise in which the answer is not so intuitive. Consider a retailer who is shipped goods on consignment.[1] A consignee holds goods under the authority of others in order to sell them, at specified prices, to third parties. Title—ownership—remains in the hands of the consignor. A consignee typically has the right to return goods without any obligation because it is an agent and not a buyer. If the goods are sold, the consignee has the obligation to remit the proceeds to the seller. This case is different from the one involving the watch in one crucial respect: the jeweler's creditors have no ability to levy on the watch while it is in the jeweler's hands, whereas if the consignor fails to jump through a number of hoops, creditors of the consignee can levy on the assets outside of bankruptcy. By returning the assets, the consignee removes them from the creditors' reach on the eve of bankruptcy. The consigned goods should therefore be considered property of the debtor for purposes of §547. The general principle was well stated in *Danning v. Bozek*: "[P]roperty belongs to the

---

[1] See, e.g., Loeb v. G. A. Gertmenian & Sons, 21 Bankr. 612 (Bankr. N.D. Ga. 1982).

debtor for purposes of §547 if its transfer will deprive the bankruptcy estate of something which could otherwise be used to satisfy the claims of creditors."[2] If a debtor holds an asset in trust, its creditors cannot reach it.[3] But if the item at issue is money in an account from which the debtor's creditors could have sought payment, it is property of the debtor. It does not matter that, for example, the funds are in an account held not by the debtor but by a related entity.[4]

Let's look at one more case dealing with the meaning of "interest of the debtor in property." A parent corporation owes money to a lender. The parent is insolvent, but one of its assets is its stock in a subsidiary and the subsidiary is solvent. The lender presses the parent for payment. Rather than use its own money, the parent has the subsidiary pay the lender. The subsidiary owes the lender nothing, so its transfer to the lender is for less than fair consideration. The subsidiary, however, is solvent and it is able to pay all *its* creditors in full. The transfer, therefore, is not a fraudulent conveyance so far as the subsidiary's creditors are concerned. Moreover, the transfer cannot be a fraudulent conveyance so far as the parent's creditors are concerned, either. The transfer is on account of an antecedent debt and thus, from the parent's perspective, is supported by fair consideration.

The transfer might appear to be a preference. It is a transfer to the lender, on account of an antecedent debt, made while the parent is insolvent, within ninety days of the filing of the bankruptcy petition, and the transfer makes the lender much better off. The parent's other creditors are made worse off. If the transfer had not taken place, the subsidiary would have more assets and the parent's equity interest in the subsidiary would be worth much more. Nevertheless, bringing a preference attack and recovering the money from the lender will not be easy. The trustee can assert that the transfer from the subsidiary to the lender is voidable and can be brought into the *parent's* bankruptcy estate only by showing that the parent transferred *its* property when it had the subsidiary make the transfer. If one looks only at form, the *parent* made no transfer. The parent's creditors were injured only because the value of one of its assets (its equity interest in the subsidiary) went down. No assets, however, actually left the parent's hands.

If one looks to substance rather than form, the transaction does amount to a transfer of property. If the parent had given some of its

---

[2] 836 F.2d 1214, 1217 (9th Cir. 1988).

[3] Begier v. Internal Revenue Service, 496 U.S. 53 (1990).

[4] See Southmark Corp. v. Grosz, 49 F.3d 1111 (5th Cir. 1995).

shares in the subsidiary to the lender and if the subsidiary had then re-purchased the shares, there would have undoubtedly been a prefer-ence. Transfer of the shares is a transfer of property of the debtor within the meaning of §547. The transaction in which the subsidiary pays the lender directly is identical in substance, though not in form, to this one. The transfer from the subsidiary to the lender is therefore a preference to the extent that one can recharacterize the transaction and treat it like one that is economically the same in substance but different in form.[5]

Secured Creditors and Voidable Preferences

You lend Jones $1,000. Jones's fortunes take a turn for the worse. You come to Jones and ask to be paid ahead of everyone else before Jones goes into bankruptcy. Jones does not have the money and so turns you down. Besides, if Jones granted your request and then en-tered bankruptcy, any cash you received would be on account of an antecedent debt and would thus be a voidable preference. Suppose Jones offers instead to give you a security interest. Can you take him up on it and not worry about the impending bankruptcy?

No. When bankruptcy is on the horizon, changing your status from general creditor to a secured creditor is itself a form of opt-out behavior. One can argue that taking a security interest should not be treated the same way as a naked seizure of assets because taking a se-curity interest affects only how the pie is divided among creditors. It does not actually destroy value in the same way that seizure of assets does. Existing law, however, treats them the same. You are improv-ing your position in anticipation of bankruptcy in the same way (al-though not to the same extent) that you would if you were paid off. In both cases, you are receiving an interest in property within the ninety-day period, while Jones is insolvent, on account of an an-tecedent debt. By receiving the transfer you are ensuring that you get paid in full, which puts you in a much better position than if you had not tried to improve your place in line. This transaction is, of course, a voidable preference. The two of you cannot use a security interest to circumvent bankruptcy's pro rata sharing rule.

Suppose Jones needs additional money to keep his unincorpo-rated business alive. Jones's existing creditors, however, refuse to throw good money after bad. Jones comes to you. You agree to lend, but only if Jones agrees to give you a security interest in his machine,

---

[5] See Harry M. Flechtner, Preferences, Postpetition Transfers, and Transactions Involving a Debtor's Downstream Affiliate, 5 Bankr. Devs. J. 1 (1987).

the only piece of equipment his business owns. Is this a voidable preference? Of course not. No gun-jumping has taken place. Jones transferred an interest in the machine to you, but did not make the transfer on account of an *antecedent* debt. Jones did it in order to get the money in the first place. You were not opting out at the time you took the security interest; you were opting *in*. Jones gave up something (an interest in the machine) but got something in return at the same time (cash). Jones's creditors cannot complain. If they think that Jones is so far gone that they should take control, they should throw Jones into bankruptcy. Until they do, Jones is free to borrow money in arm's-length transactions and encumber assets that would otherwise go to the general creditors.

A secured creditor avoids a preference attack by ensuring that the security interest is transferred to it within the meaning of §547(e) at the same time it extends value to the debtor. Remember our discussion of §544(a). If you are a secured creditor but have not perfected your interest, you are at risk. All you have done is bargain for the ability to repossess without having to go to court, provided you can repossess without a breach of the peace. Vis-à-vis other creditors, you are no better than a general creditor. You are still in a race to get a priority right. The relevant time is not the moment that you enter into a security agreement with the debtor, but rather the moment that you perfect your interest (typically through a public filing) and acquire priority over a lien creditor. So far as other creditors are concerned, a preexisting but unperfected secured creditor who perfects on the eve of bankruptcy has grabbed assets just as much as an unsecured creditor who takes a security interest and perfects on the eve of bankruptcy. The crucial factor is not the existence or the nonexistence of the security interest, but rather the existence of the priority right. If we are measuring your rights against the rights of the other creditors, it makes sense to date the time of the transfer from the time that you acquired the priority right. You should be able to enjoy your security interest only if you acquired your priority right a long time ago, or only if you acquired your priority right at the same time you extended credit.

The plight of the secured creditor who wakes up and discovers that its security interest is not perfected is a common one. A bank will make a loan and everyone will shake hands and pass out cigars. The loan documentation will be filed away and forgotten. Only when the deal starts to go sour does anyone look at it again. Indeed, the lawyers handling the workout may not even come into the deal until after it has gone sour. At this point, their first job is to check out the paperwork. Should they be able to correct the paperwork without having to worry about a voidable preference attack? Of course not. The workout lawyers have been called in because the debtor is sinking fast and bankruptcy is on the horizon. They are in the picture because the race to the assets has begun and they are trying to win it. It is exactly this kind of opt-out behavior that §547 tries to prevent.

Section 547 does allow a short grace period for perfecting the security interest. Assume that Jones is in big trouble and borrows $1,000 from you. Jones gives you a security interest in his machine, but you take five days to file the financing statement. You were not trying to opt out; it just took some time to get all the paperwork in order. In §547(e), the Bankruptcy Code tries to distinguish between the case in which you wake up and discover that your interest is not properly perfected and the case in which the filing in the ordinary course comes a little while after the security interest attaches. Section 547(e) provides for a grace period of ten days. A transfer takes place at the time it is effective between the parties, provided that you perfect within ten days. The grace period collapses only the time of perfection and the time of attachment. You still have to ask when the debt was incurred. If the debt was incurred before the security interest attached, there is a presumptive voidable preference, regardless of whether perfection took place at the same time.

Suppose Jones borrows $1,000 from you on January 1. On that day, you take a security interest in his machine, and Jones signs a written security agreement. Five days later you file your financing statement. A month later Jones files a bankruptcy petition. There is no voidable preference. The debt was incurred on January 1. Because the filing was made within ten days, §547(e) provides that the transfer of the security interest from Jones to you took place on that day as well. If you had waited until January 15 to file, there would be a voidable preference, because the act that makes the transfer good as against lien creditors took place outside the ten-day grace period. Problems also would arise if you lent the money on January 1 and filed on January 1 but Jones did not sign the security agreement until January 5. A transfer does not take place for purposes of §547(e) until it is effective between the parties and, under Article 9 of the Uniform Commercial Code, a security interest is not effective between the parties until the debtor signs a written security agreement. The transfer in this case took place on January 5, after the debt was incurred. To survive a preference attack, you would have to show that you fit under one of the exceptions to the trustee's preference power. These are in §547(c), and it is to them that we now turn.

The Safe Harbors of §547(c)

The Net Result Rule. Section 547(c)(4) protects lenders who make a new loan after an old one is paid off. The typical case is a revolving credit arrangement. Suppose you lend Jones $1,000 for thirty days, and Jones pays you back at the end of thirty days. You lend Jones $1,000 again for another thirty days, and so on. At the time Jones files a bankruptcy petition, you have been repaid a $1,000 loan three times during the ninety days before the filing of the petition. Under §547(b) each of the transfers would be preferential. Each of the repayments was on account of an antecedent debt and each made you better off than you would have been if you had not been repaid and everything else remained the same. It would not make sense, however, to allow recovery of all three $1,000 payments. The purpose of the credit arrangement was to limit your risk to $1,000 at any one time. You made the subsequent loans only because Jones paid off the earlier ones. The transfers made you better off only to the extent of $1,000, the most you would have lost if any of the transfers had not been made. You might argue that two of the $1,000 transfers are not preferential because of §547(b)(5). These two payments did not make you better off than you would have been if the payments had not been made. If the payments had not been made, you would not have extended new credit. In other words, §547(b)(5) forces us to ask what the picture would look like if Jones had not made the transfer. This is not necessarily a picture in which everything else looks the same. If Jones had not repaid the old loans, you would not have made the new loans. Thus, $2,000 of the $3,000 you received did not make you better off, because these payments induced you to extend $2,000 in new credit. You need not, however, rely on §547(b)(5) here. This case is specifically covered in §547(c)(4). One looks at the *net result*—the extent to which you were preferred, taking account of the new value you extended to Jones *after* repayments on old loans.

Section 547(c)(2). Section 547(c)(2) excepts from preference attack routine payments to creditors. These are payments that are made in ordinary course on debts incurred in ordinary course according to ordinary business terms. Without §547(c)(2), the trustee would have the power to avoid many routine transactions. You receive your phone bill on the fifth day of the month and you regularly pay it on the twentieth day of the month. Without §547(c)(2), there might be a preference action against the phone company. The transfer occurs on the day you make the payment. The debt, however, is incurred when you use the phone service, which is during the prior month. It is a transfer on account of an antecedent debt, but there is no opt-out behavior. It is the ordinary way you go about paying bills. Section 547(c)(2) serves to except these sorts of payments from the trustee's avoiding powers. Section 547(c)(2), however, deals only with *payments*. It does not apply to any transfers of property.

The §547(c)(2) exception is designed to limit the trustee's avoiding powers under the preference section to actions that, at least presumptively, are the result of conscious opt-out behavior. Section 547(c)(2) replaces the reason-to-know-of-the-insolvency test under the 1898 Act, and it may work better because it uses an objective standard and does not require an inquiry into the transferee's state of mind. Whether debts were incurred in the ordinary course and whether payments were made in the ordinary course are necessarily questions involving a number of facts, and it is easy to find cases that fall on either side of the line. Our previous example involving a telephone bill paid at the same time in the same way as the debtor and others in the same business usually pay such bills does fall within §547(c)(2). A late payment by certified check after several dunning phone calls is not made in ordinary course.

Determining whether a loan is made in the ordinary course of business, however, is not always so simple. Consider a firm with a large, long-term operating loan. Was this loan incurred in the ordinary course of business? We know that we cannot exclude the loan from the reach of §547(c)(2) simply because it is long term.[6] Nevertheless, one can argue that when the firm incurs such a loan only once in its life, the loan is not incurred in ordinary course. This interpretation of "ordinary course"—focusing on whether obtaining such a loan is an everyday event for this debtor—is consistent with the way the term is understood in §364. That section requires court approval of a postpetition loan that is not made in ordinary course, and no one thinks that the trustee could enter into such a loan without first obtaining court approval. But there is a completely different way of interpreting §547(c)(2). One can argue that "ordinary course" in the context of §547 (as opposed to §364) requires us to identify particular features of the transaction that make it suspect. So long as similar firms typically have such a loan, §547(c)(2) should apply.

Determining what payments are made in the ordinary course can also be troublesome. The decision to make timely payments to a firm's largest and most important creditor may cease to be ordinary if an implicit decision is made at the same time not to pay others. A payment made after a decision to prefer one creditor over another

---

[6] See Union Bank v. Wolas, 502 U.S. 151 (1991).

cannot be "ordinary." Such an argument is, of course, even more compelling if the debtor's president guarantees the loan and must pay it out of pocket if the debtor defaults.

The Contemporaneous Exchange for New Value. Section 547(c)(1) introduces another grace period. Suppose you buy supplies from a supplier and pay by check. You take the supplies back to your store, and the supplier deposits the check the same day. The check clears the next day. Two months later you file a bankruptcy petition. Can the trustee recapture the payment you made to the supplier? Under §547(b), the supplier did not make a transfer to you until its bank honored your check.[7] Only at this point are assets removed from the reach of the other creditors. This transfer was on account of the debt incurred when the supplier gave you the goods several days before. At that time, you already had been using the supplies for a day. For the interval between the time you took the goods and the time the check cleared, the supplier was your creditor. The supplier, however, was not engaged in opt-out behavior. There was a gap between the time the debt was incurred and the time the transfer was made, but it was too short to be opt-out behavior. We exempt an exchange that is substantially contemporaneous from voidable preference attack.

Does the contemporaneous exchange exception apply to secured transactions? Let us look at the case where it might matter. At a time when Jones is solvent, you lend Jones money and take a security interest in Jones's machine. Later, when Jones is insolvent and trying to turn the business around, Jones asks for your permission to trade in the machine in which you have a security interest for a new machine. You agree to give up your security interest in Jones's old machine in exchange for a security interest in the new one. Is that a substantially contemporaneous exchange for new value? You are giving new value because you are giving up something that is yours. Your security interest in the old machine is valuable. It would survive the sale, and if you did not give up the interest, you could still seize the old machine even though it was in the hands of the new buyer. Think of it this way: if Jones repaid the loan in full, you would not be receiving a preference. Assume that Jones sold the machine and gave you the proceeds. Jones then asked for a new loan for a new machine. You make the loan on the condition that you get a security interest in this machine as well and Jones agrees. Even if Jones is insolvent and a few weeks away from filing, the transfer of the security interest in the new machine in this case would not be preferential. Because this transac-

[7] Barnhill v. Johnson, 503 U.S. 393 (1992).

tion is not a voidable preference, why should we not allow the substitution of collateral? You are giving up a security interest instead of cash, but the economic effect is the same. The case law on this point is not clear. The less the secured creditor is involved in the details of the replacement of one machine with the other, the less likely a court is to find that the exception applies.

The Floating Lien. A creditor will commonly take a security interest in a debtor's inventory or accounts. These turn over constantly. The supplies the debtor has this month in its store are not the same supplies the debtor will have next month. When is the security interest in the debtor's new inventory transferred to the secured creditor for purposes of §547? You could make an argument that a security interest is like a Heraclitean river. There are no new transfers. The secured creditor has a continuous interest in the inventory, even though the inventory itself is constantly changing. But there is a potential for manipulation. A debtor could favor a secured creditor who was undersecured by acquiring new inventory just before going under. The Bankruptcy Code confronts this problem in §547(c)(5) and §547(e)(3). Section 547(e)(3) provides that transfers cannot take place until the debtor acquires the property, but §547(c)(5) goes on to protect the secured creditor to the extent that it did not improve its position during the preference period. We take two snapshots, one at the start of the ninety-day period (or the time of the loan if the loan was made during the ninety-day period) and one at the time of the petition. The secured creditor is protected to the extent that it has not improved its position in inventory or accounts between the first snapshot and the second.

Consider the following problem. A florist buys flowers every day from many different vendors in a wholesale market. It gives a bank a security interest in all its inventory, existing and thereafter acquired, to cover a $12,000 loan. On January 1 the loan is made, the florist signs a security agreement, and the bank files its financing statement. On February 1 the inventory is worth $5,000. Ninety days later, the florist files a petition in bankruptcy. During those ninety days, the inventory has completely turned over and the amount of the inventory has increased. When the petition is filed, the inventory is worth $15,000 and the florist still owes the bank $12,000. To what extent does the bank have a security interest that will survive the attack of the trustee?

If §547 did not exist, the bank would have a perfected security interest in the flowers that the florist has when the petition is filed. Article 9 of the Uniform Commercial Code warmly embraces the idea of the *floating lien*. The bank can take a security interest in a pool of assets and date priority back to the time it files its financing statement, even though the things in this pool are constantly changing. So long as the bank's filing is proper, the world is on notice that the bank may be claiming a security interest in the flowers. But what happens under §547? We need to determine if there has been a transfer on account of an antecedent debt, and we have to go through §547(b) before looking to §547(c). When was the debt incurred? The debt was incurred on January 1. When did the transfer of the security interest from the florist to the bank take place? We have to look at the language of §547(e)(3). It tells us that the transfer did not take place until the florist had rights in the collateral. When did this happen? We are not sure, but we know that the property changed over completely between February 1 and the date on which the petition was filed. It follows necessarily that the florist did not acquire any rights in the inventory it now has until after February 1.

Therefore, we have a transfer that took place *after* the debt was incurred (on January 1) and within ninety days of the filing of the petition. Providing that the other conditions of §547(b) are met and providing that nothing in §547(c) calls it off, we have a voidable preference. Has the bank engaged in opt-out behavior here? It may well have. The bank's position improved during the relevant time period. At the start of the ninety-day period, the flowers were worth only $5,000. Bank was undersecured to the extent of $7,000. At the time of the filing of the petition, however, the bank was comfortably oversecured. It is possible that there was some kind of side deal. It may not have been mere coincidence that the inventory increased in value. The florist could have been filling its shop with flowers because the bank threatened to pull the rug out from under it even sooner if it did not. Or the florist might have had more flowers on hand for some innocent reason. Perhaps flower shops typically have more stock on hand in May than in February. Without knowing more facts, we cannot determine whether the bank has engaged in opt-out behavior.

The Bankruptcy Code does not engage in such a case-by-case inquiry, however. Instead, it provides for a limited exception to floating liens in inventory or accounts and the proceeds of either. Section 547(b) starts by striking down all new acquisitions of inventory within the preference period, but then §547(c)(5) provides a partial safe harbor. A creditor's security interest is recognized in bankruptcy, but only to the extent that the creditor does not improve its position during the ninety days before the filing of the bankruptcy petition. In our case, the bank was undersecured to the extent of $7,000 at the start of the preference period. Section 547(c)(5) tells us that the bank is going to be an unsecured creditor to that extent, even if the value of the inventory happens to increase during the ninety-day period. The bank will therefore have a secured claim in bankruptcy for only $5,000. The bank should be no better off than it would have been before it knew that bankruptcy was on the horizon, and this date is arbitrarily set at ninety days before the filing of the petition (or the time of the loan itself if later). Section 547(c)(5) embraces what is called the *two-point net improvement test.*

To apply the two-point net improvement test, let's look at the extent to which the bank is undersecured ninety days before the filing of the petition or on the date that the loan was made, whichever is later. (The language focuses on the extent to which the creditor is undersecured rather than on the amount the creditor is owed because the debtor could opt out by increasing the amount of inventory or decreasing the amount of the debt.) If the bank is no better off on the date of bankruptcy than it was ninety days before, §547(c)(5) will protect the bank with a floating lien on inventory or accounts. The section even allows for the bank to improve its position, if the improvement is not "to the prejudice of other creditors holding unsecured claims." This language is typically interpreted narrowly, however, and applies only when the increase in inventory is attributable to changes, such as harvest cycles, that affect the whole industry and not just the debtor.

Working through the basics is essential to solving any §547 problem. Consider the following case. An automobile dealership has fifty foreign cars. On January 1 the bank lends the dealer $500,000 and simultaneously takes a security interest in the cars. The bank makes a proper Article 9 filing. The dealer sells only five cars and acquires no new ones. Exactly ninety days before bankruptcy, the dealer's inventory of foreign cars is worth $450,000. Thereafter the dealer acquires no new cars, but those the dealer already carries happen to be in short supply, and their value rises unexpectedly. As a result, the inventory is worth $500,000 on the date the bankruptcy petition is filed. The bank's position has improved by $50,000 during the ninety days before bankruptcy. Is there a voidable preference to this extent?

We should begin with the two basic questions of any preference analysis. When was the debt incurred? On January 1. When did the transfer occur? All the inventory that is at issue was in the dealer's hands on January 1. The bank's security interest was both attached and perfected on that date. Therefore, under §547(e)(2), the transfer took place on January 1. There is a transfer on account of a debt, but not a transfer on account of an *antecedent* debt. Under normal definitions of *transfer*, increases in the value of an item attributable solely to market forces are not transfers. Such a definition also fits well with the purpose behind voidable preferences—after all, no opt-out behavior is at issue if the increases are due solely to market forces. The trustee therefore lacks the power to set aside the bank's security interest under §547(b). Whether the bank could assert an exception under §547(c) is therefore irrelevant. Section 547(c)(5) applies only when inventory has turned over.

As the following example illustrates, §547(c)(5) is straightforward in its application, but at the cost of glossing over some activity that might be opt-out behavior. Suppose a bank lends a debtor $20,000 on January 1 and takes and perfects a security interest in the debtor's inventory. At that time, the inventory is worth $15,000. The value of the inventory remains at that level through January, although the inventory turns over several times, but by the middle of February, the value of the inventory plummets to $8,000. The debtor files for bankruptcy on April 1, ninety days after taking out the loan. At that time, the inventory has regained value and is worth $14,000. Because of the turnover in inventory, the bank's interest in the inventory on April 1 was "transferred" to it within ninety days of the filing of the petition. Section 547(e)(3) compels this conclusion. We turn next to the two-point test to determine whether the bank falls within the §547(c)(5) exception. That section requires us to focus on whether the transfers to the bank improved its position. Did they reduce the unsecured portion of its claim against the debtor, the portion that would not be paid in full? In this case, $5,000 of the bank's claim was unsecured ninety days before the filing of the petition. The bank, however, was in even worse shape at the time of the petition. Its loan was undercollateralized by $6,000 on the date of bankruptcy. The bank's position improved dramatically between the middle of February 10 and the filing of the petition on April 1, as the bank went from being undersecured to the extent of $12,000 to being undersecured by only $6,000. But the value of the inventory in February is irrelevant. Under the two-point test we look only at the two end points, not at what happens in the meantime. We sacrifice actual inquiries into preference-type behavior for a rule that establishes rough but cheap justice.

The floating lien is no longer litigated as much as it was under earlier law. Section 547(c)(5) eliminated some of the provisions that had generated litigation under the 1898 Act. Careful inventory financers can avoid preference attacks by ensuring that the debtor's inventory and the proceeds from the sale of inventory are always worth more than what they are owed. Moreover, inventory and accounts financing is not as large a part of the secured credit picture as it once was. The limitations that §547 places on security interests in after-acquired property matter largely with those who claim interests in types of collateral, such as equipment, that fall outside the ambit of §547(c)(5). A secured creditor faces a preference attack with respect to any equipment the debtor acquires during the ninety days before the filing of the petition, unless the secured creditor gives new value or falls within the exceptions in §547(c)(1) or §547(c)(3) for substantially contemporaneous exchanges and purchase money security interests.

The Scope of §547

The knottiest preference problems arise when there are three parties in the picture. Consider the following situation. A debtor has a long-standing relationship with a bank, and it has a credit line that it can draw on. Any obligations that the debtor owes the bank are secured by interest in all the debtor's assets. The debtor obtains most of its raw materials from one supplier. On January 1, the debtor owes the supplier $100,000. The supplier, sensing that the debtor will likely file for bankruptcy, wants to extricate itself. Rather than demanding payment, something that would subject it to a preference attack, the supplier persuades the debtor to go to the bank and have the bank issue a standby letter of credit, naming the supplier as the beneficiary. The supplier can draw on the letter of credit on March 1 to the extent of any obligations the debtor owes it. The bank knows nothing of the supplier's relationship with the debtor. It is willing to issue the standby letter of credit, however, because, under letter-of-credit doctrine, the debtor is obliged to reimburse it in the event the letter is drawn on, and this obligation, like all the debtor's other obligations to the bank, is fully secured. When March 1 arrives, the supplier draws on the letter of credit. On March 2, the debtor files a bankruptcy petition. The trustee discovers the transaction and seeks either to recover $100,000 from the supplier or reduce the bank's security interest by the same amount.

The trustee's task here is not easy. The supplier will argue that the letter-of-credit relationship between it and the bank is independent of its relationship with the debtor. The transfer of $100,000 of the bank's money under the draw on the letter of credit did not affect any of the debtor's general creditors. When the letter of credit was issued, there was the transfer of a security interest from the debtor to the bank supporting the bank's contingent obligation under the letter of credit, but this transfer took place because of the relationship between the debtor and the bank. It was independent of the relationship between the supplier and the bank.

The bank, for its part, will argue that the transfer of the security interest supporting its contingent obligation under the letter of credit was in return for issuing the letter of credit, not on account of the antecedent debt owed the supplier. In short, the supplier argues it never received anything from the debtor, while the bank argues that it never received a transfer on account of an antecedent debt.

Our instincts, however, should tell us that something is amiss here. We should not allow the bank and the supplier to fragment this transaction into its separate pieces and find that no preference took place when, if we step the various transactions together, there has been a transfer on account of the antecedent debt owed the supplier that left the general creditors worse off.

Courts have allowed preference actions against the supplier in such cases.[8] These courts reason that the transfer of the security interest to the bank was a transfer on account of the antecedent debt owed the supplier. It was not a transfer directly to the supplier, but the language in §547(b) allows preference actions when a transfer is made either to or for the benefit of a creditor on account of an antecedent debt. Section 550 allows the trustee to recover from the supplier the value of the transfer made for the supplier's benefit.

These cases, however, lead us to two additional inquiries. First, can the trustee recover from the bank instead of the supplier? The bank did not itself receive a transfer on account of an antecedent debt owed it, but it was the initial transferee, and §550 allows the trustee to recover from transferees even if they were not themselves creditors who were preferred.[9] Section 550(c) limits the trustee's power to seek repayment from initial transferees, but only in one kind of three-party case. Suppose a corporate debtor repays a general creditor that has a guarantee from an insider, such as the debtor's principal shareholder. The debtor files for bankruptcy more than ninety days after but within a year of the transfer. The transfer is a preference because it relieved the insider of her liability on the guarantee within a year of the bankruptcy petition. Section 550(c) provides that in this three-

---

[8] See Kellogg v. Blue Quail Energy, Inc., 831 F.2d 586 (1987), rehearing granted, 835 F.2d 584 (5th Cir. 1988).

[9] See Levit v. Ingersoll Rand Financial Corp., 874 F.2d 1186 (7th Cir. 1989).

party case, the trustee's only recourse is against the insider. Given the unequivocal language of §550(a), however, the trustee has unfettered rights to pursue initial transferees that were not themselves preferred in other kinds of transactions.

The example shows how preference law ensures substance prevails over form by stepping discrete transactions together to allow a preference recovery. Our second inquiry asks whether the converse is also true: Can we step transactions together to *prevent* a preference attack when the transaction as a whole is not preferential? On occasion, the proceeds of a new loan are paid directly to an existing creditor. Sometimes the debtor has discretion over the use of the proceeds and asks the new lender to direct them to the existing creditor. Other times it is the new lender who insists that the new loan be used to repay an earlier obligation. The lender's reasons vary. The new lender may, for example, want to ensure the earlier creditor's release of collateral that the debtor has pledged to the new lender. In any case, when a new lender directly pays an antecedent debt, or the debtor is obligated to use the proceeds of a new loan to repay such debt, the new loan is called an *earmarked loan*. The transaction is one in which one lender leaves the picture and another stands in its place. It is the same as if the old lender had traded its claim against the debtor to the new lender.

The trustee would like to argue that nothing requires the two transactions to be stepped together. The new lender's decision to extend credit is one transaction. The repayment to the old lender is a separate one. It should not matter that the new loan was intended or earmarked for the old lender. Although there is no explicit statutory basis for an earmarked loan exception to the voidable preference rules, courts have established such an exception, known as the *earmarking doctrine*. The doctrine applies when the amount of the new loan is no greater, and of no higher priority, than the loan to be repaid. First, one can argue that the proceeds of an earmarked loan do not constitute an interest of the debtor in property and thus are not subject to §547(b) preference rules. Second, one can argue that unpaid creditors are not injured by an earmarked loan transaction. When one creditor replaces another, the whole of the transaction does not look like the last-minute grab that preference law is designed to prevent. Thus, courts conclude, no purpose would be served by requiring reimbursement from the recipient of an earmarked loan's proceeds.[10]

---

[10] See Kaler v. Community First National Bank, 137 F.3d 1087 (8th Cir. 1998).

The way in which transactions are linked together, however, is not always clear. Consider the following case. A retailer engages a supplier to buy clothes for it from abroad. To ensure that it is paid, the supplier requires the retailer to have its bank issue a letter of credit in the supplier's favor. The letter is large enough to cover the total amount it will spend securing goods for the holiday season. The supplier is entitled to draw upon the letter up to $1 million whenever it has reasonable grounds for insecurity. First Bank issues the letter, and the retailer promises First Bank that it will cover the total amount of the draw on the letter of credit on the same day it is made. The retailer can make such a promise, because it enjoys a $1 million credit line with Second Bank.

The supplier, reasonably fearing that the retailer is in trouble, draws on the letter of credit on August 1. At this point, the supplier has not purchased any goods on the retailer's behalf and it has no claim against retailer. First Bank honors the letter of credit on August 1 and gives the supplier $1 million. Within a few minutes, the retailer transfers $1 million from Second Bank to First Bank. Two months later, before the supplier has given the retailer any goods, the retailer files a Chapter 11 petition. The retailer continues to stay in business. During the next two months, the supplier delivers $1 million worth of goods. The supplier charges the cost of each shipment against the $1 million it received as a result of the draw on the letter of credit.

In March, the case is converted to Chapter 7 and a trustee is appointed. The trustee brings a preference action against First Bank to recover the $1 million it was paid on August 1. The trustee argues that this payment was on account of the retailer's obligation to reimburse First Bank if First Bank was forced to pay on the letter of credit. First Bank will argue that the transfer of $1 million it received should be linked to the $1 million it had given the supplier a few minutes before. If the two transactions are linked, there is no preference. The supplier was never a creditor of the retailer's. Before the draw on the letter of credit, the retailer had a $1 million credit line with Second Bank. Five minutes later, after the draw on the letter of credit and the transfer from the account at Second Bank to First Bank, the retailer had a right to receive $1 million in goods from the supplier.

If the supplier had threatened to draw on the letter of credit and the retailer had simply transferred the money from Second Bank to the supplier directly, there would have been no preference. This transaction is arguably no different. Diminution of the estate is ordinarily thought to be necessary for any successful preference action.[11] Finding in First Bank's favor, however, depends on the court's willingness to step the transactions together. Letter-of-credit doctrine insists on the independence of the supplier's right to draw on its letter of creditor from whatever rights First Bank might have against the retailer and from the retailer's decision to use its credit line with Second Bank to pay First Bank.[12] But whether multiple transactions should be joined together to ask if a preference has taken place is a question of bankruptcy law, not of the law governing letters of credit.[13]

[11] See Kapela v. Newman, 649 F.2d 887 (1st Cir. 1981) (Breyer, J.).

[12] See Douglas Baird, Standby Letters of Credit in Bankruptcy, 49 U. Chi. L. Rev. 130 (1982).

[13] For a case in which the court declined to step the transactions together under these facts, see P.A. Bergner & Co. v. Bank One, 140 F.3d 1111 (7th Cir. 1998).

Chapter Nine

The Automatic Stay

The Scope of the Automatic Stay

In a perfect world, a corporate bankruptcy proceeding would be over in an instant (assuming that in a perfect world you would still have bankruptcy). The world we live in, however, is not so simple. Even a straight sale of the firm for cash takes time. We need a mechanism to preserve the status quo while we sort out the affairs of the debtor. This is the purpose of §362 and the automatic stay. The core role of §362 is stop individual creditors from taking actions that would thwart the reorganization and to allow the debtor to continue doing business with the rest of the world on ordinary terms.

The general creditors of an insolvent debtor must wait until the entire proceeding is over. They will receive only a fraction of what they are owed, and we will not know until the bankruptcy proceeding is over how large that fraction will be. Allowing creditors to take action during the bankruptcy proceeding would undermine bankruptcy's pro rata sharing rule. The justification for continuing the automatic stay against a secured party is, however, different from the one for general creditors. Someone with a property interest that prevails against both the debtor and the trustee will be paid in full at the end of the day. We still need to stay the secured creditor's hand, however. Even though we know how much the secured creditor will be paid, allowing the secured creditor to exercise its rights before the end of the case is likely to interfere with the debtor's attempt to reorganize. But if a secured creditor will receive the property in any event and if the property is not needed for the reorganization, the court will grant a motion to lift the stay.

The automatic stay extends beyond actions of creditors and also ensures that the bankruptcy court retains control over the assets of the estate. Bailors, for example, cannot retrieve property from the debtor, but in these cases the stay is short-lived. Return to the case we considered in chapter 5, in which a dry cleaner files a Chapter 7 petition after you have given it your clothes to clean. In such a case, the automatic stay should preserve the status quo only for so long as it takes to sort out whether there is a true bailment. We need to be

169

sure that the clothes are yours and not the dry cleaner's. Once that is determined, you should be able to recover your clothes.

The automatic stay, however, does not alter the debtor's interactions with the rest of the world going forward. A firm outside of bankruptcy cannot force others to do business with it. A supplier can refuse to ship goods to it for any reason or for no reason at all. In bankruptcy, it is no different. A firm in bankruptcy has no right to go to those with whom it has never dealt and insist upon a special deal or, indeed, any deal at all.

Section 362 for the most part does an effective job of ensuring that rights of prepetition creditors remain frozen in place while ongoing relations with others remain unaffected. You will never see a reported decision in which a general creditor asserts the right to levy on its debtor's assets once the bankruptcy begins. Everyone understands that this action is forbidden. So it is with many other easy cases. As we look the hard cases, do not forget that §362 does most of its work without great controversy.

Section 362(a) prevents a prepetition general creditor from enforcing a claim. The automatic stay also applies to other actions to further the pursuit of a prepetition claim. Even if one does not touch property of the estate, §362 forbids one from going ahead in another forum on a prepetition claim. The bankruptcy proceeding is designed give the debtor's assets a safe harbor. The trustee is supposed to have time to take stock of where things stand. Moreover, the trustee (or, more typically, the debtor in possession) is supposed to be able to deal with all the creditors in a single forum. The bankruptcy court is in charge of determining the size and validity of a claim. The stay allows the bankruptcy court to control where the claim is heard—in the nonbankruptcy forum, or in bankruptcy under either a §502(b) notice and hearing action or under a §502(c) estimation hearing. In addition, §362(a)(4) ensures that attempts to perfect or create liens against property also violate the automatic stay.

Section 362 does not, however, stay all debt collection. Pursuit of postpetition claims is not stayed. For example, you can sue a debtor in a nonbankruptcy forum for a postpetition tort. The automatic stay, however, prevents you from actually levying on the debtor's property. The bankruptcy judge has to be in control of the property of the estate to ensure order. This distinction is reflected in the differences between §362(a)(4) and (a)(6). The automatic stay does not prevent prepetition creditors from going against third parties or exercising control over their assets. Prepetition creditors may pursue guarantors or codefendants.[1] Some courts have found that in unusual circumstances, the automatic stay will apply to actions against third parties.[2] Courts take this extraordinary step only when allowing such actions would adversely affect the property of the estate. An example is a case in which the debtor is obliged to indemnify its officers for claims brought against them.[3] Another example is the case in which the same insurance policy covers the debtor and codefendants. Actions against codefendants could reduce the total obligations of the insurer under the policy. Hence, they might fall within the stay.[4] Cases also arise in which a court will stay actions against officers of the debtor under §105 on the ground that they need to devote their attention to the affairs of the debtor.[5]

There is one more important point about §362(a) that should be remembered. One can always ask to have the automatic stay lifted. For example, if it makes sense for the government to litigate an environmental claim against the debtor in another forum because the litigation in that forum is well under way, the government can always go to court to ask to have the stay lifted. When a policy embedded in some provision of the Bankruptcy Code requires an action to be stayed, the court has the power to issue a stay under §105 even if the action is not automatically stayed under §362(a). In the end, the automatic stay simply establishes a presumption. If one finds an action that ought to be stayed that is not within the scope of §362(a), it does not necessarily mean there is anything wrong with the way §362(a) is written. Rather, the stay is designed to cover actions so common and easy to describe that they can be stayed automatically without requiring a court to review the particulars.

One of the most difficult issues involving the automatic stay arises when a third party attempts to extricate itself from an ongoing relationship with the debtor. Consider a third party that exercises a termination clause. This would violate the automatic stay if the party's right to terminate exists only when the debtor files a bankruptcy petition or becomes insolvent. Section 363(*l*) parallels other provisions of the Bankruptcy Code, such as those in §§541, 545, and 365, that

[1] See In re Aldan Industries, 2000 WL 357719 (Bankr. E.D. Pa. 2000).

[2] McCartney v. Integra National Bank North, 106 F.3d 506 (3d Cir. 1997).

[3] See Lomas Financial Corp. v. Northern Trust, 117 Bankr. 64 (S.D.N.Y. 1990), remanded by 932 F.2d 142 (2d Cir. 1991).

[4] See A.H. Robins Co. v. Piccinin, 788 F.2d 994 (4th Cir. 1986).

[5] See, e.g., Lazarus Burman Associates v. National Westminster Bank, 161 Bankr. 891 (Bankr. E.D.N.Y. 1993); Rustic Manufacturing v. Marine Bank, 55 Bankr. 25 (Bankr. W.D. Wis. 1985).

refuse to give effect to ipso facto clauses. Bankruptcy does not respect rights that are effective in bankruptcy, but not outside.

The automatic stay can have other effects on third parties, even when they are not creditors. A third party that terminates is taking an action that "obtains possession . . . of property from the estate" within the meaning of §363(a)(3). The automatic stay should last long enough to establish that, given the third party's right to terminate, the debtor has no right to the property. Whether the stay reaches further is not clear. Consider the following case. Cahokia Downs operated a racetrack and had a prepaid fire insurance policy.[6] The racing commission denied racing dates for the season, and Cahokia Downs was pushed into bankruptcy. The insurance policy entitled the insurer to cancel for any reason on thirty days' notice. A week after the bankruptcy filing, the insurance company exercised its right to terminate.

We must decide whether, when the insurance company asks for relief from the stay, the court should grant its motion. The racetrack will be worse off if the insurance company can cancel the policy, but this seems neither here nor there. The racetrack would be better off if we all agreed to go there every day (assuming its racing season had not been canceled), but the court will not make us go to the track just because it will make the debtor better off. The insurance company may be in the same position. Like the rest of us, the insurance company is not a creditor of the racetrack. It is not owed any money. It is not trying to grab assets or opt out of the collective proceeding. Before we reach any firm conclusion, however, we need to focus more closely on the insurance company's motives and ask if, in light of them, relief from the stay is appropriate.

There are at least two explanations for what the insurance company is doing. The first (and less likely) is that the insurance company—independent of the bankruptcy filing—reevaluated the risk of fire and decided to terminate the policy. The racing season has been canceled and the track is deserted. A stray spark is likely to have greater consequences. In addition, the closing of the track and the presence of the insurance policy may combine to make fire an attractive option to people whose scruples are not what they should be. The insurance company would terminate the policy even if no bankruptcy petition had been filed. If the bankruptcy filing were utterly unconnected with the termination of the policy, it seems we should

---

[6] Holland American Insurance Co. v. Sportservice, Inc., 5 Bankr. 529 (Bankr. S.D. Ill. 1980).

let the insurance company terminate. The debtor did not pay the extra premium the insurance company would have demanded for a policy that was not terminable. No coherent bankruptcy policy suggests that the debtor should be able to obtain this kind of policy without paying for it.

The termination and the bankruptcy filing, however, may not be independent events. The insurance company may have canceled the policy only because the bankruptcy petition alerted it to the poor condition of the racetrack. In the absence of the bankruptcy petition, it would never have found out about the problem. The question we face here is the extent to which we should prevent the insurance company from taking advantage of the informational signal that bankruptcy conveys.

Most courts would agree that the trustee has no right to extend a policy beyond its term.[7] Moreover, most courts would allow parties to terminate when they are able to show that they would exercise the right apart from the bankruptcy filing.[8] In these cases, however, parties must first obtain relief from the automatic stay. Even if their ability to cancel at will is "cause" that justifies relief from the stay under §362(d), when they act unilaterally, they act at their peril.[9] Some bankruptcy judges may take an inappropriately expansive view of the automatic stay. When they do, relief must be obtained through appeal of the bankruptcy court's decision. It cannot be collaterally attacked.[10]

Government Regulations and §362(b)(4)

Bankruptcy is not an occasion to give debtors special breaks from the operation of substantive nonbankruptcy law. Consider a debtor that produces silicon chips. Let us assume that the debtor's assets are worth $2 million if they are used to make these chips. In other words, a buyer would pay $2 million for the assets free of prebankruptcy liabilities. The buyer who buys the assets at a certain price is willing to pay that price only after concluding that the net income of the pro-

[7] See Heaven Sent Ltd. v. Commercial Union Insurance Co., 37 Bankr. 597 (Bankr. E.D. Penn. 1984). But see Garnas v. American Family Mutual Insurance Co., 38 Bankr. 221 (Bankr. D.N.D. 1984) (requiring renewal of an insurance contract on the ground that renewal was routine and would have been automatic but for the filing of the bankruptcy petition).

[8] See In re M.J. & K. Co., 161 Bankr. 586 (Bankr. S.D.N.Y. 1993).

[9] See In re Elber Beerman Stores Corp., 195 Bankr. 1012 (Bankr. S.D. Ohio 1996).

[10] See Celotex Corp. v. Edwards, 514 U.S. 300 (1995).

ject offers a sufficient return on $2 million. In calculating the firm's net income, the buyer will take into account, among many other things, the costs that various legal rules impose. A law may require, for example, the installation of environmental equipment at a cost of $500,000. In arriving at a value of $2 million, the buyer has already taken this cost into account.

If the assets could be used to produce silicon chips without complying with this regulation (and assuming that pollution victims otherwise had no legal recourse), a buyer would pay $2.5 million for the assets rather than $2 million. Hence, relieving a party from the duty of complying with such a rule increases the value of the assets. Again, no bankruptcy policy suggests that the debtor in possession be able to obtain such relief. The need to free an individual from the burdens of past debt or the need to give a firm a new capital structure provides no justification for allowing the debtor to play by a different set of rules. We find the same idea at work in 28 U.S.C. §959(b):

> [A] trustee ... appointed in any cause ... including a debtor in possession, shall manage and operate the property in his possession ... according to the requirements of the valid laws of the State in which such property is situated, in the same manner that the owner or possessor thereof would be bound to do if in possession thereof.

This principle is embraced in §362(b)(4), which provides that the automatic stay does not apply to "the commencement or continuation of an action or proceeding by a governmental unit . . . to enforce such governmental unit's police or regulatory power." Debtors in bankruptcy have to play by the same rules as everyone else. For example, they cannot pollute. If a debtor is operating in violation of a state or federal statute, the government should be able to tell it to stop regardless of whether it is in bankruptcy. Spending money to comply with governmental orders is not one of the things that a firm should be able to avoid simply because it is in a collective proceeding. Section 362(b)(4) ensures that the government retains this power notwithstanding the automatic stay. This power remains even when the action will have irreversible consequences for property of the debtor, such as a city's demolition of a debtor's building after it has been condemned.[11] Congress broadened §362(b)(4) in 1998 to apply not only to the "commencement or continuation of an action or pro-

---

[11] Javens v. City of Hazel Park, 107 F.3d 359 (6th Cir. 1997).

ceeding" but also to acts "to obtain possession of property of the estate" under §362(a)(3).[12]

Section 362(b)(4) requires that we draw a line between the actions a governmental unit takes in the exercise of its police or regulatory power and those it takes as an ordinary prepetition creditor. An action does not cease to be regulatory simply because it forces the debtor to spend money. But because the government can always assert that it is advancing a police or regulatory purpose with respect to any action it takes, drawing the line is not easy. The government can argue, for example, that a debtor's obligation to clean up property it did not own at the time of the petition serves a regulatory purpose, even though the obligation predated the bankruptcy petition and even though meeting the obligation requires only paying the agency money.[13]

Consider the extreme case in which an agency auctions off a license but lends qualified buyers part of the purchase price. The agency argues that the purpose of the auction was to identify those who value the license most and it can ensure that this happens only by collecting its loans in full. One of the buyers files for bankruptcy at a time when it is current on its payments to agency. The debtor believes that, for purposes of collecting the money, the agency is a prepetition creditor rather than a regulator. The debtor ceases its payments to the agency while in bankruptcy. The agency cancels the license when the debtor stops paying and argues that the cancellation is allowed as an exercise of its regulatory power under §362(b)(4).[14] If such an action is beyond the scope of the automatic stay, however, it is difficult to imagine how the stay would halt any governmental action. When the regulator is the federal government, the power of the bankruptcy court may be limited in another way. The agency can argue that even when its actions violate the automatic stay, the bankruptcy court may still not be able to do anything about it because it has no subject matter jurisdiction over the actions of federal administrative agencies.[15] Review must be conducted through administrative law judges and then the court of appeals.

[12] A number of courts had already interpreted §362(b)(4) this broadly before the passage of the amendment. See, e.g., Yellow Cab Cooperative Association v. Metro Taxi, 132 F.3d 591 (10th Cir. 1997).

[13] See Torwico Electronics, Inc. v. New Jersey Department of Environmental Protection, 8 F.3d 146 (3d Cir. 1993).

[14] See In re Kansas Personal Communications Services, Ltd., 252 Bankr. 179 (Bankr. D. Kan. 2000).

[15] See In re Federal Communications Commission, 217 F.3d 125 (2d Cir. 2000).

When the government acts as a postpetition regulator, it is not engaging in any of the acts prohibited by the automatic stay in §362(a), at least so long as it does not assert control over the debtor's assets. One can argue that the exceptions carved out for actions of the government in §362(b) go beyond simply those actions that the government takes as a postpetition regulator. Under this view, the purpose that §362(b) serves is largely jurisdictional. The government is not obliged to resolve its prepetition disputes against the debtor in the bankruptcy forum when the dispute arises by virtue of the government's exercise of its police or regulatory power. The government, acting in this capacity, is presumptively entitled to pursue the debtor in the forum of its own choosing. In the absence of any order issued under §105, the government can pursue its claim in the nonbankruptcy forum.[16]

The Supreme Court confronted a similar problem in *Board of Governors v. MCorp Financial*.[17] Before filing for bankruptcy, MCorp caused two of its subsidiary banks to extend credit to an affiliate and engaged in other transactions that may have violated federal banking law. The Board of the Federal Reserve commenced one administrative proceeding before the bankruptcy began and then another after MCorp entered bankruptcy. The Supreme Court rejected MCorp's argument that the board was trying to enforce a prepetition claim and therefore violated the automatic stay. In the Court's view, the board's actions fell under §362(b)(4). The proceedings might culminate in a final order that would interfere with the bankruptcy court's exclusive jurisdiction over property of the estate under 28 U.S.C. §1334(d), but until that time, the board's actions did not violate the automatic stay. The Court was not persuaded that "the automatic stay provisions of the Bankruptcy Code have any application to ongoing, nonfinal administrative proceedings."[18]

MCorp and similar cases suggest that in the case of government regulations, some policies conflict with bankruptcy's goal of resolving all claims against a debtor in a single forum. One might also take the view that both §362 and nonbankruptcy federal law give the government a privileged place among those to whom the debtor owes obligations. One provision of §362(b), for example, exempts Housing and Urban Development foreclosure actions from the automatic stay.

---

[16] See United States v. Nicolet, Inc., 857 F.2d 202 (3d Cir. 1988). The argument in text is set out in Robert K. Rasmussen, Bankruptcy and the Administrative State, 42 Hastings L.J. 1567 (1991).

[17] 502 U.S. 32 (1991).

[18] Id. at 41.

The Automatic Stay and the Secured Creditor

As we have noted, bankruptcy provides the secured creditor with the value of its secured claim, but it does not allow the secured creditor to exercise the default rights it has under nonbankruptcy law. It cannot physically seize its collateral. To take such an action, the secured creditor must ask for relief from the stay. When is such relief granted? And when it is not granted, what must the trustee do to protect the secured creditor's collateral? As elsewhere in bankruptcy, there are a few basic guideposts that resolve many of the cases we are likely to encounter.

The secured creditor is entitled to have the stay lifted if its collateral is at risk. Section 362(d) provides that the stay can be lifted for cause. If the debtor is damaging the collateral or has stopped insuring it, a creditor will be able to lift the stay. If the collateral is not at risk, the secured creditor has no right to have the stay lifted when the collateral is worth more than the amount the secured creditor is owed. The debtor is the one who stands to gain or lose when the property is sold. The secured creditor is the wrong person to conduct the sale. The secured creditor has nothing to gain from getting more than the amount it is owed. Hence, it will be unlikely to sell it in a way that maximizes its value. We do have rules that require the secured creditor to act reasonably, but we are going to be better off if the person conducting the sale has the incentive to get the best price. The Bankruptcy Code recognizes this idea in §362(d)(2). In the absence of cause, the secured creditor cannot lift the stay if the debtor has any equity in the property. Sometimes a secured creditor's collateral is worth more than it is owed, but other creditors also have security interests in the property, and all these interests together exceed the value of the property. One needs to ask whether the debtor lacks equity in the property within the meaning of §362(d)(2). Most courts have concluded that the debtor has no equity in the property in such a case.[19] This seems a defensible interpretation of the language of the Bankruptcy Code, but it may not make sense as a matter of first principle. If the property is worth more than the secured creditor is owed, the secured creditor may not have the right incentives to obtain the best price for it.

When the debtor lacks equity in the property, it can keep the collateral only if the collateral is necessary for an effective reorganization. When the collateral is worth more in the debtor's business than

---

[19] Nantucket Investors II v. California Federal Bank, 61 F.3d 197 (3d Cir. 1995); Stewart v. Gurley, 745 F.2d 1194 (9th Cir. 1984).

anywhere else, the secured creditor is not allowed to repossess it. This principle might seem to apply when the debtor is liquidating and the assets are worth more sold together as a unit. The language of §362(d)(2)(B), however, speaks of a "reorganization," and hence the secured creditor may be able to insist on retrieving its collateral unless the debtor is reorganizing. Indeed, in *United Savings Association v. Timbers of Inwood Forest Associates* the Supreme Court found that a secured creditor should be able to lift the stay where there is no "reasonable possibility of a successful reorganization within a reasonable time." [20]

The lift-stay motion forces the debtor to set up a timetable. To persuade a court to deny a lift-stay motion, the debtor has to show how it will reorganize itself and why the amount of time it will take is reasonable. The court can then use the debtor's own timetable to hold it to account at the next juncture in the case, which might be another lift-stay motion, a request to extend the exclusivity period, or a motion to convert the case to Chapter 7. Lift-stay motions, like these others, are the discrete points in a case when the court must decide whether to continue the business or shut it down. Just as the venture capitalist tells the entrepreneur that a new round of funding is assured only if the prototype works by a certain date, the bankruptcy judge will demand that the debtor present objective indicia of the firm's prospects.

While the automatic stay is in force, the secured creditor is protected in a number of ways. Often the secured creditor asserts an interest not only in an asset such as a piece of real property but also in the revenue stream that the property generates. Section 552 relieves the secured creditor of the burden of showing that its interest in rents is perfected under nonbankruptcy law. Unlike a security interest in after-acquired personal property, state law sometimes does not allow for automatic perfection of rents (and analogous income streams from hotels). Section 552 reflects the judgment that the notice the bankruptcy process provides obviates the need to demand simultaneous compliance with perfection requirements under state law.

More generally, we require the trustee to ensure that the value of the secured creditor's rights are adequately protected throughout the bankruptcy process. Failure to offer adequate protection is itself cause that requires lifting the automatic stay under §362(d)(1). The meaning of *adequate protection* is illustrated (although not quite defined) in §361. First, the debtor may periodically make cash pay-

[20] 484 U.S. 365, 376 (1988).

ments to the creditor, to the extent that the stay decreases the value of the secured creditor's interest in the property. Second, the debtor may provide an additional or replacement lien under the same circumstances. Finally, the debtor may give some other kind of protection (other than giving administrative expense priority) that will result in the "indubitable equivalent" of the right that the secured creditor is asserting.[21]

Even though adequate protection cannot be in the form of an administrative priority, the secured creditor is entitled to an administrative expense claim that trumps others if what is offered as adequate protection turns out to be inadequate. Assume that the secured creditor is entitled to $100 at the end of the bankruptcy proceeding, but is given a lien on an asset that proves to be worth only $80 at that time. The secured creditor is entitled to be paid the $20 shortfall before any other administrative expenses are paid. This includes the fees for the trustee and the trustee's lawyers. §507(b). The value of this super-administrative priority lies largely in the incentives it gives the trustee and others. They will ensure that the secured creditor's protection is adequate, because they will not be paid until after the secured creditor's right to adequate protection is vindicated.

In a single-asset real estate case, §362(d)(3) requires that the debtor make monthly payments to secured creditors unless it has filed within ninety days a reorganization plan that has a reasonable possibility of being confirmed within a reasonable time. Even if a bank is undersecured (its mortgage on Blackacre secures a $100 loan, but Blackacre is worth only $60), the debtor must make payments that protect the time value of the bank's secured claim (that is, to the extent of $60). The costs of imposing this requirement on the debtor seem light in the single-asset real estate case. There are no jobs at risk and there is no going-concern value to be protected.

Other secured creditors are not entitled to adequate protection for the time value of their claims.[22] Assume a bank has lent $100 and has a security interest in a machine that is worth $60 at the time the bankruptcy petition is filed. The bankruptcy will take several years. The bank is entitled to insist only on receiving protection on account of its $60 secured claim sufficient to ensure that, two years hence, it will receive $60 in nominal dollars. Receiving $60 in two years is not the same as receiving $60 today. The effect of interpreting adequate

---

[21] The idea of the indubitable equivalent is repeated in §1129 and comes from Learned Hand's opinion in In re Murel Holding Corp., 75 F.2d 941 (2d Cir. 1935).

[22] United Savings Association v. Timbers of Inwood Forest Association, 484 U.S. 365 (1988).

protection in this fashion is to require the bank to make a forced, in-terest-free loan for the duration of the bankruptcy.

This rule creates a number of inconsistencies. As noted, a single-asset real estate lender does enjoy protection for the time value of its secured claim. The rule also treats different secured creditors differ-ently depending on how their collateral is used. If a debtor owns a machine and leases it out, the secured creditor gets the rental pay-ments under §552 so long as it would have received them under appli-cable law or under its contract. If the debtor owns a machine and uses it in its business, the secured creditor receives nothing on account of the debtor's use of the property. The streams of income a capital as-set produces are economically identical.

While denying time value gives those who are junior to the se-cured creditor an incentive to procrastinate, these bad effects may be greatly offset if the bankruptcy judge is willing to lift the stay should the debtor start dragging things out. Denying time value may also reduce the amount that a secured creditor lends in the first place. Section 506(b) allows an oversecured creditor to recover interest as well as principal. When the time value is not protected, the secured creditor has an incentive to lend less than the value of the collateral and thus be able to enjoy postpetition interest to the extent of the difference between the value of the collateral and the amount of the loan.

Sometimes, the secured creditor repossesses before the bankrupt-cy petition is filed. Suppose a solvent debtor takes out a loan to buy a drill press, but falls behind on its payments to the bank. The bank repossesses the press and sells it before the debtor files for bank-ruptcy. In this case, the debtor is simply out of luck. It cannot bring a voidable preference action against the bank because a preference ac-tion does not lie against a fully secured creditor who repossesses or is paid off. (Recall that the transfer does not make the bank better off within the meaning of §547(b)(5), another anomaly given the treat-ment of time value in the bankruptcy case.) Nor can the debtor re-cover the property from a third-party buyer. Because the buyer is a bona fide purchaser for value, the trustee cannot retrieve the ma-chine. The debtor no longer has any cognizable interest in the drill press, nor do any of the creditors. The person who now owns the drill press is a stranger to the process.

What if the bank repossesses but does not sell the drill press be-fore the debtor files the petition? In this case, we do not have a bona fide purchaser for value in the picture. Let's look first at how this situation is handled outside of bankruptcy. Normally the debtor could recover the machine provided it pays the entire amount of the debt, not simply the value of the machine. The debtor continues to have a property interest in the machine, but its only interest is its right to redeem the property upon payment of the debt, not a right to the machine itself. Now let's examine how the situation is handled inside bankruptcy. Section 542 requires those holding property that the trustee can use, sell, or lease to turn it over. Under §363 the trustee can sell, use, or lease property of the estate, which is defined in §541 as the debtor's interest in the property. It might seem that §542 does not apply to the case in which a secured creditor has repossessed before the petition, because after the repossession the debtor's interest in the machine is only its right to redeem the property by forking over the full amount that the bank is owed. The trustee can use, sell, or lease that right of redemption, but not the collateral itself. The Supreme Court, however, interpreted this problem more broadly in *United States v. Whiting Pools, Inc.*:

> Although these statutes could be read to limit the estate to those "interests of the debtor in property" at the time of the filing of the petition, we view them as a definition of what is included in the estate, rather than as a limitation.[23]

Although this interpretation has an ipse dixit quality, it makes sense as a matter of first principle. The trustee can keep the machine after it is turned over only if the bank is not entitled to have the automatic stay lifted under §362(d). Hence, the only cases in which the issue is important are those in which the repossessed property is essential for an effective reorganization. If the bank were allowed to keep the collateral, the debtor would be forced to pay the bank all of what it is owed, even if the bank were undersecured. The bank, however, should not be entitled to have the unsecured portion of its claim paid in full. So long as the trustee ensures that the value of the bank's rights is adequately protected, the bank is not made worse off if the debtor gets the property back and the general creditors are made better off. Allowing the debtor to take the property back is not much different from curing a default on an executory contract.

[23] 462 U.S. 198, 203 (1983).

Chapter Ten

The Debtor in Possession

Continuing the Business Under §363

If a firm in Chapter 11 is to survive as a going concern, it must continue to operate during the bankruptcy proceeding. It takes time to restructure the financing of the firm, and the world is not going to stand still. Still, it is necessary to supervise the decisions that are made. In most Chapter 11 cases, no trustee is appointed, and the debtor in possession, the prebankruptcy manager of the firm, is likely to have interests closely aligned with the shareholders. Indeed, in many closely held firms, the two may be identical. Nevertheless, nonbankruptcy law requires that directors shift their fiduciary duties to the creditors when the firm becomes insolvent.[1] The trustee (and by inference the debtor in possession) must maximize the value of the estate rather than promote the interests of any particular group.[2] Chapter 11 does not rely entirely on the debtor in possession's selflessness to ensure this outcome, however. Creditors are given their own representative in reorganization proceedings through the creditors committee, and equity owners ordinarily have no such representative. Moreover, courts have increasingly measured the performance of professionals in connection with fee requests by whether they have advanced the interests of the estate as a whole.[3]

The Bankruptcy Code puts in place oversight mechanisms to ensure that the managers are looking out for everyone's interests, not just their own. These procedures, embodied in §363, begin with the idea that many day-to-day business decisions are not controversial. The trustee (and hence the debtor in possession) has the general authority to use, sell, or lease property of the estate.[4] It would be crazy to require a retailer to go to court every time a customer came

---

[1] See, e.g., Geyer v. Ingersoll Publications Co., 621 A.2d 784, 787 (Del. Ch. 1992); FDIC v. Sea Pines Co., 692 F.2d 973, 976–77 (4th Cir. 1982) ("[W]hen the corporation becomes insolvent, the fiduciary duty of the directors shifts from the stockholders to the creditors.").

[2] In re Central Ice Cream, 836 F.2d 1068 (7th Cir. 1987).

[3] See Everett v. Perez, 30 F.3d 1209 (9th Cir. 1994).

[4] The trustee has this power only if the trustee has the authority to run the business, but such authority is presumed in Chapter 11 cases.

into the store to buy something. The debtor in possession has to be able to buy raw materials and sell finished products. If the debtor in possession cannot be relied upon to do at least that, a trustee should be appointed. If a transaction falls outside the ordinary course of business, it is subject to judicial scrutiny. The trustee can act only after there has been notice and a hearing.[5]

The usual checks that keep the managers of a firm in line—the prospects of profits from their equity interests, the default clauses in the loan agreement, the ability of the shareholders to throw them out—are displaced once a bankruptcy petition is filed. Nonetheless, nonbankruptcy law often offers a useful benchmark to which courts often turn. In looking at the approaches of different courts, it might seem that they have dramatically different views of how to translate nonbankruptcy principles to the bankruptcy forum. Courts might, for example, seem to take different views of whether the business judgment rule applies in bankruptcy.[6]

In most cases, however, the differences stem more from the facts of the cases themselves than from any fundamental difference in the nature of the inquiry. Bankruptcy courts must always ask whether the decisionmaking process itself was likely to further the welfare of all the parties, notwithstanding their diverse interests. In the nonbankruptcy forum, often it is sufficient to note that the directors' interests do not depart from those of the shareholders. In bankruptcy, courts must take greater care to ensure the absence of self-dealing and a process that is likely to "obtain the highest price or greatest overall benefit possible for the estate."[7] The diverse interests that require the bankruptcy proceeding in the first place also require the court to ensure that they have not colored the decision at hand. At the same time, the bankruptcy judge must take care not to rely on his own judgment when market mechanisms are available.[8] Hence, it should come as no surprise to find bankruptcy courts less likely to accept

[5] Requiring notice and a hearing within the meaning of the Bankruptcy Code is not the same, of course, as requiring a hearing. Recall our discussion of §102 on pp. 6–7 *supra*.

[6] Compare Official Committee of Subordinated Bondholders v. Integrated Resources, 147 Bankr. 650 (S.D.N.Y. 1992), with Calpine Corp. v. O'Brien Environmental Energy, 181 F.3d 527, 535 (3d Cir. 1999); In re America West Airlines, 166 Bankr. 908 (Bankr. D. Ariz. 1994).

[7] Cello Bag Co. v. Champion International Corp., 99 Bankr. 124, 130 (Bankr. N.D. Ga. 1988).

[8] See Bank of America v. 203 North LaSalle Street Partnership, 526 U.S. 434 (1999).

doctrines such as the business judgment rule when the debtor's actions have circumvented the marketplace.[9]

Section 363 limits the debtor in possession's ability to make some sales in the ordinary course of business. If the money derived from such sales goes toward buying more inventory, the secured creditor has no cause to complain, but the cash might be used for something else. To protect a creditor with a security interest in inventory, we must be sure that proceeds from the sale of inventory do not go toward paying off other creditors or toward buying airplane tickets to Rio. Under §364(e), parties with a security interest in inventory can insist that their interest be adequately protected. The right to sell goods in ordinary course does not free the trustee or the debtor in possession from this obligation. The court also may limit the ability to sell in the ordinary course as circumstances warrant.

When a business is in trouble, it may be hemorrhaging cash. The trustee may be paying off suppliers and making all sorts of decisions that may be irrevocable. A secured creditor may be left short if it is unable to do anything other than go to court and ask for adequate protection. For this reason, §363 limits the powers of the trustee with respect to cash collateral. Even if the use of the cash collateral (cash, negotiable instruments, bank accounts, and other cash equivalents) is in the ordinary course, the trustee (and hence the debtor in possession) cannot use them without going to court first and giving the party with the security interest adequate protection.

The debtor in possession, like the trustee, is liable to meet all its postpetition obligations in full before the general creditors receive anything. These are "administrative expenses," the "actual, necessary costs and expenses of preserving the estate." They are given a priority over the unsecured claims of the debtor under §507(a)(1). Money spent to increase the value of the estate inures to the benefit of the general creditors. The rule is necessary to ensure that people do business with the debtor, but its reach is broader. It ensures, for example, that those whose tort claims arise after the filing of the petition are paid before the prepetition general creditors.[10] The risk of incurring tort liability is one of the necessary costs incident to taking time to sort out the affairs of the debtor. We can ensure that those who benefit from the bankruptcy proceeding internalize this cost by giving postpetition tort claims priority over unsecured claims.

[9] See, e.g., In re Bidermann Industries U.S.A., 203 Bankr. 547 (Bankr. S.D.N.Y. 1997).

[10] Reading Co. v. Brown, 391 U.S. 471 (1968).

One should not infer, however, that those who do business with a debtor in Chapter II can count on being paid. Secured credit has become so pervasive that in many cases there are no unencumbered assets. In such a case, administrative expense priority is of little value. The trustee (and the debtor in possession) has the power under §506(c) to charge against the collateral the reasonable, necessary costs and expenses of preserving the property, but a third party has no right to reach such assets in the event that the trustee refuses to pay for them.[11] Those who lend to the debtor postpetition have to ensure that the money is there and are well advised to reach an explicit agreement with the secured creditor or postpetition financer before extending credit themselves.

It might seem that secured creditors would be unwilling to give up some of their collateral when not compelled to do so. But often in practice they are willing to reach deals with postpetition suppliers when the suppliers are engaging in transactions with the debtor that serve to maximize the value of the assets. Many modern Chapter II cases involving ongoing enterprises are in effect being run for the benefit of the secured party. The bankruptcy forum makes it easier for the secured party and the debtor in possession to work together to find a buyer of the assets because the buyer can be confident of obtaining assets free and clear in a sale under §363. As noted in our discussion of claims, successor liability under state law may limit the ability of the bankruptcy judge to give clean title, but buyers may be found when this risk is the only one they face.[12]

Distinguishing between the rights of pre- and postpetition creditors is difficult in the case of obligations that arise under environmental law. An obligation to clean up past pollution is a prepetition claim if the debtor committed the relevant acts and the environmental claimant was on notice of the environmental hazard before the petition is filed. Some courts have expanded the idea of a prepetition claim even more, requiring only that the acts were committed prepetition.[13] In the case of an individual, the question of when a claim arises matters because only prepetition claims are discharged. Section 727(b) provides that the discharge extends to debts that arose "before the date of the order for relief," and §301 provides that

[11] See *Hartford Underwriters Insurance v. Union Planters Bank*, 530 U.S. ••• (2000).

[12] See, e.g., *New National Gypsum Co. v. New National Gypsum Co. Settlement Trust*, 219 F.3d 478 (5th Cir. 2000).

[13] Compare *California Department of Health Services v. Jensen*, 995 F.2d 925 (9th Cir. 1993), with *United States v. The LTV Corp.*, 944 F.2d 997 (2d Cir. 1991).

the commencement of a voluntary case "constitutes an order for relief."

When a firm continues as a going concern, the question of when the claim arises may not matter much. If the obligation gives rise to a prepetition claim, then the prepetition claim is discharged. But liability for the violation of environmental law arises from many sources. Even if a debtor can extinguish a prepetition claim, it may remain liable nevertheless. The toxic waste dump poses an ongoing hazard, and anyone who owns the dump at a particular moment may be liable to clean it up, even if they took no part in creating the hazard in the first place. Some courts are reluctant to force the trustee to clean up if there are no unencumbered assets to pay for the cleanup.[14] Nevertheless, if any current owner would be obliged to clean it up outside of bankruptcy, it would seem the trustee would have this obligation inside. The trustee must comply with applicable laws and, by virtue of owning the property, the trustee has a legal duty to clean up the property. Under this view, the duty to clean up sites that pose a continuing hazard is an actual, necessary expense of preserving the estate within the meaning of §503(b).[15] The obligation arises independently of the debtor's prepetition conduct, so the discharge of any liability that arises from that conduct is irrelevant.

Some courts have suggested that the trustee can limit the estate's clean-up obligations by virtue of her ability to abandon property under §554.[16] This is wrong. Section 554 empowers the trustee to turn over collateral to secured creditors that is of no use to the estate. It does not give the trustee a license to do something that those running the business could not do outside of bankruptcy. The trustee should not be able, by invoking §554, to rid the estate of an obligation that arises out of the debtor's postpetition ownership of the property. The debtor in possession, like the trustee, is obliged to obey applicable nonbankruptcy law, and this duty implicitly qualifies the powers that the debtor in possession enjoys under provisions such as §363. If you run over someone with a car, you do not escape liability by ridding yourself of the car. By the same measure, whatever obligations the trustee has—whether by virtue of prepetition torts of the debtor or postpetition ownership by the trustee—the abandonment of an asset should not change them.

---

[14] See Borden, Inc. v. Wells Fargo Business Credit, 856 F.2d 12 (4th Cir. 1988).

[15] See United States v. The LTV Corp., 944 F.2d 997 (2d Cir. 1991).

[16] A case that tends to lead courts astray, not because of its holding but because of its use of balancing language in dictum, is Midlantic National Bank v. New Jersey Department of Environmental Protection, 474 U.S. 494 (1986).

Ownership brings with it benefits and burdens. The result in these environmental cases seems odd only because the benefits of ownership usually exceed the costs. This is not always the case. Sometimes that which we own sells for a negative price. Sometimes we have to pay someone to take the property off our hands, as "two desperate men" unhappily discovered in "The Ransom of Red Chief."

Financing the Debtor in Possession

We have long since passed the day when businesses could exist without debt. Suppose, for example, you get a contract with a customer. To fill the order, you need to buy supplies. Ordinarily, you can find a bank that is willing to lend on the basis of the customer's promise to pay. Alternatively, your supplier may be willing to ship you the goods on open account and wait until you convert the raw materials into finished goods and sell them. Neither the supplier nor the bank, however, is going to extend you credit if your liabilities exceed your assets and they have to share pro rata with the other creditors. Rational lenders do not extend credit if they know in advance that repayment will be at ten cents on the dollar. They will do business only with those who can pay them. The bank or the supplier has to be given a priority over the general creditors if the debtor is to survive as a going concern.

Section 364 allows the trustee to borrow on an unsecured basis in the ordinary course of its business, unless the court orders otherwise. Because new lenders will extend credit only if they are confident they will be repaid, these loans enjoy a priority over prepetition claims. If the trustee wants to borrow outside the ordinary course or do anything fancy, such as giving a security interest to the new creditor, the old creditors must be given a chance to be heard. Moreover, before approving credit on any other basis, the judge must find that credit is not available with administrative priority. There are several possible kinds of protection that are greater than administrative priority. First, the judge can grant an administrative priority that beats out other administrative priorities. There are in effect three levels of administrative priority. At the highest level is the special priority for some postpetition loans. §364(c)(1). Just beneath it are the claims of secured creditors to the extent that the protection extended them turns out to be less than adequate. §507(b). At the lowest level are the various expenses of administration like the fees of the trustee and the lawyers. §503(b).

In addition to administrative priority, the court can place a lien on property that is not otherwise encumbered or a junior lien on property that already is encumbered. In the scheme of things, this should not be different from the special administrative priority as far as the payout is concerned. (You are still sandwiched between secured creditors and administrative expense priority claims.) Your ability to look to particular property, however, may give you additional advantages. The final option is for the court to approve a lien that primes even a secured creditor. §364(d). The trustee can take advantage of this provision only if two conditions are satisfied. First, the trustee (or debtor in possession) must be unable to obtain credit in any other way. Second, the trustee has to give adequate protection to the secured creditor. It will be a rare case in which both requirements can be met simultaneously. A trustee who cannot find anyone to lend without taking priority over a secured creditor will find it hard to give that creditor protection that is truly adequate.

Obtaining postpetition financing is one of the first tasks a debtor faces after filing for Chapter 11. It is called debtor-in-possession (or dip) financing. When dip financing is done with a new lender under active review by the creditors committee, few problems arise. In many cases, however, this financing has been negotiated before the bankruptcy petition is filed. All that remains to be done is for the bankruptcy judge to put her seal of approval on the deal. Moreover, the dip lender is often the debtor's principal source of credit before bankruptcy. The debtor will often need to turn to this lender because there is not enough time to find another one. The general creditors are unlikely to be able to propose alternative sources of credit, and time is of the essence if the firm is to stay in business.

In dip financing, the lack of careful review and the absence of an arm's-length relationship with the lender create the potential for abuse. Judge Henry J. Friendly struck down part of a dip financing in *In re Texlon Corp.*, a case under the old Bankruptcy Act.[17] In that case, the prepetition lender insisted that it be granted a security interest both for the prepetition loan as well as the new one. Judge Friendly did not find that the bankruptcy law flatly prohibited such clauses (commonly called *cross-collateralization clauses*), but he emphasized the need to give the creditors a chance to object to them when they arose in postpetition loans. A deal between a debtor in possession and its existing lender is not an arm's-length transaction. In *Texlon*, the deal was struck in an ex parte hearing before the credi-

[17] Otte v. Manufacturers Hanover Commercial Corp. (In re Texlon), 596 F.2d 1092 (2d Cir. 1979).

tors committee got together. No one else was notified. As Judge Friendly observed, "The debtor in possession is hardly neutral."

In addition to cross-collateralization clauses, prepetition lenders ask for waivers of lender liability actions, as well as waivers of the trustee's ability to assess a lender with the costs of maintaining collateral.[18] Often these financing orders include carve-outs for attorney's fees. Under one view, the prepetition lender who demands such terms for extending a postpetition line of credit is likely to lend even if it does not obtain them. The lender often has a strong interest in having the debtor survive as a going concern. Such a lender also fears that another lender might prime its loan or that, in any event, it would have a hard time showing which assets acquired postpetition were subject to its security interest under §552. Banning cross-collateralization clauses and other favorable terms, in other words, is a way of keeping the lender from taking advantage of the chaos that exists at the start of the bankruptcy case. Courts, however, typically resist per se rules and look instead to the exigencies of the moment. Courts are especially apt to approve these clauses when the lender's prepetition loans seem to be fully secured and its prepetition conduct consistent with established norms. Here the secured creditor's interests are aligned with those of the firm. The secured creditor wants the clause to make bookkeeping easier and to avoid strike suits when some creditor searches for a deep pocket.[19] Courts may also pay attention to whether the general creditors as a group object.[20] They are the ones who will ultimately pay for the dip loan.

Under the Bankruptcy Code, one of the fighting issues is whether such clauses can be challenged on appeal. Section 364(e) provides that the reversal or modification on appeal of an authorization under §364 "to obtain credit or incur debt, or of a grant under this section [§364] of a priority or a lien, does not affect the validity of any debt so incurred, or any priority or lien so granted, to an entity that extended such credit in good faith." If another judge can second-guess the first one on whether a loan is authorized, a lender will not be willing to make a loan until all issues concerning it have been fully litigated. Section 364(e) is designed to put the other creditors to the test. They

[18] See, e.g., In re Molten Metal Technology, 244 Bankr. 515 (Bankr. D. Mass. 2000).

[19] See In re Vanguard Diversified, Inc., 31 Bankr. 364 (Bankr. E.D.N.Y. 1983).

[20] See In re Beker Industries Corp., 58 Bankr. 725, 742 (Bankr. S.D.N.Y. 1986) ("In these instances, the view of unsecured creditors is of paramount importance for it is they who are able to contest whether other financing is available and it is they, the victims of unequal treatment . . . .").

have a chance to object, but they cannot second-guess the decision if the money is lent in good faith. The general creditors should not be able to have it both ways, complaining about the deal if things go badly and also enjoying the benefits if things go well.

Section 364(e) responds to the urgency that usually surrounds dip financing. The scope of the protection given a postpetition lender under §364(e), however, is not clear. The Eleventh Circuit held that a cross-collateralization clause is not authorized under §364 and cannot be considered a "grant under this section" that is protected from attack on appeal.[21] The Ninth Circuit, however, found that loans with cross-collateralization clauses fall within the safe harbor of §364(e). For this reason, it did not reach the question of whether the Bankruptcy Code prohibits them altogether.[22] Given this division of opinion in the appellate courts, the postpetition lender cannot completely rely on the safe harbor under §364(e). It should be prepared to defend the various provisions of the dip financing agreement on their merits.

Postpetition Bargaining with Prepetition Creditors

In Chapter 11 proceedings involving closely held firms, the largest creditors may be suppliers of goods and services to the debtor. In many cases, the debtor may want to continue to do business with these suppliers, but these suppliers may want to take advantage of the debtor's need for new supplies to obtain payment of their prepetition debts. These suppliers wear two hats. They are both prepetition creditors and postpetition suppliers. The extent to which they can exploit the debtor's continuing need for them remains unclear. The question is usually not formally litigated, but is the subject of heated negotiations that take place at the start of the case at the same time as the order concerning dip financing.

In many cases, large suppliers who are also prepetition creditors do not threaten to stop deliveries, so long as the reorganization has a good chance of succeeding. The important suppliers are usually content to be paid for any new supplies in cash. A supplier may have little holdup power. When the debtor specializes in dealing with a par-

---

[21] See Clinton Marine Products v. Saybrook Manufacturing Co., 963 F.2d 1490 (11th Cir. 1992). Charles Tabb, Lender Preference Clauses and the Destruction of Appealability and Finality: Resolving a Chapter 11 Dilemma, 50 Ohio St. L.J. 109 (1989).

[22] See Burchinal v. Central Washington Bank (In re Adams Apple, Inc.), 829 F.2d 1484 (9th Cir. 1987).

ticular supplier's line of goods, it is usually the beneficiary of an executory contract. Its ability to assume the contract limits the holdup power the supplier enjoys. Even if the executory contract is terminable at will outside of bankruptcy, termination without first going to court may be an exercise of control over property of the debtor within the meaning of §362(a)(3).[23] A supplier risks the sanctions that follow from violating the automatic stay if it makes such a demand. In most cases, the holdup power is not likely to loom that large. Other suppliers are usually out there who are willing to deliver for cash, and the size of the prepetition debt may be large relative to the costs of finding another supplier.

In theory, one way of limiting such tactics is to limit the trustee's power to respond to demands from prepetition creditors. A demand does no good if the trustee or the debtor in possession is disabled from succumbing to it, and some courts have found that the Bankruptcy Code forbids payments to prepetition creditors.[24] One court refused to allow the debtor to pay tort victims for surgery before the confirmation of the reorganization plan. If performed, the surgery would have likely reduced the estate's liability significantly and thus made everyone else better off.[25] It might seem that those who objected would not be acting rationally, but those challenging the payments might fear that the valuations are suspect and that the payments do not in fact make everyone better off. More troubling are those who object merely to establish their reputations as tough negotiators before bargaining over the reorganization plan begins in earnest.[26]

When suppliers of critical inputs have holdup power and are willing to use it, they are not likely to be dissuaded by such limitations on the trustee's power. Payments to creditors before confirmation of the reorganization plan do happen in Chapter 11. For example, payment of prepetition wages to workers is an ordinary event in the typical Chapter 11 reorganization of a large firm. Even if the bankruptcy judge would not authorize the payment in the face of objec-

---

[23] See, e.g., In re Elber Beerman Stores Corp., 195 Bankr. 1012 (Bankr. S.D. Ohio 1996). Once in court, the supplier may be hard put to explain why it is not willing to take cash for its goods.

[24] See, e.g., In re Timberhouse Post & Beam, Ltd., 196 Bankr. 547 (Bankr. D. Mont. 1996); In re FCX, Inc., 60 Bankr. 405 (E.D.N.C. 1986).

[25] See Official Committee of Equity Security Holders v. Mabey, 832 F.2d 299 (3d Cir. 1987).

[26] For an account of the A.H. Robins bankruptcy, see Richard B. Sobol, Bending the Law: The Story of the Dalkon Shield Bankruptcy (1991).

tion, no one may object. Some of the real-world dynamics can be intuited by imagining a trucking firm that has just filed a Chapter 11 petition. The payroll checks that were issued yesterday are going to bounce unless postpetition financing is found. From a theoretical perspective, you might think that all the payroll checks *should* bounce. The workers, after all, have only prepetition claims. They should not be paid until the end of the case. But the creditors actively participating in the bankruptcy will likely take a more practical view. If the checks bounce, the workers will not work anymore and the firm will have to close down.

Even if the refusal to work violates §362(a)(6) because it is an act to obtain payment on a prepetition claim, the Norris-LaGuardia Act prevents the bankruptcy court from issuing an injunction against the workers.[27] The workers are diverse and in many cases judgment-proof. Tracking each of them down is costly, and, in any event, the threat of monetary sanctions for violating the automatic stay will not work against those who have little to lose. Moreover, because wages are entitled to a priority under §507(a), there may be little danger that they will receive more at the outset than they would have received at the end of the process. The debtor may need to borrow money to meet the payroll, but the bank with a security interest in the firm's trucks may be willing to extend credit. The value of its collateral (the trucks) may decline if the paychecks bounce. Self-help is a time-honored remedy.

When courts are asked to approve payments to prepetition creditors, they are hard put to find a provision in the Bankruptcy Code that authorizes them to act. One possibility is to look toward §363. The trustee is allowed to spend resources to maintain the value of the firm's assets. The trustee can spend money to repair machines or buy insurance. Such expenses are entitled to priority because in theory they ultimately increase the value of the assets and hence the distribution to the general creditors. When a payment to a prepetition creditor will increase the return to general creditors, it is arguably a use of assets within the ambit of §363. Such a payment is not an ordinary course expenditure to be sure, but §363 requires in such cases only that there be notice and a hearing. One might fear that the payment, especially done at the outset of the case by the debtor in possession, might in fact not make the general creditors better off. But one might account for this by placing a heavy burden on the party

---

[27] See *Crowe & Associates v. Bricklayers & Masons Union Local No. 2*, 713 F.2d 211 (6th Cir. 1983).

proposing the payment or requiring that the payment be supported by a third party such as an examiner.

In addition to relying on §363, courts might invoke two rules developed in the era of equity receiverships.[28] The first was usually called the *six-month rule*.[29] When secured creditors chose to have a railroad placed in receivership, they typically offered to pay debts incurred in the ordinary course during the previous six months for labor and other supplies to the extent allowed by the operating income of the railroad.[30] One can think of the six-month rule as an expanded version of §547(c)(2). Ordinary course payments made to those who provided goods or services to the debtor on the eve of bankruptcy do not violate bankruptcy's norm of pro rata sharing. One can argue that paying those who provide such goods or services out of the income that their goods or services may have generated postbankruptcy does not, either. These people agreed to bear only the risk that the operating income of the firm would not be sufficient to pay them. They did not agree to become participants in the restructuring of a firm that would remain intact as a going concern. Under the old Bankruptcy Act, the six-month rule was extended on occasion to firms other than railroads.[31] It has not, however, been applied to cases other than railroads under the Bankruptcy Code.[32]

Although sometimes confused with the six-month rule, the *doctrine of necessity* (or the *necessity-of-payment rule*) is quite different.[33] The six-month rule applies to all creditors who fall within its scope. Any supplier who sells goods or services in ordinary course within six months of the reorganization can insist on payment in full, as of right, from the income the firm produces. The doctrine of necessity allows the debtor to make payments. It does not give any creditor a right to insist on payment. Moreover, it authorizes the debtor to make only those payments that are necessary to keep the business going *during* the equity receivership. In *Gregg v. Metropolitan Trust Company*, for example, Justice Oliver Wendell Holmes refused to apply the doctrine of necessity to a prepetition creditor who wanted payment for railway ties that were supplied pre-receivership and that were neces-

---

[28] Miltenberger v. Logansport, C. & S.W. Railway Co., 106 U.S. 286 (1882).

[29] See In re Boston & Maine Corp., 634 F.2d 1359 (1st Cir. 1980).

[30] See Fosdick v. Schall, 99 U.S. 235 (1878).

[31] See, e.g., Dudley v. Mealey, 147 F.2d 268 (2d Cir. 1945) (hotel).

[32] For example, the Ninth Circuit expressly declined to apply it to nonrailroad cases in B & W Enterprises v. Goodman Oil Co., 713 F.2d 534 (9th Cir. 1983).

[33] The doctrine of necessity was first set forth in Miltenberger v. Logansport, C. & S.W. Railway Co., 106 U.S. 286 (1882).

sary to the continued operation of the railroad.[34] Because the ties were delivered before the receivership began, paying this creditor in priority to others during the proceeding would not have benefited the owners of the railroad as a group.

The doctrine of necessity gives no *rights* to suppliers or others who are owed money. It merely gives the debtor the power to respond to credible threats. The doctrine of necessity can be found in §1171(b), a part of the Bankruptcy Code limited to railroads. For this reason courts are reluctant to rely on it in other cases, but there are exceptions.[35] Most recently, the bankruptcy court in Delaware applied the doctrine of necessity and allowed the debtor to pay a critical supplier.[36] Over the past decade, Delaware has increasingly become the venue of choice for large Chapter 11 reorganizations, so its decisions may take on the same importance in bankruptcy as the decisions of Delaware state courts do in corporate law outside of bankruptcy. Nevertheless, the status of the doctrine of necessity is uncertain; this uncertainty has often led courts to decide such matters without issuing written opinions, and the decisions often become moot before they can be appealed.[37]

Bankruptcy Decisionmaking

Often the issues faced by the bankruptcy court force it to decide whether resources should be committed to keep a firm going. For example, a debtor might come forward with an employee compensation program designed to keep key personnel from jumping ship. The compensation program is consistent with those of other firms that have reorganized under Chapter 11, and denying the debtor's request to put it in place might be tantamount to shutting the firm down.[38] The plan, however, would make little sense if the firm were destined to fail anyway.

The bankruptcy judge finds herself in the same position as the venture capitalist who must decide whether to inject new funding into a firm or whether to walk away from her investment. The ven-

---

[34] 197 U.S. 183, 186 (1905).

[35] See In re Ionosphere Clubs, 98 Bankr. 174 (Bankr. S.D.N.Y. 1989); In re Structurlite Plastics Corp., 86 Bankr. 922 (Bankr. S.D. Ohio 1988).

[36] In re Just for Feet, 242 Bankr. 821 (D. Del. 1999).

[37] See Russell Eisenberg & Frances Gecker, The Doctrine of Necessity and Its Parameters, 73 Marq. L. Rev. 1 (1989).

[38] See Dai-Ichi Kangyo Bank v. Montgomery Ward Holding Corp., 242 Bankr. 147 (D. Del. 1999).

ture capitalist, however, has not only expertise in the industry but also intimate knowledge of the firm. The bankruptcy judge has no such knowledge. Indeed, she is not called on to act until a disagreement arises among the players.

To make this decision effectively, the bankruptcy judge often creates discrete milestones that she then uses to assess the firm's future. One of the best bits of evidence that a firm has a viable future is the presence of third parties willing to buy it. Bankruptcy judges are making increasing use of this objective measure, and as a result the debtor in possession is essentially charged with searching for someone to buy the firm. An illustration of such a case is Iridium.

Iridium was the first full-service wireless global communications network. After more than a decade of planning, it began operations in late 1997. As a user you could call people any time you wanted no matter where you were or where they were. The system worked through a constellation of sixty-six satellites in low-earth orbit. The harbinger of a new era in telecommunications, a spare Iridium satellite joined the Wright Brothers 1903 *Flyer*, *Apollo* 13, and the *Spirit of St. Louis* at the Smithsonian Institution. In early 1999 the network was going strong, and Iridium raised an additional quarter of billion dollars in equity funding.

Six months later, however, Iridium filed for Chapter 11. Most of Iridium's bankruptcy proceeding has been consumed with the search for a buyer of the entire firm. None appeared at the outset of the case. Less than a year after the filing of the petition, the bankruptcy judge decided to give up. The proliferation of cell phones and other changes in technology prevented Iridium from even meeting its operating costs. The absence of buyers was strong evidence this would not change. The judge ordered Iridium to turn off its network, sell its ground-based assets, and command each of its satellites to fire their thrusters and burn up in the earth's atmosphere. In many bankruptcy courts, the days when debtors could stall indefinitely until their fortunes turned are over, if they ever existed at all.

Section 363 authorizes the trustee or the debtor in possession to engage in transactions outside the ordinary course of business, provided creditors are given notice and a hearing. The nonbankruptcy principles likely to provide the best guidance here are those that operate when a corporation is "in play" outside of bankruptcy.[39] Under the *Revlon* doctrine, once a takeover becomes inevitable, the board of

[39] See Josef S. Athanas, Using Bankruptcy Law to Implement or Combat Hostile Takeovers of Targets in Chapter 11, 55 Business Lawyer 593 (2000).

directors "has a duty to maximize the company's value at a sale." They become "auctioneers" with a duty to get the best price.[40]

In *Committee of Equity Security Holders v. Lionel Corporation*, the Second Circuit set out a standard for the sale of a major asset under §363.[41] One of Lionel's most important assets was its 82 percent ownership interest in Dale Electronics, a healthy, publicly traded firm. The debtor in possession and the creditors committee wanted to sell the stock immediately under §363. The committee of equity-holders wanted the sale to wait. The Second Circuit found that the sale could go forward in the face of an objection only if a "good business reason" justified the sale.[42] The Second Circuit stopped the sale of Lionel's equity interest in Dale because the only justification that the debtor in possession offered was that the creditors committee wanted the sale: "Such is insufficient as a matter of fact because it is not a sound business reason and insufficient as a matter of law because it ignores the equity interest required to be weighed and considered under Chapter 11."[43] The general standard put forth in *Lionel* has generated widespread approval.[44]

Bankruptcy judges are typically not well equipped to assess whether any particular sale objectively leads to a fair price. If sufficient doubt exists, the bankruptcy judge can insist that the sale take place as part of a formal reorganization plan with its procedural protections. In other instances, the bankruptcy judge will rely on objective, process-oriented measures. If a firm has been extensively shopped and bids have been solicited from an array of different buyers, the bankruptcy judge is likely to have more confidence in the sale than if the sale leaves the firm in the hands of insiders.

One of the most difficult issues arises when the debtor in possession seeks court approval of a deal that has short-term costs but potential long-term benefits. A frequently litigated question of this nature concerns breakup fees. No buyer wants to become a "stalking horse," doing the due diligence and satisfying itself that the firm is worth keeping intact as a going concern only to watch another firm, one that could enjoy a free ride on its research, make a slightly higher bid and walk away with the company. Outside of bankruptcy, the

[40] Revlon, Inc. v. MacAndrews & Forbes Holdings, 506 A.2d 173, 182 (Del. 1986).

[41] 722 F.2d 1063 (2d Cir. 1983).

[42] Id. at 1071.

[43] Id.

[44] See, e.g., Stephens Industries v. McClung, 789 F.2d 386 (6th Cir. 1986); In re Abbotts Dairies, 788 F.2d 143 (3d Cir. 1986).

first bidder commonly insists on being paid a fixed amount if the firm is ultimately sold to someone else. This breakup fee can have a chilling effect on the bidding. Alternatively, it might be a useful device to entice someone to making a solid bid that generates additional bids. Many bankruptcy courts have not been as deferential to breakup fees as courts outside of bankruptcy.[45] Nevertheless, courts have been willing to approve them when their purpose and effect was to increase the sale price.[46] The bankruptcy judge should not be in the business of second-guessing market mechanisms, but he must be vigilant in ensuring that that they are working. In small markets, it is often not easy to tell the difference. Potential buyers may be insiders. Potential buyers may acquire major positions in a firm's debt or equity to ensure themselves a place at the bargaining table. The mechanism that ignites bidding in one case can smother it in another. Here, as elsewhere, the court is charged with a high-wire act.

[45] See, e.g., Calpine Corp. v. O'Brien Environmental Energy, 181 F.3d 527, 535 (3d Cir. 1999). For the argument that bankruptcy procedures make breakup fees unnecessary, see Bruce A. Markell, The Case Against Break-up Fees in Bankruptcy, 66 Am. Bankr. L.J. 349 (1992).

[46] Official Committee of Subordinated Bondholders v. Integrated Resources, 147 Bankr. 650 (S.D.N.Y. 1992).

Chapter Eleven

Forming the Plan of Reorganization

The Opt-Out Problem

The reorganization of a corporation is, at its heart, a question of corporate governance. By accident of history, however, it is controlled by federal rather than state law. Most provisions of corporate law operate by default, so investors can craft special provisions to their liking. Chapter 11 is strikingly different. As a general rule, a debtor cannot waive the right to file for bankruptcy. This rule has been applied not only to individual debtors, for whom such a waiver would eliminate the fresh start, but also to corporate debtors, whose individual owners are protected by limited liability under state corporate law and are not obligated to pay the debts of the corporation.[1]

Courts have permitted the functional equivalent of the bankruptcy waiver for corporate debtors in some circumstances. A firm can transfer account receivables—obligations that customers owe the firm—to a special purpose vehicle (SPV). Providers of capital to the firm then purchase interests in the vehicle. The firm might retain a residual interest in the SPV and perform the vehicle's ministerial functions. But the firm no longer holds a significant economic interest in the receivables. If the firm later entered bankruptcy, a court might be unlikely to subject the SPV's assets to the firm's bankruptcy, or permit a voluntary petition by the SPV, in violation of an agreement to keep the SPV independent of the firm and out of bankruptcy. The SPV itself might not even be eligible for bankruptcy if, for example, it was a trust.

Whatever the successes of SPVs, one should be wary of drawing broad lessons from them. An SPV is, in essence, merely a vehicle that allows the sale of receivables. The SPV has no business operation and no employees. Courts are considerably more skeptical when

---

[1] See United States v. Royal Business Funds Corp., 724 F.2d 12 (2d Cir. 1983) (stating, in dicta, that such waivers "generally" were not enforceable, while holding, in the case before it, that a corporation had effectively waived its right to file bankruptcy by stipulating that the Small Business Administration would be its receiver).

creditors try to change an operating firm into a "bankruptcy remote vehicle."[2] Sometimes, however, courts are sympathetic to more narrow limitations, especially when they are part of a nonbankruptcy workout.[3] During a workout, for example, the debtor may accede to a drop-dead clause, in which it promises not to contest a creditor's motion to lift the automatic stay in the event of a bankruptcy filing.

One should not assume from this discussion, however, that sophisticated investors can do little to avoid the risk of finding themselves in Chapter 11. Investors are often free, in the case of a start-up firm, to fashion a capital structure that contains no debt, but rather multiple tiers of equity. Through such structures, they can enjoy the priority of debt and, through the ability to convert the shares into common stock, the higher potential returns of equity as well. Regardless of whether they succeed or fail, many high-tech start-ups will never have a significant amount of debt in their capital structures.

Overview of the Reorganization Process

We now turn to the plan of reorganization and the reorganization process. The ideal sequence as envisioned by the drafters is as follows. A corporation that is unable to make its loan payments, but is worth keeping intact, files a Chapter 11 petition. The old managers continue to run the business. They may make some non–ordinary course decisions after notice and a hearing, but they mostly stick to business as usual. The rest of the world continues to do business with the corporation the same way as before. Shortly after the petition is filed, the United States Trustee appoints a committee of creditors. This committee usually consists of the creditors with the seven largest unsecured claims who are willing to serve or the creditors who formed the committee that tried to do the nonbankruptcy workout. This committee may hire professionals to look into the debtor's affairs, and it provides a vehicle for negotiations between the debtor and the creditors.

While the debtor's business continues, the debtor tries to come up with a reorganization plan. Even when one or more groups of claimholders oppose a plan, the debtor may still be able to confirm it if the plan meets, in addition to all the usual tests, the special ones set out in §1129(b). The process of obtaining confirmation of a plan over the objection of a class is called *cramdown*. But cramdown requires

---

[2] See, e.g., In re Kingston Square Associates, 214 Bankr. 713 (Bankr. S.D.N.Y. 1997).

[3] See In re Colonial Ford, 24 Bankr. 1014 (Bankr. D. Utah 1982).

outside valuations, and these are expensive and unreliable. Ideally you want a plan each class of claimholders can live with. Even if you could cram down a plan on the general creditors, you would prefer not to have to do so. General creditors typically will insist on receiving something. They will make a calculation of what they would receive in the event of liquidation. If those pickings are small enough, they may be willing to accept a small amount. The firm may be in a high-tech industry, and much of its value may lie in projects that only the shareholder-manager knows how to finish. The representatives of the general creditors, however, must worry about their reputations in future negotiations with different debtors but the same lawyers. At some point they will draw a line. Many an old-time bankruptcy veteran can recall (now fondly) a particular creditor's lawyer in the garment trade who always stood on principle—and his principle was 50 cents on the dollar.

The Bankruptcy Code assumes that the debtor will propose a reorganization plan within 120 days of filing the Chapter 11 petition. During this period, the right to propose a reorganization plan belongs exclusively to the debtor. The plan divides the claims of the creditors into various classes and proposes a treatment for each class. After the debtor files the plan, the debtor must try to get the plan accepted. The debtor must write a *disclosure statement* and persuade the court to approve it. The purpose of the disclosure statement is to explain the plan to those who must vote on it. Once the disclosure statement is approved, the debtor may begin seeking acceptance of the plan from the various classes. The debtor may obtain approval in one of two ways. First, those whose claims are in a given class can approve the plan. A majority of the creditors holding claims in the class who vote must vote in favor of the plan, and their claims must have a value equal to at least two-thirds of the value of the claims of those who are voting. In the case of equity interests, the debtor simply needs two-thirds of the shares being voted. This is consistent with state corporate law in that the number of shareholders does not matter, just the number of shares. Second, the debtor can receive constructive approval from a class if that class is *unimpaired* within the meaning of §1124. Generally speaking, a class is unimpaired if it consists only of claims that the plan does not restructure. A creditor's claim, for example, is unimpaired if the original terms of the loan are reinstated (and all defaults are cured).

After the votes are received, the debtor can ask the court to approve the reorganization plan. The court must satisfy itself that the plan meets all the requirements of Chapter 11. Many are spelled out in

§1129(a). The plan must, for example, pay off administrative expense claims in cash. §1129(a)(9)(A). This requirement may not be burdensome for a large firm that has ready access to capital markets, and practices have emerged that make this requirement less rigid than it might first appear even for those that lack such access. Administrative creditors are free to scale back or modify their claims in a side deal. Their willingness to do so depends on their past and future relationship with the debtor. For example, among the largest administrative claims may be payments owed to debtor's counsel, and these are often structured initially with a schedule over time.

Nevertheless, §1129(a)(9)(A) sets a baseline that matters, particularly for smaller firms. The success of some Chapter 11 reorganizations depends on the debtor's ability to bring a preference or fraudulent conveyance action. Failing that, the only source of new cash may be the old equityholder. For such a firm, a reorganization may be possible only if the old equityholder has at least enough cash to pay administrative expenses. The longer the reorganization lasts, the greater this amount will be and the harder it will be for the debtor to confirm a reorganization plan, at least without extraordinarily patient accountants and lawyers. Professional fees for even a closely held firm in Chapter 11 routinely run into hundreds of thousands of dollars.

Similarly, §1129(a)(9)(B) requires that a plan provide cash for specified prebankruptcy claims afforded high priority by §507(a)(3)–(7). These include, for example, specified obligations to employees and employee benefit plans. Immediate full payment is required for such claims if the class of claims has not accepted the plan. If the class has accepted the plan, an individual creditor cannot demand immediate payment, but may insist on full payment over time, including appropriate interest. This is the case even if the claim is not of a high enough priority to have warranted payment in full under Chapter 7. Other obligations to employees, retiree benefits as opposed to contributions, are also given special treatment. Section 1129(a)(13) requires that the plan provide for the continued full payment of such obligations.

Perhaps the most important of these requirements is the condition stated in §1129(a)(9)(c) that a plan provide for the deferred cash payment of those taxes afforded priority by §507(a)(8), including income, excise, and withholding taxes. These cash payments must be made within a six-year period and must have a value, as of the date of the plan, equal to the amount of taxes owing, whether or not the claim would have been paid in full under Chapter 7. These provisions are clear and give rise to few reported decisions. Nevertheless, tax claims may dominate the landscape of many debtor firms. A debtor in bankruptcy may not have been earning enough before bankruptcy to become liable for significant corporate income tax, but even an unprofitable firm owes or must withhold taxes related to the firm's role as an employer. A firm often fails to meet these obligations when it encounters trouble, notwithstanding the risk of criminal liability to the firm's managers. (Tax laws treat the failure to turn over taxes withheld from employees' paychecks much more seriously than a failure to pay the firm's own taxes.) Negotiations over how these tax obligations will be paid are often the primary focus of Chapter 11 when the debtor is a small, family-run business.

Another requirement that is not often litigated but can affect the plan is in §1129(a)(10). Even if a plan meets the absolute priority rule, a court cannot confirm it unless at least one class of impaired claims approves the plan. A Chapter 11 plan is supposed to be a product of negotiations among the interested parties. To show that there were negotiations and at least some give and take, you must gain the approval of one class that has the right to reject. Although there is rarely a dispute about whether a class has accepted, there has been a great deal of litigation over whether the initial classification of claims was manipulated to create one class that would accept the plan. The greater the debtor's ability to divide claims into many separate classes, the more likely it is that one class will vote in favor of the plan.

A number of requirements do generate substantial litigation. Section 1129(b) embodies the substantive component of the absolute priority rule. When a class (as opposed to a minority within a class) dissents and a class junior to it is receiving something under the plan, the court must ask whether the dissenting class is being paid in full. As reviewed below, determining whether a plan satisfies §1129(b) requires a valuation that uses marketplace benchmarks. By contrast, courts tend to use a less rigorous method when an objection is brought by an individual creditor. Under §1129(a)(7) the court must be satisfied that each individual creditor either consents to the plan or is getting as much as it would have received in a Chapter 7 liquidation. This is commonly called the *best-interests-of-creditors test*. When a firm can be sold as a going concern, the value that might be realizable in Chapter 7 may be the same as the value of the firm reorganized in Chapter 11. The less rigorous valuation methods, however, make §1129(a)(7) much easier to meet than §1129(b).

There is one other important requirement that is frequently the focus of litigation. The court must be satisfied that the firm will not end up in a reorganization again. §1129(a)(11). This is commonly called the *feasibility test*. It is subjective, but the court can give it some hard edges by comparing the capital structure of the reorganized firm with other firms in the same industry. A reorganization plan that leaves a firm too highly leveraged relative to other firms in the same industry may not be feasible within the meaning of the Bankruptcy Code.

If the court confirms the plan, the plan is carried out according to its terms. Under §1141, confirmation of the plan discharges *all* debts (that arose prior to confirmation) except for (and insofar as) those debts that are dealt with in the plan. On its face, Chapter 11 permits the discharge of all corporate debts. Due process, however, mandates a minimum level of notice, and this ultimately places a check on the scope of the bankruptcy discharge in Chapter 11.[4] The discharge does not abrogate any obligations that arise after the plan is confirmed. Recall, for example, the debtor that owns property on which it (or someone else) had dumped toxic wastes before the filing of the bankruptcy petition. The environmental claims that arose before confirmation are discharged, but the discharge of these claims is not sufficient to insulate the debtor from cleanup obligations if it remains the owner of the property and incurs obligations in that capacity. Such a debtor remains liable for environmental cleanup obligations that arise by virtue of postbankruptcy ownership in the same way that someone to whom the debtor sold the property would be liable.[5]

In sum, for the prototypical Chapter 11 case, the old claims against the firm disappear with the discharge and the new obligations of the firm take their place. The firm sails off happily into the future. A financial reorganization of the firm takes place in such a way that the firm survives as a going concern. This scenario is common with respect to large firms that file for Chapter 11. Most of these emerge from bankruptcy and continue as going concerns. While they involve a substantial portion of the assets that are reorganized in Chapter 11 and most of the jobs, these cases are but a small minority of the Chapter 11 cases filed each year. More than half of the firms that file for Chapter 11 reorganization have assets of less than $500,000 and two-thirds have less than $1 million. Of these, most never leave Chapter 11

---

[4] See Reliable Electric Co. v. Olson Construction Co., 726 F.2d 620 (10th Cir. 1984).

[5] See In re CMC Heartland Partners, 966 F.2d 1143 (7th Cir. 1992).

as going concerns. Hence, it is important not to equate the course of an abstract case through Chapter 11 as we have sketched out above with the day-to-day realities of Chapter 11 in practice.

Chapter 11 is often the forum of choice for sorting out the problems of a failed business that has little value as a going concern. State law may not provide a procedure that allows a firm to wind up its affairs in an orderly way. The debtor and the relevant creditors may both want the flexibility that Chapter 11 offers. If they are content to remain there, a bankruptcy judge is unlikely to force them out—even if ultimate reorganization is unlikely. Firms that enter Chapter 11 are not necessarily even in serious *unresolved* financial trouble. Parties may use Chapter 11 as a way of facilitating a deal that has already been agreed on ahead of time by almost all involved. (Such cases are called *prepackaged bankruptcies*, or *prepacks*.)

All too commonly, however, a firm will be in Chapter 11 only after dealings with creditors turned sour outside of bankruptcy. Bankruptcy filings typically happen too late rather than too soon. The firm is already in desperate straits, and the inability to cut a deal outside of bankruptcy does not bode well for the bargaining process inside of bankruptcy. Proponents of the reorganization plan often find it impossible to overcome an impasse in bargaining. Even where proponents can gain the consent of a single impaired class as required by §1129(a)(10), a court may be skeptical of a plan that requires a cramdown against other impaired classes. As we shall see, the Supreme Court has recently required bankruptcy judges to become even tougher in testing valuations when a debtor seeks to cram down a plan and retain an equity interest in exchange for new cash.

In too many cases, a Chapter 11 filing is simply a play for time. The managers or the debtor's shareholders hope for a miraculous reversal of fortune. By their nature, however, miracles are rare. Section 1112(b) authorizes the bankruptcy judge to dismiss a bankruptcy proceeding for want of good faith. "The clearest case of bad faith is where the debtor enters Chapter 11 knowing that there is no chance to reorganize his business and hoping merely to stave off the evil day when the creditors take control of his property."[6] Still, hope springs eternal and debtors frequently file doomed petitions, after which resources are wasted (mostly to the detriment of creditors) until the evil day finally arrives.

Bankruptcy judges are growing less tolerant of Chapter 11 cases that seem to be headed nowhere. They are more reluctant to grant

[6] In re James Wilson Associates, 965 F.2d 160, 170 (7th Cir. 1992).

routine extensions of the exclusivity period and more willing to convert a Chapter II case to Chapter 7 or to dismiss it entirely. Bankruptcy judges are especially likely to take such action (assuming some creditor asks for it) if the debtor cannot generate revenues sufficient to meet operating expenses or if it fails to pay postpetition taxes or allows its insurance policies to lapse. In many cases, however, the firm languishes in bankruptcy because there is no active creditors committee and no single creditor with enough at stake to move the case forward. Some bankruptcy judges have established "fast-tracking" procedures for small cases.

For its part, Congress has taken a number of steps to reshape Chapter II in recent years. One area in which Congress has taken action concerns the single-asset real estate case. In 1994 Congress added §362(d)(3) and corresponding definitions in §101. If a court denies relief from the stay to a creditor with a security interest in single-asset real estate, the debtor must expedite the reorganization or make monthly payments. Being impatient in these situations may make sense. In a single-asset real estate case, a management company usually runs the day-to-day operations. The general partner might run the management company, but the debtor itself has no employees to speak of. No jobs are at issue. There is no going concern. The only creditor of any consequence is a bank that holds a nonrecourse mortgage on the land. The collective action problem that drives bankruptcy policy does not exist. The only problem is the inability of the lender and the partners to reach a deal.

Congress has also taken some steps to recognize formally the fast-tracking procedures that bankruptcy judges had instituted on their own for small cases. Amendments to §105 allowed bankruptcy judges to call status conferences on their own motion and otherwise keep the case moving. The 1994 amendments to the Bankruptcy Code also permit a qualified small business debtor to elect an expedited reorganization process. This process eliminates the requirement of a creditors committee, shortens the exclusivity period, and relaxes disclosure and solicitation requirements. See §§1121(e) and §1125(f). These provisions operate only when the debtor elects to be put on a fast track; they do little to advance the case when the debtor wants Chapter II merely to play for time.

To address perceived shortcomings of the bankruptcy process, particularly for small firms, Congress is actively considering additional reforms that would expedite the treatment of small Chapter II debtors. The proponents of these reforms argue that the costs of a longer Chapter II process outweigh the benefits of giving debtors additional time. The affairs of a firm that has only a few hundred thousand dollars in debt are sufficiently straightforward, this reasoning goes, that if the firm cannot reorganize within a short time, it is unlikely ever to do so.

Not all recent developments involve small firms. At the same time that bankruptcy judges and Congress have reshaped Chapter 11, practitioners who specialize in large cases have taken increasing advantage of bankruptcy's venue rules and have filed their cases in Delaware when the debtor is a Delaware corporation. (Most publicly traded firms are Delaware corporations.) Like their state court counterparts, Delaware's bankruptcy judges have made themselves an attractive forum for debtors in large cases. It is commonly said that fee awards are contested less often in a bankruptcy court in Delaware. Moreover, the court's handling of the case, especially its willingness to approve debtor-in-possession financing, is more predictable. Most large firms file their Chapter 11 petitions in Delaware, but few small businesses can.

Taken together, these developments suggest two distinct trajectories for large and small firms in Chapter 11. While the substantive rules of Chapter 11 will be largely identical for both, the process itself will be altogether different. Large firms will go forward with elaborate procedures at a leisurely pace in the predictable hands of a bankruptcy judge in Delaware. Small firms, lacking such uniform treatment, will experience a faster and less predictable course through bankruptcy. Their fate will depend largely on the norms of each jurisdiction and the abilities of each bankruptcy judge.

As we have noted before, the procedures of Chapter 11 are available to individual debtors as well. Consider an individual debtor who runs a business as a sole proprietor and files for Chapter 11. The individual might be a lawyer or a doctor. She does not do business in corporate form, and her personal finances have become intertwined with those of her practice. If no trustee is appointed, it is the individual debtor, rather than the debtor in possession, who runs the business and proposes a plan for a new set of obligations to replace the old. The rules for confirmation are the same. Unlike the corporate debtor, however, the individual maintains an identity separate from the productive assets she owns. Thus, an individual debtor under Chapter 11 commits only that future income promised by the plan. Through discharge, she retains the rest of her human capital and achieves a fresh start as she would in Chapter 7. Correspondingly, as in Chapter 7, there are exceptions to discharge for certain obligations, such as child support and some taxes.

Classification

A plan of reorganization must sort the claims of the various creditors and the interests of the various equityholders into different classes. In the language of the Bankruptcy Code, creditors have claims and equityholders have interests. All claims or interests in a class must be treated the same unless the holder of a claim agrees to less favorable treatment. See §1123(a)(4). A plan cannot give one claim in a class ten cents on the dollar and another five cents on the dollar. Nor can it provide that some claims in a class be paid in cash and others with long-term promissory notes.

The Bankruptcy Code does not set out in detail how much freedom the debtor or any other plan proponent enjoys in the way in which claims are sorted into different classes. Section 1122(a) provides that only substantially similar claims or interests can occupy a single class. This provision requires at least that claims with different legal rights be classified separately. For this reason, each secured claim is typically in a class by itself. Two claims are not substantially similar if they are secured by different collateral, for example, nor are they substantially similar when they are secured by the same collateral if one claim enjoys priority over the other. Other determinations are harder to make. Consider, on one hand, a deficiency claim held by a secured creditor for the difference between the amount it is owed and the value of its collateral and, on the other hand, the claim of a trade creditor who looks forward to continuing business with the reorganized debtor. When these two claims are put in one class, the ability of one of them to invoke the absolute priority may turn on whether the other wants to as well.

The bankruptcy judge must decide whether a plan proponent can put different claims in the same class, must put them in separate classes, or can enjoy the freedom to do either. Section 1122(a) tells us that we can put together substantially similar claims "except as provided by subsection (b)." The latter subsection allows a plan to designate a separate class of unsecured claims below a plan-specified threshold if necessary for administrative convenience. The "except as provided subsection (b)" language in §1122(a), therefore, suggests that except for administrative convenience claims, substantially similar claims *must* be put into the same class. One can go on to argue that unsecured claims are, by their nature, substantially similar because their legal attributes under nonbankruptcy law are identical.[7]

---

[7] See Granada Wines, Inc. v. New England Teamsters & Trucking Industry Pension Fund, 748 F.2d 42, 46 (1st Cir. 1984).

Another way to read §1122(a) starts with the observation that substantially similar claims *may* be put in the same class but are not *required* to be.[8] But even then we still need to decide whether the claims are indeed substantially similar. Returning to our example of creditors with trade and deficiency claims, one could argue that the claims are substantially similar because both are unsecured claims and neither enjoys priority over the other. But one can also adopt a different view. Consider a real estate case involving a nonrecourse mortgage. If the debtor defaults outside of bankruptcy, the creditor can look only to the real property to satisfy the obligation. Even if the property proves to be worth much less than the amount of the loan, the creditor cannot go against the debtor's other assets for the deficiency. A different rule applies to the debtor in bankruptcy. As we discuss in greater detail below, §1111(b)(1) of the Bankruptcy Code permits an undersecured creditor with a nonrecourse loan to treat the loan as if it were recourse in Chapter 11 (but not in Chapter 7). Thus, in Chapter 11 a creditor holds both a secured claim equal to the value of the collateral and an unsecured claim for the balance of its loan. One can argue that the legal rights of this real estate lender's unsecured claim are not identical to those of a trade creditor. The real estate lender's unsecured claim is worthless in Chapter 7 and hence it receives no protection from the best-interests test, while the trade creditor does. The Seventh Circuit found that this and other differences kept the two from being substantially similar and hence mandated that they be placed in separate classes.[9] Other courts, however, have found that these differences are not sufficient to mandate putting such claims in separate classes.

If those whose claims are in the same class have differing interests, one cannot be sure that the majority will in fact make a decision that is in the best interests of the group. The possibility of manipulation if unsecured claims could be placed in a class with secured claims is obvious. Secured creditors should be paid in full and general creditors only a few cents on the dollar. It makes no sense for those holding one kind of claim to be able to speak on behalf of those holding another. If they were classified together, dissent from one group or the other is likely to be suppressed. In the typical bankruptcy, their interests are

[8] See, e.g., Barakat v. Life Insurance Co. of Virginia, 99 F.3d 1520 (9th Cir. 1996); Boston Post Road Ltd. Partnership v. FDIC, 21 F.3d 477 (2d Cir. 1994); Phoenix Mutual Life Insurance Co. v. Greystone III Joint Venture, 995 F.2d 1274 (5th Cir. 1991). For a useful summary of the case law, see In re Dow Corning Corp., 244 Bankr. 634 (Bankr. E.D. Mich. 1999).

[9] See In re Woodbrook Associates, 19 F.3d 312 (7th Cir. 1994).

adverse to each other. One can argue that the claim of a creditor who is also a shareholder should not be in the same class as the claim of someone who is simply a creditor. A shareholder-creditor's approval of the plan does not accurately reflect what is in the interest of creditors who are not shareholders.

Consider the question whether the claims of trade creditors can be put in the same class as the claim of a bank that has made an unsecured loan to a debtor. The bank may be anxious to cut its losses and may intend to have no future dealings with the debtor. By contrast, the trade creditors may look forward to future dealings. They have much more to gain from a successful reorganization and may be more inclined to vote in favor of a plan that gives creditors less and leaves the firm better capitalized. The bank and the trade creditors have interests that differ radically, even though their legal rights—those of unsecured creditors—are the same. There are, however, no ready benchmarks by which to judge whether a creditor is *sufficiently* different to justify its claim being put in a separate class. It may be that the bank is not different enough from the trade creditors. The usual presumption is that creditors holding claims that have the same legal status should be placed in the same class. The claims of the trade creditors and the bank would ordinarily be grouped together.

Creating two or more classes increases the chance that the plan will have to meet the absolute priority rule. Only if a class dissents must a plan satisfy the absolute priority rule in order to be confirmed. Therefore, the smaller each class, the larger the role each dissenting creditor has. Forcing the debtor to put creditors into separate classes increases the chance that dissenters will be able to keep their class from approving a plan. In the face of the rejection of this class of creditors, the debtor has to show that, as to them, the absolute priority rule is satisfied. But this effect can be offset, as we have already noted. A court can confirm a plan only if one class of impaired claims approves the plan. Just as increasing the number of classes increases the chance that one of them will dissent, it may also increase the chance that one of them will approve.

Many of the classification cases arise when the debtor's only asset is a single parcel of real estate. In these cases, the court will ask whether the separate classification has been undertaken solely for the purpose of creating an impaired class that will vote in favor of the plan. As the court put it in *Greystone*, there is "one clear rule that emerges from the otherwise muddled caselaw on §1122 claims classification: thou shalt not classify similar claims differently in order to gerrymander an affirmative vote on a reorganization plan."[10] Separate classification is easier to justify outside of the single-asset real estate case.[11]

Section 1123(a)(4) provides that everyone in the same class be treated the same. The person proposing the plan cannot escape the absolute priority rule by being generous to a bare majority that holds two-thirds of the claims and giving short shrift to the claims of the rest. Similarly, the "unfair discrimination" component of the absolute priority rule in §1129(b) protects creditors from the temptation the debtor may have to put creditors into different classes and treat some more favorably than the others. A plan cannot be confirmed if an objecting class can point to another class containing the same legal claims that the plan treats more favorably. The protections of §1129(b), however, may not go far enough toward ensuring that creditors put in different classes are treated equally. A debtor may be able to put creditors into separate classes and provide for complex payout schemes that are difficult to value. (One class might get one type of preferred stock and another might receive a convertible debenture.) The debtor might assert that creditors in each class received rights that gave them the equivalent of ten cents on the dollar for their claims, and disproving this assertion can be hard. Forcing creditors into the same class wherever possible (and hence forcing the same kind of payout to each under §1123(a)(4)) makes this problem disappear.

Voting on the Plan of Reorganization

Next we look at the process of plan confirmation. After a plan is drafted, its proponents must prepare a disclosure statement for distribution to eligible holders of claims and interests. §1125. The disclosure statement resembles a securities prospectus. Section 1125(b) provides that proponents may not solicit acceptances until a court determines, after notice and a hearing, that the disclosure statement contains adequate information.

---

[10] Phoenix Mutual Life Insurance Co. v. Greystone III Joint Venture, 995 F.2d 1274, 1279 (5th Cir. 1991); Boston Post Road Ltd. Partnership v. FDIC, 21 F.3d 477 (2d Cir. 1994).

[11] See, e.g., In re Jersey City Medical Center, 817 F.2d 1055 (3d Cir. 1987) (separating claims of physicians, medical malpractice victims, employee benefit plan participants, and trade creditors); Teamsters National Freight Industry Negotiating Committee v. U.S. Truck Co., 800 F.2d 581 (6th Cir. 1986) (separating claims of collective bargaining unit members).

This burden is lessened somewhat if the debtor elects to be treated as a small business under §1121(e). The debtor may obtain conditional approval of a disclosure statement, solicit acceptances, and combine the hearing on the disclosure statement with a hearing on confirmation of the plan. See §1125(f). Even for debtors that have not formally elected to be treated as small businesses, a number of bankruptcy judges have adopted a similar practice in straightforward cases, such as those involving plans that call for liquidating the assets and distributing the proceeds to the creditors. Moreover, bankruptcy judges can expedite the process informally through their power to hold status conferences under §105(d). These most often prove useful when the United States Trustee takes an active role in small cases and is able to flag problems for the bankruptcy judge. These procedures are effective when everyone is working cooperatively. In a contested or complex case, efforts to expedite matters and combine procedures can backfire.

The hearing on the disclosure statement replaces the scrutiny that the securities laws require outside of bankruptcy. See §1145. This hearing is an important event in the life of the reorganization provides an opportunity to resolve many issues. These include whether exclusivity should be lifted, allowing a creditor to propose its own plan. The information in the disclosure statement itself, however, may not be as useful as one might expect. Section 1125(b) explicitly states that "[t]he court may approve a disclosure statement without a valuation of the debtor or an appraisal of the debtor's assets." A creditor that has to vote on a plan should want to know at least whether it is being treated better than it would be under a liquidation. That seems to require some sort of valuation. In addition, if one is receiving stock, it may not be possible to know the value of what one is receiving under a plan without taking account of how much the debtor's assets are worth. To ensure that the rights of creditors are protected, the bankruptcy court may insist that the plan itself operate in such a way to minimize valuation issues. Senior creditors, for example, do not have to fear undercompensation if the participation of those junior to them takes the form of an option to buy them out for the amount of their claim.[12]

The requirement that the court approve a disclosure statement before the proponents of a plan may solicit acceptances is significant when a creditor has an alternative plan of reorganization that it will

[12] See Lucian Arye Bebchuk, A New Approach to Corporate Reorganizations, 101 Harv. L. Rev. 775 (1988).

put forward if the debtor's plan is rejected and the exclusivity period is terminated. This creditor may want to talk with other creditors about its plan in the course of trying to persuade them to vote against the debtor's plan. The Third Circuit has allowed creditors to talk about their own plans under these conditions without obtaining court approval of a disclosure statement under §1125(b), and a number of courts have followed its lead.[13] Other courts, however, limit creditors to offering their views of the proposed plan of reorganization. When the debtor's case is in such a court, creditors are not permitted to present alternative plans of reorganization, and if they do so anyway they risk having their claims subordinated.[14]

Sections 1124 and 1126(f) take the right to vote away from classes of claims or interests when they are not being compromised in the reorganization. To use the language of the Bankruptcy Code, such claims are not "impaired." If a class of claims receives the same set of rights in the reorganization that it had before the reorganization, those who hold such claims have nothing to complain about. §1124(1). A loan is unimpaired if the debtor is willing to continue to make the same payments and accept the same terms. A loan may also be deemed unimpaired under §1124 even if the loan is in default. Section 1124 confronts a problem we encountered before in the context of executory contracts. Just as a debtor may breach an executory contract on the eve of bankruptcy only because it has too little incentive to watch out for the interests of others, a debtor may also allow a favorable loan to go into default. Like §365, §1124 overcomes this problem by allowing past defaults to be cured and the original loan reinstated. Just as the trustee can keep an executory contract in place by curing defaults and assuming its obligations, the trustee can reinstate a loan. The principal difference is that this power to assume a loan that is in default exists only when the firm is being reorganized in Chapter 11, while an executory contract can be assumed in Chapter 7 as well.

Making a creditor unimpaired is one way of avoiding a cramdown. The trustee (or, more likely, the debtor in possession) will favor reinstatement when it allows the firm to enjoy the benefits of a below-market loan from a fully secured creditor. Assume a bank has lent $1 million on a long-term basis at an interest rate that is now substantially below the market rate. The debtor, however, is now in default.

---

[13] Century Glove, Inc. v. First American Bank, 860 F.2d 94 (3d Cir. 1988). But see In re Apex Oil Co., 111 Bankr. 245 (Bankr. E.D. Mo. 1990).

[14] See In re Clamp-All Corp., 233 Bankr. 198 (Bankr. D. Mass. 1999). For a case in which a creditor is held in contempt, fined, and assessed fees, see Colorado Mountain Express v. Aspen Limousine Service, 198 Bankr. 341 (D. Colo. 1996).

Unless the debtor takes advantage of §1124, the default accelerates the loan and makes the entire $1 million in principal due and owing. Under §502, the bank has a claim for $1 million. The best-interests-of-creditors test would entitle the bank to a bundle of rights with a present value of $1 million. Section 1124(2), however, allows the bank's claim to be "de-accelerated." The terms of its contract are reinstated, and the bank is deemed unimpaired. The bank is deemed to have accepted the plan, and hence the bank cannot invoke the best-interests-of-creditors test, let alone the absolute priority rule, even though the present value of the stream of payments the bank will now get is significantly less than $1 million. As in this example, continuing a below-market loan makes the most sense when the loan is oversecured. The oversecured creditor is entitled to interest under §506(b) and therefore will be paid in full in any event. There is no cost associated with taking advantage of the loan's favorable terms.

As noted, creditors with unimpaired claims are deemed to have accepted the plan, and no solicitation of them is required. §1126(f). The reorganization plan is not affecting these creditors, thus their approval of the plan is irrelevant. By similar reasoning, a class that receives nothing under the plan is deemed to have rejected it. §1126(g). There is no reason to ask whether the plan gives them enough. (Rejection, of course, brings the absolute priority rule into play.)

For classes that do vote, approval is determined by §1126. That provision requires positive votes by those who hold two-thirds in amount and a majority by number of the allowed claims duly voted in a class. In the case of equity interests, actual approval requires positive votes by those who hold two-thirds in amount of the shares duly voted. Whether a claim or interest is duly voted depends on §1126(e), which allows the court to disqualify votes not procured and exercised in good faith.

In *Young v. Higbee Company*, the Supreme Court suggested that bad faith could be attributed to those "whose selfish purpose was to obstruct a fair and feasible reorganization in the hope that someone would pay them more than the ratable equivalent of their proportionate part of the bankrupt assets."[15] This definition reflects a problem that arose under prior law. Under the 1898 Act, the absolute priority rule could be invoked by single creditors, and some bought claims in bankruptcy merely to hold up the reorganization unless they were paid more than others holding the same securities. Courts

[15] 324 U.S. 204, 211 (1945).

have also found bad faith when a company purchased a claim for the purpose of blocking an action against it, or where creditors associated with a competing business were voting to advance the interests of their businesses at the expense of the debtor's. Similarly, if old equityholders or those close to them buy claims in order to promote or block a plan because of the way it treats their equity interests, courts have found bad faith as well.[16]

In recent cases, the problem is much more likely to arise when an outsider enters and seeks to gain control of a class in order to put its own reorganization plan in place. Imagine that a debtor proposes a reorganization plan within the exclusivity period and solicits acceptance of the plan. In the meantime, a prebankruptcy creditor, or an outsider, purchases claims at a discount. The purchaser hopes to gain complete control of the debtor and substitute its own plan for the debtor's plan. The purchaser also hopes to substitute its management for current management. Like any other corporate acquirer, the purchaser hopes ultimately to profit from its acquisitions. One might argue that this anticipated profit is not a legitimate creditor's attempt to protect its rights as a creditor but instead advances a different, and illegitimate, interest. This was the court's view, for example, in *In re Allegheny International*.[17] In that case the court found that a would-be acquirer acted in bad faith under §1126(e) and decided not to permit the acquirer to vote its purchased claims.

Under one view, those who buy up claims of firms in Chapter 11 disrupt the bargaining process that is at the core of Chapter 11. It is hard to gain acceptance of a reorganization plan if the owners of the claims shift constantly. But one can take a more generous view of these "vulture" investors, as they are sometimes called. They assemble dispersed claims and thus mitigate the problem that makes bankruptcy necessary in the first place. The negotiation and conflict inherent in the reorganization process would vanish or greatly diminish if a single entity owned all or most of the claims against a debtor. A sole or majority owner of claims has a strong incentive to maximize the value of the debtor's assets. Moreover, the other creditors are protected in bankruptcy by the best-interests test of §1129(a)(7). Finally, by creating a market for claims in distressed firms, these investors create competition for the claims. This competition may increase the amount that prebankruptcy creditors can realize on their claims if they are not able to wait until the conclusion of the case.

[16] For a discussion, see Figter, Ltd. v. Teachers Insurance & Annuity Association, 118 F.3d 635 (9th Cir. 1997).

[17] 118 Bankr. 282, 289–90 (Bankr. W.D. Pa. 1990)

While the structured negotiation inherent in the reorganization process may be desirable when markets do not function properly, one might well argue that the process itself should not keep a market from coming into being. From this perspective, the prospect of profiting by trading in claims should not without more be considered an illicit ulterior motive and should not constitute lack of good faith or disqualify votes of purchased claims.

Confirmation of the Plan

After the vote on the plan, the court must decide whether to confirm the plan. The court must satisfy itself that a plan meets the requirements of Chapter 11, particularly §1129. Section 1129(a)(1) requires a court to review a plan to make sure it complies with "the applicable provisions of this title." Thus, the court is supposed to review things such as classification sua sponte. Two of the more important items the court reviews are the substantive standards for confirmation—the best-interests-of-creditors test and the absolute priority rule. As we have noted, §1129(a)(7) requires that for a plan to be confirmed, either every member of every class must have accepted it or each member that voted against it must receive at least the liquidation value of its claim. Given the costs of asserting its rights under §1129(a)(7), a creditor may be better off consenting to a plan, even if the creditor would have done better in Chapter 7. Moreover, as we have already observed, the valuation procedures under §1129(a)(7) are not rigorous. Section 1129(a)(7) requires us to posit the counterfactual world in which a firm that properly belongs in Chapter 11 finds itself in Chapter 7 under the control of a trustee, and courts tend to assume that any liquidation that takes place in Chapter 7 involves the piecemeal sale of the firm's assets. Finally, bankruptcy judges may use different and less careful valuation procedures than under §1129(b). More casual valuations can work against the creditors' interests, especially if the judge believes that finding in favor of a dissenter will undermine the firm's prospects for a successful reorganization.

Assume that §1129(a)(7) is satisfied (perhaps because we can avoid rigorous valuations). The plan still has to satisfy the absolute priority rule if a class rejects a plan. Section 1129(a)(8) prevents the plan from being confirmed unless the plan meets the tests set out in §1129(b). Section 1129(b)(2) provides that each class must be paid in full before a class junior to it can get anything. During the era of the equity receiverships, the absolute priority rule was a right that each creditor enjoyed. Under the Bankruptcy Code, however, it applies only to dissenting classes. Section 1129(b)(2) contains three different glosses on the rule, and the one to be applied depends on the nature of the claim or interest of the class on whom the plan is being crammed down. Section 1129(b)(2)(A) deals with the issue of secured claims, §1129(b)(2)(B) with unsecured claims, and §1129(b)(2)(C) with interests. (As noted, the difference between "claim" and "interest" is the difference between debt and equity.) The basic point is this: either the claimants in the senior class must get the full amount of their claims as of the effective date of the plan—a present value concept—or junior classes must get nothing. Junior classes can receive something on account of their former rights against the firm only if one of two conditions are met: (1) the senior classes, by class-wide vote, consent to their participation; or (2) the senior classes receive payment in full.

Junior classes, however, have the right to invoke the procedures of Chapter 11 (and particularly the valuation procedures) in every case. This right can dramatically alter the positions of junior parties from what they would be if the firm were sold for cash and the cash parceled out according to nonbankruptcy priorities. Senior creditors may prefer a plan that does not fully compensate them rather than incur the costs of the procedures to which the junior parties would be entitled if they opposed the plan. So long as a class approves the plan, of course, it no longer matters whether the dictates of the absolute priority rule are being met. Even if the best-interest-of-creditors test and absolute priority rule are satisfied, the court under §1129(a)(11) must be confident that the firm will not need to be reorganized again. This requirement is usually called the *feasibility test*.

The §1111(b) Election

Understanding the rights of a secured creditor under §1129(b) requires a close examination of the special rights the secured creditor is given under §1111(b). Nonrecourse claims are made recourse, and a secured creditor can waive its unsecured claim and have its entire claim treated as secured. Much is unknown about the consequences of making the §1111(b) election, but identifying what is at stake is not difficult. Consider a bank that lends a debtor $1 million. The loan is secured by Blackacre. The loan is nonrecourse. Outside of bankruptcy, the bank can look only to Blackacre for satisfaction of its claim. If Blackacre sells at a foreclosure sale for only $600,000, the bank is out of luck on the remaining $400,000. What would happen in bankruptcy if §1111(b) did not exist? The bankruptcy judge would put a value on the bank's claim. If the judge valued it at $600,000, the bank could be crammed down with a package of rights having a present value of $600,000. The bank would have no unsecured claim because of the nonrecourse nature of the loan. The $400,000 deficiency would simply disappear. Congress introduced the §1111(b) election because it thought that a bankruptcy judge should not be able to eliminate the bank's deficiency with the stroke of a valuation pen.

The problem that Congress addressed in §1111(b) gained wide attention after *Great National Life Insurance Company v. Pine Gate Associates*, a decision under the old 1898 Act.[18] In that case, a nonrecourse secured creditor unsuccessfully objected to a plan in which its collateral would be appraised and the creditor would be paid the appraised value. The secured creditor wanted either to be paid in full or to have the property surrendered to it. If the appraisal was done correctly, of course, the secured creditor would have been paid as much as it would have received if it sold the property, but the secured creditor may have feared that the appraisal would not be done correctly. Because its claim was nonrecourse, it had no unsecured claim for any deficiency and hence no vote in the reorganization. Section 1111(b) responds to this situation—known as the *Pine Gate* problem—first by saying that all loans, whether or not they are recourse outside of bankruptcy, are recourse in Chapter 11. Thus, the bank mentioned in our example above will always (unless it elects differently) have a $400,000 unsecured deficiency in the above scenario. To the extent that the bankruptcy court undervalues Blackacre, the bank can vote with the unsecured creditors.

Section 1111(b) also gives the secured creditor an *election*. If the election is made, the creditor is deemed to have a secured claim for the entire amount of the debt, irrespective of the collateral's value. Thus, in the above example, the bank would have a secured claim of $1 million, not $600,000. The bank does not, however, receive a stream of payments worth $1 million. Under §1129(b)(2)(A)(i)(II) the bank would be given a stream of payments with a *present value* of $600,000. (The section provides that the stream of payments must equal "the value of such holder's interest in the estate's interest in such property." The court has valued the property at $600,000.) In this respect, the bank is treated no better or worse than if it had not made the election. By making the election, the bank gives up its deficiency claim of $400,000, and in return it receives the right to a stream of payments with a face amount equal to $1 million. Moreover, the stream of payments is secured by a *lien* of $1 million instead of

[18] 2 B.C.D. 1478 (Bankr. N.D. Ga. 1976).

$600,000. In many cases, the term of the loan is long enough that a note can have a present value of $600,000 and still have a stream of payments over $1 million. In such a case, the §1111(b) election benefits a secured creditor only if the court undervalued the property *and* there is likely to be either a default in the near future or a sale that would accelerate the $1 million obligation.

Implementing the Absolute Priority Rule

The Supreme Court set out the contours of the absolute priority rule in *Bank of America v. 203 North LaSalle Street Partnership*.[19] In that case a group of real estate investors acquired fifteen floors of an office building in downtown Chicago and obtained a nonrecourse mortgage from a bank. Real estate values dropped in the early 1990s, and the partners sought to restructure the bank's loan in Chapter 11. The partnership offered a plan that, in its view, left the bank with more than it would receive through a state law foreclosure, yet allowed the prebankruptcy investors in the partnership to remain as owners and enjoy significant tax benefits. When the bank turned down the partnership's plan, the bankruptcy court had to decide whether the plan could be confirmed over the bank's objection. The precise legal issue can be set out simply. To the extent that it was owed more than its collateral was worth, the bank held an unsecured deficiency claim in addition to its secured claim. The Seventh Circuit had already decided that the bank's §1111(b) deficiency had to be put in a class by itself.[20] Hence, when the bank voted against the plan, a class of unsecured claims necessarily voted against it as well. Section 1129(b)(2) of the Bankruptcy Code provides that when a class of unsecured claims dissents from a reorganization plan, the bankruptcy court can confirm the plan only if the plan is fair and equitable:

> [T]he condition that a plan be fair and equitable . . . includes the following requirement[ ]: . . . the holder of any [junior] interest . . . will not receive or retain under the plan on account of such junior . . . interest any property.

In other words, to confirm a plan, the court has to find that the plan was fair and equitable, which, at a minimum, requires that the old investors not receive any "property" "on account of" their old interests. In writing for the Court, Justice David Souter found that this language required adherence to "absolute priority." Under a regime

[19] 526 U.S. 434 (1999).
[20] See In re Woodbrook Associates, 19 F.3d 312 (7th Cir 1994).

of absolute priority, old equity cannot receive any "property" if a dissenting class was not being paid in full. A plan that gives old equity the exclusive right to acquire the old equity gives them property within the meaning of §1129(b). As Justice Clarence Thomas recognized in his concurring opinion, the plan, in substance, gave the old equityholders the exclusive right to the equity of the reorganized entity. Such an exclusive right was a stock option, something ordinarily regarded as property and thus property within the meaning of the statute. Hence, equity could not participate without the process being opened up.

If old equity could participate at all, it had to contribute an infusion of new capital. Moreover, old equity could not be given any breaks. Old equity had to pay top dollar for the new interest. As we have noted elsewhere, *LaSalle* requires that bankruptcy judges implement the Bankruptcy Code in a way that ensures—by the use of market-based and other mechanisms—that the value of nonbankruptcy rights is preserved. In practice, bankruptcy judges now lift exclusivity when the debtor files a plan in which old equity contributes new value in return for a share of the reorganized firm. Often the senior lender is a bank that has a security interest in all of the debtor's assets, and lifting exclusivity allows the bank to file its own plan. The bank's plan might propose a sale of the assets to the highest bidder. Because it has the senior security interest, the bank is entitled to the proceeds of the sale up to the amount of its claim. Hence, the bank can effortlessly offer a cash bid equal to its claim as any money it pays in will be returned instantly. As a matter of practice, at such sales the bank is allowed to *credit bid*. It can bid the amount of its claim without having to produce the cash that would come back to it anyway.

When multiple plans on the table satisfy §1129, the Bankruptcy Code charges the bankruptcy judge with choosing a plan after considering "the preferences of creditors and equity security holders." This provision is not helpful, as such preferences will likely go in opposite directions in cases of any moment. *LaSalle* itself also gives no guidance for the judge to follow in choosing among multiple plans. An interesting situation arises when a firm has a future as a going concern only if its current owner-manager remains in place. A senior creditor typically will be owed more than the assets are worth, but if the senior creditor and the owner-manager could have reached a deal, the firm would not be in Chapter 11. In many cases, the problem turns on valuation issues. The plan promises a package of rights that is hard to value. If the external market tests *LaSalle* requires are ignored, there is a built-in bias even when judges give accurate valuations. A judge in reviewing the plan might give an unbiased estimate of the value of the assets, but the debtor would systematically benefit as it loses nothing if the judge sets the value too high and profits if the value is set too low.[21] A serious conceptual issue exists, however, even if there is no dispute about valuations.

Consider the following case. There is a dinner theater in the suburbs of a large city. Its manager is the sole shareholder. He had only a modest career in Hollywood, but his gregarious good nature allowed him to develop many contacts with famous entertainers. He is able to persuade many of them to appear at the dinner theater, but construction cost overruns and lackluster ticket sales lead the dinner theater to file under Chapter 11. Bank has a security interest in all of the dinner theater's assets, both tangible and intangible. It is owed $10 million. A number of trade creditors are owed a total of $4 million. During the reorganization, the dinner theater's assets are appraised at between $5 and $6 million. The dinner theater has no long-term contract with the manager, and he has made it clear that he will continue to run the dinner theater only if he owns the equity.

The manager proposes a reorganization plan. He has found an investor who is willing to invest $6 million cash in the business. The manager will put up $2 million of his own money, also in cash. Under the plan, the bank will receive a one-time cash payment of $7 million. The remaining $1 million will be reinvested in the business. The general creditors will receive a $1 million note, secured by all of the dinner theater's assets. The investor will take an unsecured $6 million note, and the manager will retain the equity. In most plans, of course, we would not find an outside investor willing to put up cash. To focus on the conceptual problem, however, we want to eliminate the disputes that arise whenever payment takes a form other than cash.

The bank objects to the confirmation of this plan. It asks the judge to lift exclusivity and allow it to propose a plan in which the property is auctioned off. Because it is the most senior creditor, the bank will receive the proceeds of the auction. Hence, the bank can either make a cash bid equal to its secured claim or—in what amounts to the same thing—credit bid the amount of its claim. The bank is not in fact putting $10 million on the line even though it is ostensibly making a cash bid. Any amount it bids in excess of the manager's bid and less than its claim will give it control of the assets without requiring it to make any additional contribution to the ven-

---

[21] See Kham & Nate's Shoes No. 2 v. First Bank, 908 F.2d 1351, 1360 (7th Cir. 1990).

ture. An auction of the assets under these circumstances is no different from lifting the stay and allowing the bank to repossess.

Some might find the bank's behavior troubling. The manager is bringing something of value to the party. Old equity in *LaSalle* had tax benefits they wanted to preserve. For this reason, they were willing to give the bank any amount greater than it could hope to realize upon foreclosure. Similarly, in this case, the manager values the assets more than anyone else. (He is willing to pay $8 million in cash for them when no one else is willing to pay more than $6 million.) In many Chapter 11 cases, the debtor's plan on its face appears to give more to the creditors than a liquidating plan but its valuations are soft. Here, as in *LaSalle*, they are not. Indeed, after *LaSalle*, someone in the manager's position has to be able to show it is willing to pay top dollar. At a minimum, there has to be something that he is bringing to the party that makes him willing to pay more for the assets, whether it is contacts in show business or, as in *LaSalle*, tax benefits that only old equity could enjoy.

There are several possible explanations for the bank's behavior. First, the bank might want the ability to insist on its own right to take control of the property so it can strike a better deal with the old investors. The manager was willing to pay $2 million over the liquidation value to keep the dinner theater. If the bank can insist on the ability to liquidate, it might get the manager to pay even more. Similarly, in *LaSalle*, old equity offered $4.1 million over the value of the property because they were getting $20 million in tax benefits. The bank might have thought that by being hard-nosed it could get more. Alternatively, the bank may want to establish its reputation as a tough negotiator in future cases. Financial institutions are repeat players in bankruptcy and will be negotiating with the same lawyers and professionals in other cases. There is also the possibility that the bank (or its employees) are not negotiating rationally. Under our assumptions, for whatever reason, the bank and the manager have been unable to reach a deal even though agreement would be in their mutual self-interest.

We can approach this problem two different ways. One way is to note that outside of bankruptcy, few think it appropriate for a court to force a deal on large financial institutions and entrepreneurs on the ground that it is in their own self-interest. Given the lenders' ability to obtain blanket security interests, many reorganizations involve, for practical purposes, only two parties. Two sophisticated professionals have been unable to reach agreement, even though a mutually beneficial bargain between them seems possible. Such a situation may be a poor candidate for judicial intervention. Modern Chapter II cases are not like the nineteenth-century railroad reorganizations with dozens of different types of secured creditors. Two parties will sometimes fail to reach a deal with each other, through either avarice, stupidity, or miscalculation, but courts are likely to make matters worse rather than better if they intervene, whether inside or outside of bankruptcy.

We might take a different approach. A judge who confirms the dinner theater's plan makes not only the manager but also the general creditors better off than they would be under the bank's plan. The added value is coming not at the expense of the bank, but because of an asset (the manager's connections and expertise) in which the bank has no security interest. Under this view, it is emphatically the mission of bankruptcy law to bring about value-enhancing restructurings when multiple people have claims against assets. This debate over the fundamental purpose of bankruptcy remains unresolved.

In understanding this problem, as with any other that lacks an easy answer, we must return to first principles, but in doing this, we should understand both bankruptcy law and its limits. Legal rules cannot cure nonlegal problems. Legal rules cannot make the imprudent wise and the unlucky fortunate. Nor can they insulate a poorly run business from the realities of the marketplace. The goals of bankruptcy are necessarily modest. Honest but unfortunate individuals should be given a fresh start. Corporations that have value as going concerns should be able to acquire a new capital structure, and those that cannot survive should be able to wrap up their affairs expeditiously. Bankruptcy law cannot work miracles, and more harm than good comes from seeking that which cannot be had. We should, in our effort to understand and apply the law, recall what my colleague and mentor Walter Blum reminded me and others on many occasions: in law, 95 percent is perfection.

Table of Cases

Table of Statutes

Index

601	395	2411

Joe/Beth